Early Brahmanical Cults and Associated Iconography

(*c.* 400 B.C. to A.D. 600)

Early Brahmanical Cults and Associated Iconography

(*c.* 400 B.C. to A.D. 600)

Richa Sikri

2002

Kaveri Books

New Delhi-110002

First Published in 2002
ISBN 81-7479-044-6

Published by : **Rakesh Goel**
Kaveri Books
4697/5-21A, Ansari Road,
New Delhi-110002 (India).
Tel : 328 8140, 324 5799 Fax : 011 719 9029
e-mail: kaveribooks@vsnl.com

Laser Typeset by : Delite Interprises, Delhi-110 035.

Printed at : Chawla Offset Press, Delhi-110052.

PRINTED IN INDIA

Acknowledgements

In the present work an attempt has been made to trace the developmental stages of various cults and iconic forms from c. 400 B.C. to 600 A.D. in a historical perspective with reference to north India. In this endeavour the works of earlier scholars and art historians have been fruitfully utilized for which I feel indebted to them.

I am indebted to the Indian Council of Historial Research, New Delhi for granting me fellowship which gave me financial support.

I owe my deep respect and gratitude to Professor S. P. Shukla, my supervisor for his help and guidance and without his co-operation it would not have been possible for me to complete this research work.

I am grateful to the Library staff of the Jawaharlal Nehru Library, Kurukshetra, Institute of Sanskrit and Indological Studies Library, Kurukshetra. The Government Museum Library, Mathurā, the State Museum Library, Lucknow and American Institute of Indian Studies, Gurgaon.

I have no words to thank Ms. Gian Gupta, Deputy Librarian Kurukshetra University, for all her support and help. I also want to thank Mr. S. P. Bali, Mr. Surinder Kumar Vashisth, Mr. Naresh Kumar and Vijay Sharma for their kind help.

I am grateful to my parents and other family members who gave me an opportunity to do the research. I also want to mention Gian didi, Amber bhaiya, Nishu behna, and Sharad for their support and co-operation.

Richa Sikri

(RICHA SIKRI)

Foreword

It is indeed a pleasure for me to write a foreward to this book on Early Brahmanical Cults and Associated Iconography by Dr. Richa Sikri who has made significant contribution in the field of Indian religion and art.

Earlier studies on ancient Indian art are mostly related to iconography, identifications of forms and their co-relation with textual details. And as such these deal with only one aspect of art and throw little light on cultic developments. In the present study Dr. Sikri has studied archaeological and literary sources to reconstruct the growth of the Brahmanical cults in a chronological framework highlighting the historical development stages. She has rightly pointed out that the Brahmanical cults and their iconography is an outcome of a long gestation of ideas. The higher cults initially has a humble beginning at folk level. With the passage of time through patronage and followings, assimilation and absorption the folk cults acquired complex identity. This process began around c. 400 BC and was completed by AD 600. The visual forms found in the Gupta art and iconographic features detailed in contemporary texts amply prove it. The mode of worship (rituals and temples) also tell the same story.

The work of Dr. Sikri has served as an important fill-up in the field of the study of ancient Indian religion and art, which I hope, will go a long way to inspire further researches in this direction. I congratulate Dr. Richa Sikri for her researches.

Prof. S. P. Shukla
Deptartment of Ancient Indian History,
Culture and Archaeology,
Kurukshetra University, Kurukshetra.

Foreword

It is indeed a pleasure for me to write a foreword to this book on Early Brahmanical Cults and Associated Iconography by Dr. Rekha Sikri who has made a significant contribution in the field of iconography and art.

Earlier studies on ancient Indian art are mostly related to iconographic identifications of forms and their co-relation with textual details. And as such these deal with only one aspect of art and throw little light on cultic development. In the present study Dr. Sikri has studied archaeological and literary sources to examine the growth of the Brahmanical cults in a chronological framework highlighting the historical development stages. She has rightly pointed out that the Brahmanical cults and their iconography is an outcome of a long evolution of ideas. The Brahmanical cults initially has a humble beginning at folk level. With the passage of time through patronage and followings, assimilation and absorption the folk cults acquired complex identity. The process began around c. 400 BC and was completed by AD 600. The cultic forms found in the Gupta art and iconographic features detailed in contemporary texts support this. The mode of worship, rituals and temples also reflect the same step.
century

The work of Dr. Sikri has served as an important landmark in the field of the study of ancient Indian religion and art which I hope will go a long way to inspire further researches in this direction. I congratulate Dr. Rekha Sikri for her researches.

Prof. S. P. Shukla
Department of Ancient Indian History,
Culture and Archaeology,
Kurukshetra University, Kurukshetra

Contents

Abbreviations

ASI	Archaeological Survey of India, Reports (Cunningham Series)
ASIR	Archaeological Survey of India, Annual Reports
BMC	Bulletin of Museums and Archaeology in U.P.
CGE	Coinage of Gupta Empire
CII	Corpus Inscriptionum Indicarum
DHI	The Development of Hindu Iconography
EHI	Elements of Hindu Iconography
EI	Epigraphia Indica
JNSI	Journal of Numismatic Society of India
SB	Śatapatha Brāhmaṇa
SI	Select Inscription
VP	Viṣṇudharmottara Purāṇa

Transliteration

a	अ	ā	आ	i	इ	ī	ई	u	उ
ū	ऊ	ṛ	ऋ	e	ए	ai	ऐ	o	ओ
au	औ	k	क	kh	ख	g	ग	gh	घ
ṇ	ङ	ch	च	chh	छ	j	ज	jh	झ
ñ	ञ	ṭ	ट	ṭh	ठ	ḍ	ड	ḍh	ढ
ṇ	ण	t	त	th	थ	d	द	dh	ध
n	न	p	प	ph	फ	b	ब	bh	भ
m	म	y	य	r	र	l	ल	v	व
ś	श	ṣ	ष	s	स	h	ह		
kṣ	क्षा	tr	त्र	jñ	ज्ञ				

List of Figures

List of Plates

Introduction

1

All the worldly as well as spiritual progress is the outcome of human desire to know. Man has conquered the space, earth and sea but is not able to know how the world came into existence and who moves it on. This search for ultimate has led him into the realm of 'Religion' i.e. the belief in some supernatural power which is styled as God. Various types of ideas about the deity or god has given birth to cults and cult practices. In the times of calamity and distress the man has found answers and solace and has approached for protection and blessing to the deity of his choice. The changes in socio-economic and cultural life have affected the origin, growth and decline of various cults in the past societies.

The history of the development of religious cults in India began from the proto-historic times. The existence of a few deities, both malevolent and benevolent, is traceable in the relics of the Harappan Civilization. The Vedic literature attests that as many as thirty three deities were known at that time. The *Brāhmaṇas* complicated the rituals centering around the deities. And every one was craving for some simpler form of worship. The solutions were sought which we find in the philosophy of the *Upaniṣads* heralding a social as well as intellectual revolt against the existing environment.

The emergence of two heterodox sects, Buddhism and Jainism, during the six century B.C. made the revolt more vigorous. The main motive of these sects was to free the society from the clutches of Vedic practices, and show them simpler ways of religious life. All these upheavals forced Brahmanism to change its mode and form to survive. The sustenance of it was in less ritualistic as well as less intelligible ways towards religion. This actually brought forth the notion of cult practices, the seeds of which had earlier been sown in proto-historic India.

A cult is basically a form or system of worship centered around a deity of one's own choice and can be called a religious cult when it gets wedded to the vitality of philosophy and metaphysics. The cult practices, which started with the folk divinities, the Yakṣas and Yakṣis, Nāgas and Nāgis, reached to its highest watermarks with the emergence of the great gods and goddesses viz. Viṣṇu, Śiva, Mother-goddess, Sūrya,

Skanda of the epics and the *Purāṇas.* The highlights of the *Purāṇas* were the cults of Viṣṇu and Śiva with their family members as divinities. This converted the Brahmanism into Purāṇic Hinduism. And it is more or less the Purāṇic practices that are still prevalent in our society.

The practice of image-making (the chief object of cult worship) started in proto-historic times as the seals of the Indus civilization proofs of it. As the cults gained momentum the practice of image-making followed. The treaties on iconography were written, which laid the rules for making the perfect images of various gods.

Historiography of Earlier Studies

The earlier studies, that have been made regarding the cults and associated iconography, are of T.A.G. Rao, A.K. Coomaraswamy, J. Gonda and J.N. Banerjea.

T.A.G. Rao produced a pioneer work *The Elements of Hindu Iconography* (Madras, 1914, Reprint 1968, 1971) dealing with the iconography of all the major and minor cult deities. But the work has many shortcomings. First of all, it mainly relies upon the south Indian sculptures to illustrate the features of iconography and he did not even think necessary to study the sculptures of the pre-Kuṣāṇa, Kuṣāṇa and Gupta periods. Secondly, it is based on myths and fables, and thirdly the author did not pay attention to coins and seals which played a prominent part in the development of iconography.

A.K. Coomaraswamy, a notable art historian, devoted all his life in the pursuit and study of the Indian art, religion and philosophy, wrote many essays and books on Indian art. His most notable work is on the *Yakṣas* (Washington D.C., 1928 and 1931, New Delhi 1971). He treated the subject in critical and comprehensive way by giving literary and archaeological proofs to prove that Yakṣas, the minor deity of later periods, must have once enjoyed the status of major cult deity. It is for the first time he tried to show how a cult developed around a particular deity. In view of new finds it need to be revised. His another work *History of Indian and Indonesian Art* (U.S.A., 1927, Dover ed., New York, 1965) made an attempt to show the development of Indian art from prehistoric to Medieval times. It not only concentrated on the study of architecture and sculpture but also encompasses painting, jewellery, textile and metal works. It lacks in giving a complete development of religious cults and iconography. Moreover in view of new findings the work has become out of date.

J. Gonda has thrown light on Viṣṇu's connection with fertility and his relations with Indra and the character of the goddess Śrī-Lakṣmī in his *Aspects of Early Viṣṇuism* (Utrecht, 1954). But his more reliance on the literary sources and complete disregard to chronological consideration has made it a futile attempt.

The Development of the Hindu Iconography (Calcutta, 1956, Rep. New Delhi, 1974) is classical work by J. N. Banerjea. It is for the first time that the author has tried to exhaust the archaeological sources and also made an attempt to show the development of all the major and minor cults and their iconography. One another notable quality of the work is that for the first time the author has described icons in the light of śastric treatises. But he has, however, not traced the development of cults in chronological order and does not use the archaeological sources in coherent way.

The recent works on the subject are those of Kalpana Desai, S.B. Singh, Suvira Jaiswal and R.N. Mishra. Kalpana Desai's work *Iconography of Viṣṇu* (New Delhi, 1973) is a fairly comprehensive manual on the iconography of Viṣṇu in Northern India. It has discussed a variety of Viṣṇu images and tried to deal with various forms of Viṣṇu in separate sections viz. Śeṣa-Nārāyaṇa, Lakṣmī-Nārāyaṇa. Vaikuṇṭha etc. *(Lalit Kalā*, No. 18, 1977, p. 47). Though the author categorically mentions the period from the earliest times to medieval times yet she totally neglects the works of Kuṣāṇa period and has made no attempt to study the coins of that period to show the iconographic development of Viṣṇu images.

The Brahmanical Icons in Northern India (New Delhi, 1977) of S.B. Singh is confined to the studies of icons of Śiva, Viṣṇu, Sūrya, Vināyaka-Gaṇapati, Devī and syncretic icons in Northern India. The author writes with precision and brevity a quite fascinating account of the development of the worship of deities by utilising epigraphs, sculptures and literary references, *(Lalit Kalā,* No. 20, 1982, p. 55). But first of all, its brevity becomes a shortcoming and secondly the work is not able to show clearly how the cults start penetrating the regions of Northern India.

The most outstanding work *The Origin and Development of Vaiṣṇavism* (Delhi, 1967, second ed. 1981) is done by Suvira Jaiswal. In this work she has made an attempt to study all the aspects of Vaiṣṇavism viz. its pantheon, doctrines, rituals and extent of influence by thoroughly consulting the previous works and related literature and archaeological sources. But the work does not indicate the development of cult in chronological order.

The Yaksha Cult and Iconography (Delhi, 1984) of R.N. Mishra is a significant work after that of Coomaraswamy's work on the 'dwellers of the forests' and 'guardians of cities' better known as Yakṣas. In the present work the author has tried to show the career graph of these demi-gods who once had a lower status in Vedic times but suddenly in post-vedic times a cult centred around them grew up and remained till Medieval times. The development of Yakṣa cult in Buddhism and Jainism is also dealt with. The author has used a large number of excellent photographs of varied forms of Yakṣas and Yakṣīs to show the development of Yakṣa iconography. Each image is dealt with in detail with regard to its attributes and its significance.

Hypothesis and Research Methodology

1. The Brahmanical cults and their iconography is an outcome of a long gestation of ideas. Therefore, in the present research work it is intended to study the evolution of the Brahmanical cults and associated iconography (c. 400 B.C. to 600 A.D.) in northern India under various historical developmental phases focussing on socio-cultural milieu.•
2. The folk cults have played important role in the development of higher religious cults which need to be thoroughly investigated.
3. A marked difference is noticeable between the early cult images and the description of iconographic texts. It appears that the images of various cult-deities in their early developmental stage were conceived in rudimentary form and it was after the popularity of a particular cult that the iconographic traits were fixed through śāstric injuctions. At what stage śāstric injunctions for making cult images were made will be exmained by a thorough study of iconographic texts.
4. Brahmanical cults and the iconography of different deities as we find in the *Viṣṇudharmottara Purāṇa,* datable to 6th century A.D., was the result of gradual development of religious cults under various socio-religious cross currents. It needs to be thoroughly studied.
5. Various religious cults have influenced the iconography of different divinities of the Brahmanical cults at different stages of development.

In the present study an attempt has been made to show the development of cults and associated iconography in chronological order through an extensive use of literally as well as archaeological sources.

The basic nature of the material related to the present study is literary. But time to time additions and interpolations raise a question mark on the authenticity of literary sources. So to check the genuinity or trustworthiness of literary sources preference has been given to archaeological sources consisting of epigraphy, coins, seals, sculptures, buildings etc. Thus the study is based upon facts not on fiction. The development of cults as well as of iconography is shown, classifying in the chronological phases, which throws sufficient light on the issue as how changes take place in the position of cults with the passing of time. The effects of time factor can further be observed on iconography, which gives an insight to find out the answer, how the rudimentary art of proto-historic times reached to its zenith in Gupta period. The material or data that has been collected and scrutinised in analytical manner to make the present study.

Sources

2

LITERARY SOURCES

The evidence regarding the Brahmanical cults and related iconography for the period under review is scattered in literary and archaeological sources. The literary works are related to religious and secular themes while the archaeological sources include epigraphy, coins, sculpture and excavated relics. A brief survey of these sources, which have been fruitfully utilised for the reconsideration of the development of the Brahmanical cults and associated iconography, is given here.

Aṣṭādhyāyī

Pāṇini, who is placed in 4th century B.C., wrote a book on grammar named the *Aṣṭādhyāyī*. The aphorisms of its sixth chapter deal with religion and philosophy. It throws light on the concept of *bhakti* and references to Yakṣa, Nāga, Bhūta, Piśācha, Graha, Rudra, Devī, Vṛkṣa (tree), river and mountain. The worship of Kṛṣṇa in the form of Nara-Nārāyaṇa, *chatur-vyūha* and *Pañcharāṛa* had come into vogue by his time.

Arthaśāstra

The *Arthaśāstra* of Kauṭilya is associated with three aims of life *(trivarga)* i.e., *dharma, artha* and *kāma*.[1] It is a compendium on politics and economics. The author is supposed to be related to Chandragupta Maurya as Prime Minister who was also called Chāṇakya and Viṣṇugupta. The *Arthaśāstra* in its present form was compiled between 4th century B.C. and 4th century A.D. Shamasastry was of the view that Kauṭilya lived and wrote his famous work, somewhere, between 321 and 300 B.C.[2] The text is divided in 15 books, 150 chapters, 180 sections and 6,000 stanzas.[3] In its second book (Chapter V) which deals with 'buildings within the fort' and refers to divinities.

Mahābhāṣya

Another work which throws light on early cults is the *Mahābhāṣya*, a commentary on Pāṇini's *Aṣṭādhyāyī,* by Patañjali. He was courtier of Puṣyamitra Śuṅga and also believed as an incarnation of Ādiśeṣa.[4] He is also credited with the authorship of the *Yoga-sūtras* and the *Nidāna-sūtras.* This has led scholars to believe the existence of more than one Patañjali.[5] The *Mahābhāṣya* in the present form is placed in c. 200 B.C. At the time of Patañjali the Vaiṣṇava and the Śaiva cults with their family members had been formalized and the worship of the Yakṣas and Nāgas with their female counterparts had become popular in the society.

Jātakas

The *Jātakas,* the stories of previous births of the Buddha, are related to the tradition of folk tales. The Bodhisattva doctrine of the *Hīnayāna* Buddhists had inspired the creation of extensive *Jātaka* literature.[6] *Jātakas,* a collection of 547 Pāli stories, are parts of the *Khuddaka Nikāya,* which is one of the five *Nikāyas* (group) of the *Sutta Piṭaka.* Though Buddhist in nature, these also deal with characters that are dealt in the epics and the *Purāṇasd.*[7] The *Daśaratha Jātaka* (No. 461) gives a version of the *Rāmāyaṇa* legend though the story has a different colour from that of Vālmiki's *Rāmāyaṇa.*

The Kṛṣṇa legend is told by a parrot in another *Jātaka* (No. 546). Yakkhas (Yakṣas) Nāgas, Gandhabbas (Gandharvas), Kinnaras are also referred in the *Jātakas.*

Rāmāyaṇa

The *Rāmāyaṇa,* literally the history of Rāma, is the immortal poem of Vālmiki,[8] considered to be the first *kavi* (*ādikavi*), the author of ornate poetry.[9] It does not treat Rāma as an incarnation of Viṣṇu but as a prince. In it, the gods have come down as men, but men, by dint of their virtues, have become gods.[10] The *Rāmāyaṇa* is a poem of 24,000 verses divided into seven *kāṇḍas* or sections, which is further divided in 500 *sargas* or chapters. It was composed in the third century B.C. The western scholars hold the view that the part of *Bālakāṇḍa* and the whole *Uttarakāṇḍa* are the interpolations of a later date.[11]

Mahābhārata

The second epic, the *Mahābhārata,* which is great narrative of the battle of the Bharatas[12] written by Vyāsa, or Kṛṣṇa Dvaipāyana. He himself played a part in the story as he was the cause of further growth of the Kuru generation which might have stopped after the death of Vichitravīrya. The *Mahābhārata* is divided in 18 *parvas* (sections) with a *khila* (i.e. a supplement) called the *Harivaṁśa Purāṇa.*[13] The latter deals with the geneology and birth of Kṛṣṇa and details of his early life.[14]

The *Mahābhārata* consists of 1,00,000 verses. There is controversy regarding the authorship by a single person and the date of its composition. Historian assign the *Mahābhārata*, in its present form, between c. 4th century B.C. and 4th century A.D.

Manusmṛti

A code of conduct written by Manu which is also called the *Mānavadharmaśāstra* has a unique place in *Smṛti* literature. The work is divided into 12 chapters. The introductory chapter's tenth *śloka* holds Nārāyaṇa responsible for the creation of the universe.[15] Again in twelfth chapter Nārāyaṇa and Śiva have been given the places in the human body.[16] It refers to Vaiṣṇavism and Śaivism. Believed to be the father of mankind he wrote this work for the harmonious existence of a social life.[17] It was composed between 2nd century B.C. and 2nd century A.D.

Buddhacharita

Aśvaghoṣa, the celebrated author of Sanskrit literature, belonged to Ist century A.D. and was one of the leaders, if not the founders of the Mahāyāna doctrine of Buddhism.[18] His famous work the *Buddhacharita* is found in 28 cantos in Chinese translation but at present its original Sanskrit of 17 cantos are available. The *Buddhacharita* is for the Buddhist what the *Rāmāyaṇa* is for the Hindus.[19] Though it is woven around the life of the Buddha yet we come across many legendry deities such as Brahmā, Kārttikeya, Rāma, Kālī, Śachī, Indra and Kṛṣṇa.

Saundarānanda

The *Saundarānanda* is a *Mahā-kāvya* of Aśvaghoṣa in 18 cantos. It gives the story of the conversion of Buddha's half brother Nanda. In it Aśvaghoṣa also refers to the Brahmanical deities like Ādityas, Arjuna, Kṛṣṇa, Veda Vyāsa, Kālī, Kubera, Madana, Sarasvatī and Sāmba.

Yājñavalkya Smṛti

This *Smṛti* is placed in first or second century A.D. In its books II, a chapter is devoted to the worship of goddess Saṣṭhī. It also refers to the worship of Gaṇapati, Śiva, Pārvatī, Kārttikeya, Viṣṇu, Lakṣmī and Balarāma.

Charaka-saṁhitā

It is a treatise on *Āyurveda* by Charaka, the royal physician of Kaniṣka, who is placed in Ist century A.D. The text is divided into 8 sections and 120 chapters. Its second section *Nidānasthānas,* (first Chapter's thirty fifth śloka) describes the cause of the fever as the anger of Maheśa.[20]

Nāṭyaśātra

Bharatamuni's *Nāṭayśāstra* is probably the earlier extensive work on drama, music and dancing. The *Nāṭyaśāstra* has 37 chapters, according to the southern version earlier texts contained 36 chapters. The third chapter of this work is devoted to the prayer of deities such as Viṣṇu, Śiva, Śri, Brahmā, Kārttikeya, Indra, Sarasvatī, Sūrya, Maruts, Lokapālas, Agni, Rudra, Gandharva, Yakṣa etc. The date of its composition is c. 200 A.D.

Viṣṇu Smṛti

The *Viṣṇu Smṛti* seems to have been originally a *dharma sūtra* of Kāṭhaka school which was recast by some adherent Vaiṣṇava in the c. 3rd century A.D.[21] the entire work is presented in the form of a dialogue between Viṣṇu and the goddess Earth.[22] The work is divided into one hundred chapters or *adhyāyas* and its chapter 65 and 66 contain the details about the daily worship of God Vāsudeva, and provides an earliest reference to ritualistic worship of the deity.

Drama's of Bhāsa

Bhāsa was one of the greatest dramatist of Sanskrit literature. He was a predecessor of Kālidāsa and flourished in c. 3rd century A.D. Bhāsa has written a large number of plays for which he has chosen his themes from the *Rāmāyaṇa*, the *Mahābhārata* and popular tales.[23] His drama, the *Pratimānāṭakam*, a seven acts play, is inspired by the *Rāmāyaṇa*. The plot is the same but the story is woven in a different texture. The *Abhiṣekanāṭākam* is another play of Bhāsa which is based on the story of the *Rāmāyaṇa*. It begins with the fight of Rāma with Bāli and ends with the fall of Rāvaṇa and Sītā's ordeal of fire. In the *Bālacharita* Bhāsa describes the birth of Kṛṣṇa and his miraculous performances related to the killing of the Daityas and Kaṁsa and the coronation of Ugrasena. The *Dūtavākya* is a one act play by Bhāsa inspired by the *Mahābhārata's* story of Kṛṣṇa acting as an ambassador of the Pāṇḍavas.

Purāṇas

The *Purāṇas* are 18 in number and their authorship is ascribed to Veda Vyāsa. The early Purāṇas include the following :

The *Mārkaṇḍeya Purāṇa* takes its name from ancient sage Mārkaṇḍeya. The date of its composition is 3rd century A.D. or little earlier. Neither Viṣṇu nor Śiva occupies a prominent position but Vedic deities especially Āditya is held in high esteem in this Purāṇa.

In the *Viṣṇu Purāṇa,* Viṣṇu is praised and glorified as the highest being. It was composed in the last quarter of the third or the first quarter of the fourth century.

The *Matsya Purāṇa* commences with the story of great flood out of which Viṣṇu in the form of Matsya saves Manu.[24] It deals with Viṣṇu's incarnations, festivals, rites and also throws a sufficient light on Śiva legend.

In some lists the *Vāyu Purāṇa* appears under the name of the *Śiva Purāṇa* dedicated to the worship of Śiva. The *Vāyu Purāṇa* is quoted in the *Mahābhārata* as well as in the *Harivaṁśa Purāṇa.* It is considered to be a work of 4th century A.D.

In the list of *Purāṇas* given in the *Kūrma Purāṇa* the eighteenth Purāṇa is called the *Brahmāṇḍa.* But the original *Brāhmāṇḍa* was an earlier version of the *Vāyu Purāṇa.*[25]

The *Viṣṇudharmottara Purāṇa,* occasionally given out as a part of the *Garuḍa Purāṇa,* is counted as an independent *Upa-Purāṇa.*[26] This *Purāṇa* is divided into three sections and its third section deals with the making of the images of the deities and construction of temples. This *Purāṇa* is assigned between 4th century B.C. and 4th century A.D.

Plays of Kālidāsa

The works of great dramatist and poet of Sanskrit literature Kālidāsa are assigned to the Gupta period.[27] The author is considered to have graced the court of Chandragupta Vikramāditya (*c.* 380-413 A.D).

Kālidāsa wrote the *Raghuvaṁśa,* an epic, in 19 cantos narrating the history of the race of Raghu, the five cantos (X to XV) recount the story of Rāma. The *Kumārasaṁbhavam* deals with the birth story of war god, Kumāra.

The *Meghadūta,* a lyrical poem of 115 stanzas, describes the story of Yakṣa, who was sent in exile at Rāmagiri hills, for the neglect of his duties. He requests the cloud (Megha) to carry his message to his beloved. In this context places related to divinities and divine characters find their mention.

Jaina Literature

A variety of early Jaina literature is available to us which contains valuable records about the existence of religious cults of the period under review. The *Aṅgas i.e.* limbs (of the body of the religion) are twelve in number and written in *prākrit* language. The eighth *Aṅga* describes a Jinistic form of the legend of the destruction of the city of Dvārāvatī and the death of Kṛṣṇa.[28]

Uttarajjhayana or Uttarādhyana Sūtra

The Uttarajjhayana is a religious poem of the Jainas which forms a valuable portion of the *Kalpa-sūtras* written by Bhadrabāhu in 3rd century B.C. The work gives information about the Kṛṣṇa legend.

Paumachariya

The earliest poem on Rāma legend is the *Paumachariya*, of Vimala Sūri who flourished in Ist century A.D. The Pauma or Padma is the name of Rāma in the poem along with his name Rāma frequently occurs in the work. The story is partially in agreement with the *Rāmāyaṇa*.

Amarakośa

Amarasiṁha was the earliest lexicon who wrote the *Amarakośa* or the *Nāmaliṅgānuśāsana*. This work on lexicography is divided into three books containing separate chapters. The first chapter of Book (1) entitled *svargavarga* mentions the synonymous names for Asura, Buddha, Viṣṇu, Baladeva, Kāmadeva, Aniruddha, Lakṣmī, Śiva, Pārvatī, Gaṇeśa, Kārttikeya, Indra, Indrāṇī, Agni, Yama and Varuṇa.

Bṛhat Saṁhitā

Varāhamihira, the famous astronomer and mathematician, was considered as an incarnation of Sun-god.[29] The *Bṛhat Saṁhitā* is an encyclopaedic work on astronomy and other subjects of human interest. The text is divided into 18 chapters. Its tenth chapter deals with town planning, architecture and also gives a vivid account of the making of idols of Mahāvīra, Nārāyaṇa, Buddha, Rāma, Ekānaṁśā, Balarāma, Divine-mothers, Sun-god, Kubera, Yama, Gaṇeśa and Indra. The text was composed in 505 A.D.[30]

ARCHAEOLOGICAL SOURCES

Besides literary sources the extant archaeological relics of the period under review not only provide the authenticity of the existing cults but also help us to know the reliability of the literary tradition. The archaeological data includes epigraphy, numismatic, sculptural art and excavated remains.

The Besnagar pillar inscription, which mentions the setting up of the Garuḍa column *(Garuḍadhvaja)* of Vāsudeva, the god of gods (*devādeva*) by Heliodorus, a *Bhāgavata*, and son of Dion and an inhabitant of Taxila, is of foremost importance for knowing the development of early Vaiṣṇavism. The Greek Ambassador from King Antialcidas had gone to Kāśīputra King Bhāgabhadra.[31] This inscription on the paleographic grounds belongs to the earlier part of the second century before the Christian era.[32]

A fragment of the shaft of another octagonal column found in a narrow street at Bhilsā, evidently from Besnagar, bears a Brāhmī inscription recording the erection of the Garuḍa column of the excellent temple of the Bhāgavata (*Bhāgavatahprāsādo*) by Gautamīputra, a Bhāgavata.[33]

The next inscription is the Ghosundi stone slab found 4 Kms. north-east of Nāgarī in the Udaipur state (Rajāsthān). It is engraved in Brāhmī characters of the second century B.C. and records the erection of a stone enclosure for the worship of *Bhāgavata* Saṁkarṣaṇa and Vāsudeva, within the enclosure of Nārāyaṇa (temple or place of worship), by Bhāgavata Gājāyana, son of Parāśarī.[34]

The Nānāghāṭa cave inscription mentions Saṁkarṣaṇa and Vāsudeva along with other deities. This inscription belongs to the first century B.C.[35]

The importance of Morā stone slab inscription, placed in the early part of first century A.D., lies in the fact that it refers to the five heroes of Vṛṣṇi family.[36]

The Mathurā inscription of the time of the great *Kṣatrapa* Soḍāsa, son of Rājuvula, also refers to the shrine of *Bhāgavata* Vāsudeva in this connection.[37]

The Udaigiri Cave inscription of 4th century A.D. of Chandragupta II is engraved over the two figures, one is of the *Chaturbhuja* Viṣṇu, attended by his two consorts and the other is of *Dvādaśbhujā* Devī.[38]

The Bhītarī pillar inscription (Ghāzīpur district of U.P.) records the installation of an image of Śāringīn and the grant of a village for its worship by Skandagupta (A.D. 454 and 464 A.D.)[39]

The Junāgarh inscription of the time of Skandagupta refers to a temple of Viṣṇu, which was constructed in 456 A.D. by Chakrapālita, son of Parṇadatta, who was appointed as viceroy of Saurāṣṭra (Kathiavad) by Skandagupta. The inscription opens with an invocation to Vāmana Viṣṇu.[40]

An inscrption from Eran (Sāgar, district, M.P) of the reign of Buddhagupta (GE 165-A.D. 483) refers that Mātṛviṣnu and his younger brother Dhanyaviṣṇu who got erected a flag-staff *(dhvajastambha)* in honour of the god Janārdana. Mātṛviṣṇu is called a great Vaiṣṇava devotee (*atyanta Bhāgavata bhakta*).[41]

A copper plate inscription of A.D. 495, found near the village of Khoh (Baghelkhand) records the grant of a village by the *Mahārāja* Jayanātha, for the purpose of a temple of the god Viṣṇu under the name Bhāgavata.[42]

The inscription on the iron pillar at Mehraulī near Kutab Minar in Delhi refers to pillar as a flag-staff to Viṣṇu erected by a great king named Chandra, who enjoyed universal sovereignty and was a great devotee of Viṣṇu. The inscription is not dated, but if Chandra is equated with Chandragupta II, it belongs to the latter part of the 4th century or beginning of the 5th century A.D.[43]

The Mathurā pillar inscription of Chandragupta II (380 A.D) mentions Uditāchārya, as a follower of the Śaivism.[44]

The Udaigiri cave inscription of Chandragupta II is Śaiva in character.[45]

The Karamdanda inscription (437 A.D) refers to the dedication of a temple to the lord Śiva.[46]

The Chammak copper plate inscription of Pravarasena II mentions him as a devout worshipper of (the god) Maheśvara.[47]

The Junāgarh rock inscription of Skandagupta refers of Viṣṇu as the permanent abode of Lakṣmī.[48]

The Gwālior stone inscription of the time of Mihirakula speaks of Viṣṇu as one who bears the goddess Śrī on the bosom.[49]

The Sārnāth inscription of Prakṭāditya and the Aphasad inscription of Ādityasena mention Śrī as the wife of Vāsudeva.[50]

The Gaṅgādhar stone inscription of Viśvavarman (480 A.D.) records that Mayurarakṣaka built a temple of divine mothers.[51]

An inscription of Mandasor reports that a guild of silk weavers, who had migrated to Daśapur, built a temple of the Sun-god at that place in 437 A.D. And when temple partly collapsed it was again repaired by the same guild in 473 A.D.[52]

A copper-plate found at Iṇdore mentions an endowment of Devaviṣṇu in 464 A.D. for lighting a lamp in a temple of a Sun.[53]

The Bilsād inscription of Kumāragupta I speaks of the construction of a temple of Kārttikeya.[54]

The Allahabad pillar inscription of Samudragupta describes the journey of Gaṅgā and Yamunā from heaven to earth.[55]

Coins

The study of numismatics is important to gauge the early religious cults and related iconographic development. The various religious systems and superstitions that prevailed in the fourth century B.C. are given in the *Niddeśa*.[56] These included a number of deities, including animals. The deities depicted on early coins both in their theriomorphic and anthropomorphic forms attest to above contention.

Śiva is depicted in theriomorphic, anthropomorphic and liṅga form. The most common theriomorphic representation of Śiva on coins has been the bull. In the *Viṣṇudharmottara Purāṇa* Śiva is said to be *Dharma* in the shape of a bull. Bull has also been represented on the tribal coins of ancient India. It appears on the coins of Ujjainī, Arjunayānas, Audumbaras, Yaudheyas, Mālavas and Śibis. Apart from the bull, a tree-in-railing which is also associated with the worship of tree as *Sthala-vṛkṣa* is sacred to Śiva, and also appears on these coins. Śiva (or *Oesho*) has been represented in anthropomorphic form on the coins of all the four Kuṣāṇa rulers viz. Wema Kadphises, Kaniṣka, Huviṣka and Vāsudeva. Wema Kadphises coins have the human representation of Śiva with his mount bull and the Kuṣāṇa ruler is found to have used the epithet *mahīśvara* (i.e. skt. *maheśvara*) or devotee of Śiva.[57] The coins of Huviṣka, also represent the *ardhanārīśvara* form of Śiva. It is interesting that the deity has not been depicted on the Gupta coins.

There is no iconic representation of Viṣṇu assignable earlier than the beginning of Christian era. On the coins of Viṣṇumitra and Rāmadatta, the rulers of Mathurā, Viṣṇu is depicted in the form of lotus a variant of *chakra*. Vāsudeva-Viṣṇu is depicted on a Kuṣāṇa seal attributed to Huviṣka. The Gupta rulers were largely responsible for the spread of Vaiṣṇavism. Chandragupta II started the 'Chakravikrama' type coins. It is strange that there is no anthropomorphic representation of Viṣṇu, the principal deity of the Vaiṣṇava cult on the Gupta coins. Only his attribute *chakra*, is represented in anthropomorphic form.

Sūrya is rarely depicted in human form on early indigenous coins. The wheel, the lotus, the rayed-disc, six-armed device, the *svastika* and taurine symbols are usually taken to represent the Sun god. The wheel is one of the most common symbols found on Punch-marked coins. The anthropomorphic representation of Sūrya comes from Avantī placed between 2nd century B.C. and 2nd century A.D. The depiction of Sūrya is also not found on Gupta coins but historians have contradictory views regarding *chakra* which is associated with Vaiṣṇava as well as Saura cults.

The symbols of peacock on hill or cock on the top of a post are related to Kārttikeya. The coins of Huviṣka depicted the figures of Skanda, Mahāsena, Kumāra and Viśākha with their names in Greek script. The new iconographic trait is added by the Yaudheyas, who depicted him as six-headed deity. Kumāragupta I was the first Gupta ruler to issue the 'peacock type' gold coins on which he is seen feeding grapes to peacock. He was named after Kumāra, the commander-in-chief of the gods.

The goddess Lakṣmī is depicted first time anthropomorphically on the coins of Azes I. She is usually found carrying lotus in her hands. She is represented on the coins of Kuṇindas and Yaudheyas. On the coins of Chandragupta I and Samudragupta she is depicted with noose in right hand and a lotus-bud in left hand, on the coins of Chandragupta II sometimes she is found with the lion.

The other form in which goddess is found is Gaja-Lakṣmī. In this style two elephants standing on lotus on either side of her are seen sprinkling water. She is found on tribal coins discovered from Ujjainī and Ayodhyā. She is also depicted on the coins of alien rulers Azilises, Rājuvula and Soḍāsa. Two forms were started by Guptas for the first time. These included Garuḍa and Gaṅgā. The coins of Guptas depicted the Garuḍa in a bird form. A new style is ushered with Chandragupta II, in which Garuḍa is depicted as half-bird and half-human form. The Guptas were the first to depict Gaṅgā in anthropomorphic form, as is seen on the coins of Samudragupta and Kumāragupta I.

Sculpture

The images attest the development of the religious cults through rituals. The reference to image-making is traced as early as the *Ṛgveda* but actual images began to be fashioned during the historical period.

Early images datable prior to c. 3rd century B.C. are not available. It is possible because of wooden images they may have perished. The early extant cult images, datable to Mauryan period, consist of Besnagar Yakṣī (now in the Indian Museum, Calcutta) Pārkham Yakṣa (the Mathurā Museum) and Dīdārganj Yakṣī (the Patna Museum) which attest the existence and popularity of Yakṣa cult.

The rule of Śuṅgas, patrons of Brahmanical order, proved to be an epochmaking so far as the fashioning of the Brahmanical images are concerned. The images of goddess and Yakṣī Chulakoka, Yakṣa Supavāsa, Sirima Devatā (probably representing the ancient mother-goddesses, now in the Indian Museum).[58] Yakṣī Sudarasana, Yakṣa Kubera is attested from Bharhut. The goddess of fortune Gaja-Lakṣmī is found depicted on eastern gateway of Sāñchī and Yakṣī holding the trunk and branches of the tree on the Northern gate. The representation of Sun-god in his characteristic four horse chariot is found at Bodh-Gayā.

The most important images of this period are of Viṣṇu from Malhār and Saṁkarṣaṇa from Mathurā. The other famous images is that of Śrī-Lakṣmī with *Kalpadruma* recovered from Besnagar, and is now housed in the Indian Museum, Calcutta.

In Kuṣāṇa period two schools, Gandhāra and Mathurā, flourished. The latter school is famous for fashioning Brahmanical, Buddhist and Jaina images. The credit for making the images of Viṣṇu in human form goes to the sculptor of this school. It is strange that excepting the reliefs showing Vāsudeva transporting the newly born Kṛṣṇa to Gokula,[59] and Keśina-vadha the depiction of Kṛṣṇa have not come to light.

The other Brahmanical images of this period from Mathura are those of Brahmā, Mukha-liṅga, Ardhanārīśvara, Pārvatī, Kārttikeya, Gaṇapati, Viṣṇu, Sūrya, Indra-Vajrapāṇi, Kāmadeva, Balarāma, Sarasvatī, Lakṣmī, Durgā, Siṁhavāhinī and Mahiṣāsuramardinī and Sapta-mātṛkās.

The Kuṣāṇa plastic art was influenced by the foreign art but by the time of the Guptas the foreign inspiration was eliminated and sculptural art became more indigenous and aesthetically more beautiful. The best examples of it are the images of Viṣṇu and Buddha. The most notable figure of fifth century is a Viṣṇu from Mathurā, marked with contemplative serenity.

The other sculpture is of gigantic image of Varāha from Udaigiri and *Eka-mukh* Śiva-liṅga from Khoh are worthy of mention.

The Daśāvatara temple at Deogarh depicts scenes related to Viṣṇu legend. Śeṣaśayi, Nara-Nārāyaṇa and Gajendramokṣa attest the supremacy of Viṣṇu cult over other divinities.

The beautiful sculpture of Gaṅgā on Makara and Yamunā on Kūrma are found on the door-frames of Udaigiri, Tigāwā, Bhūmarā, Nachnā-Kuṭhārā, Deogarh and Ahichchhatrā. The images of Yama, Sūrya, Indra and Mahiṣāsuramardinī are depicted at Bhūmarā.

References

1. Winternitz, M., *A History of Indian Literature*, Vol. III, p. 608.
2. Shamasastry, R., *Kautilya's Arthaśāstra*, Preface, p. viii.
3. *Ibid.*, Preface, p. ix.
4. Mani, Vettam, *Purāṇic Encyclopaedia*, p. 583.
5. Jacobi rightly summed up that since the author of the *Yogasūtras* does not conform to the grammatical rules taught by the author of the *Mahābhāṣya* and because latter is ignorant about the philosophical views of the former (Puri, B. N., *India in the Time of Patañjali*, p. 13). Again an inscription from Narendra of the time of Vikaramāditya and the Kadamba ruler Jayakeśin II dated A.D. 1125 refers to Patañjali, the grammarian, by way of comparing and eulogising the qualities cf the ruler... so it necessarily suggests that there were two or more Patañjali. (Puri, B. N., *op. cit.*, pp. 14-15).
6. Dwivedi and Bhatt, *The Jātakamālā of Āryaśūra, p. Intro. xi.*
7. Sen, Benoychandra, *Studies in the Buddhist Jātakas* (Tradition and Policy), p. 5.
8. Krishnamachariar, M., *History of Classical Sanskrit Literature*, p. 3.
9. Winternitz, M., *A History of Indian Literature, Epics and Purāṇas*, Vol. I, Part II, p. 417.
10. Sadhu Ram, *Essays on Sanskrit Literature*, p. 121.
11. Mani, Vettam, *Purāṇic Encyclopaedia*, p. 389.
12. Winternitz, M., A *History of Indian Literature, Epics and Purāṇas*. Vol. I, Part II, p. 389.
13. *Ibid*, p. 364.
14. Krishnamachariar, M., *loc. cit.*, p. 35.
15. *Manusmṛti*, 1, 10, 11.
16. *Ibid.*, 12, 120, 121.
17. Mani, Vettam, *Purāṇic Enyclopaedia*, p. 481.
18. Nariman, J.K., *Literary History of Sanskrit Buddhism*, p. 28.
19. Khosala, Sarla, *Aśvaghoṣa and His Times*, p. 15.
20. *Charaka-Saṁhitā*, ed. by Sharma, P. V., p. 257.
21. Jaiswal, S., *The Origin and Development of Vaiṣṇavism*, p. 20.
22. Winternitz, M., *A History of Indian Literature*, Vol. III, p. 20.
23. Sadhu Ram, *Eassay on Sanskrit Literature*, p. 184.
24. Winternitz, M., *A History of Indian Literature*, Vol. I, Part II, p. 504.
25. *Ibid.*, p. 507.
26. *Ibid.*, p. 508.
27. The evidence adduced from Aihole inscription and the *Harṣacharita* of Bāṇa favours Kālidāsa to be placed in sixth century A.D. or to a later date.(Ram Gopal, *Kālidāsa, His Art and Culture*, p. 12). He is also regarded to a contemporary of Śuṅga king Agnimitra (2nd century B.C.) on the basis of his play the *Mālavikāgnimitram*. The tradition also associates Kālidāsa with king Vikramāditya of Ujjaini, the founder of *Vikram* Era (57 B.C.), as one among the nine jewels of Vikramāditya's court. The prominent view about

the date of Kālidāsa is that he flourished during the reign of king Chandragupta II (*c.* 380-413 A.D.), who assumed the title of *Vikramāditya* after conquering north-west parts of India.

28. Winternitz, M., *A History of Sanskrit Literature*, Vol. II, p. 467.
29. Bhat, Ramakrishna, M., *Varāhamihira's Bṛhat Saṁhitā*, p. Intro, xi.
30. Shastri, Ajay Mitra, *India as seen in the Bṛhat Saṁhitā of Varāhmihira*, p. 9.
31. Lüder, H., *Appendix to EI and Record of the ASI, A List of Brāhmi Inscriptions*, Vol. X, No. 669.
32. Sircar, D. C., *Select Inscriptions*, Vol. I, No. 2, p. 88.
33. A.S.I. Annual Report, 1913-14, Pt. II, P. 190. Cf. Puri, B. N., *India in the Time of Patañjali*, p. 185.
34. Lüder, H., *Appendix to EL and Record of the ASI, A List of Brāhmi Inscriptions*, Vol X, No. 6, See also Sircar, D. C., *SI*. Vol. I, No. 3, p. 90.
35. *Lüder, H., loc. cit.* No. 1112, Sircar, D. C., *SI*, Vol. I, No. 82, p. 192.
36. *Ibid.*, No. 14
37. Sircar, D. C. *loc. cit.*, No. 26A, p. 122.
38. *Ibid.*, No. 3, Pt. 11. B, p.21 ff.
39. *Ibid.*, No. 13, Pt. VII, p. 52 ff.
40. Fleet, J. F., *CII*, Vol. III, No. 14, Pl. VII, p. 56 ff.
41. *Ibid.*, No. 19, Pl. XIIA, p. 88 ff.
42. *Ibid.*, No. 27 Pl. XVII, p. 121 ff.
43. *Ibid.*, No. 32, Pl. XX 1A. p. 139 ff.
44. Sircar, *SI.*, Vol. I, No. 9, p. 277.
45. Fleet, *CII.*, Vol II, No. 6, 21, IVA, pp. 34-35.
46. Sircar, *loc. cit.*, No. 17, p. 289.
47. Fleet, *loc., cot.*, No. 55, Pl XXXIV, p. 235.
48. *Ibid.*, No. 14, Pl. VIII, p. 56 ff.
49. *Ibid.*, No. 37, Pl. XXIIB, p. 161
50. *Ibid.*, No. 42, Pl. XXVIII, p. 200.
51. *Ibid.*, No. 79, p. 284, Pl. XLIIIC.
52. *Ibid.*, No. 17, Pl. X. 72.
53. *Ibid.*, No. 16, Pl. IXB, p. 68 ff.
54. *Ibid.*, No. 10, Pl. V. p. 42.
55. *Ibid.*, No. 1, Pl. I, p. 1, Line 30.
56. Bhandarkar, R.G., *Vaiṣṇaviasm, Śaivism and other Minor Religious Systems*, p. 165.
57. Chattopadhyay, B., *Coins and Icons, A Study of Myths and Symbols in IndianNumismatics Art*, p. 11.
58. Kar, Chintamoni, *Classical Indian Sculpture*, p. 29.
59. Agrawala, V. S., *Studies in Indian Art*, p. 183.

Development of the Brahmanical Cults

3

c. 4th to 2nd Century B.C.

A cult or sect does not come into existence suddenly as it is culmination of the beliefs, traditions, and practices of many centuries. In the fourth century B.C. an air of change was prevailing in the society as far as the sphere of religion is concerned. The heterodox sects like Buddhism and Jainism were penetrating the previous faiths of the people. Vedic religion was gradually losing its hold because of its rigidity and people were waiting for a simple faith which could satisfy their inner craving as well as less ritualistic and elaborate. Above all, the notion of *bhakti* is namely a cordial adoration or prayer to the god of one's choice.[1]

In Pre-Maurayan age, by the time of Pāṇini, the folk cults of Yakṣa, Nāga, Bhūta, Piśācha, Graha (planet), Rudra, Devī, Vṛkṣa, river, mountain etc. started gaining momentum. The reference of these we also find in the *Ṛgveda.* The word Yakṣa occurs several time in the *Ṛgveda*[2] but the meaning is doubtful.[3] But it is in the *Jaiminīya Brāhmaṇa* [4] where Yakṣa means nothing more than a wonderful thing.[5] In later literature the Yakṣas are usually bracketed with the Asuras, Rākṣasas and Piśāchas and placed by lexicons in the category of demi-gods like Vidyādharas, Gandharvas, Kinnaras, Guhyakas, Siddhas and Bhūtas.[6]

Though the Nāgas or serpents are mentioned in the *Ṛgveda* yet no reference to snake worship is made there.[7] In the later *Saṁhitās*[8] the serpents are found as a class of semi-divine beings beside the Gandharvas and others.[9] In the age of *sūtras*[10] the people used to make offerings to serpents on different occasions. It was, however, not due to any veneration for serpents but due to the belief that if serpents were propitiated by means of offerings they would not bite the worshippers.[11] It proves that the serpents were worshipped because of their hurtfulness.

Mountains (*Parvata*) are often in the *Ṛgveda* conceived as divinely animate being invoked as deities nearly twenty times in the plural and four times in the singular number. In this capacity they never appear alone, but only with other natural objects such as waters, rivers, plants, trees, heaven and earth or with gods like Savitṛ, Indra and others.[12] Parvata is even three times lauded with Indra in the dual compound

Indra-parvata.[13] The pair are spoken of as driving in a great car and besought to come to the offering. Here, Parvata seems to be a mountain god, conceived anthropomorphically as a companion of Indra.[14]

The evidence about sacredness of the tree can be cited from Indus valley civilization. The worship of trees or the tree-spirits is the characteristic manifestation of animistic belief. Many seals in the Indus Valley sites show the presence of two forms of tree worship among the people of the locality 'one in which the tree itself is worshipped in its natural form, the other in which the tree spirit is personified and endowed with human shape and human attributes.[15] In Vedic period large trees, called Vanaspati, 'Lord of the forest' are a few times addressed as deities, either in the plural or singular, chiefly among with waters and mountains.[16]

The cult of Vāsudeva also flourished in this period. His worship started in two forms-one with Arjuna[17] as Nara and Nārāyaṇa and other with his family members in the shape of *Chatur-vyūha* consisting of Saṁkarṣaṇa, Vāsudeva, Pradyumna and Aniruddha and at times including Sāmba converting the same into *Pañcha-vira* system. R.G. Bhandarkar is of the view that by the time of Pāṇini Vāsudeva-Kṛṣṇa merged as a deity with Vedic Viṣṇu.[18] Western scholars also hold this view.[19] Viṣṇu occupies a subordinate position in the *Ṛgveda* being celebrated in only five or six hymns.[20] While his name occurs only about 100 times. The essential feature of his character is that he takes three strides, which are referred to a dozen times. His epithets *Urugāya*, wide-going and *Urukrama* wide-striding, with these three steps Viṣṇu is described as traversing the earth or the terrestrial spaces. Two of these steps or spaces are visible to men, but the third or highest step is beyond the flight of birds and mortal ken.[21]

Viṣṇu is also associated with the sun and his three steps are considered by western scholars as rising, culminating and setting of the Sun. Viṣṇu is related to the Sun in another way also. Imagine if there would be no Sun, what would happen to the earth in the same way if there would not be Viṣṇu, there would be disorder on the earth because it is the duty of Viṣṇu, being as a preserver to protect and sustain the lives of the created beings. Even Viṣṇu's favourite vehicle, in the later Purāṇic mythology Garuḍa, has his original in the Vedic Suparṇa, which is on its part the Sun-bird itself. The fight between Garuḍa and the Serpents is symbolic of the conflict between light and the demons of darkness.[22]

In all the Brāhmaṇa texts sacrifice (*Yajña*) has been identified with Viṣṇu.[23] The expression 'sacrifice is Viṣṇu' occurs again and again.[24] This identification ultimately resulted in the stimulation of the status of Viṣṇu.

A story referred in the *Śatapatha Brāhmaṇa*[25] and the *Taittirīya Āraṇyaka* vividly reflects this. The sacrifical session was held by the gods for the attainment of splendour, glory and food. They proposed themselves that he amongst them, who by his deeds reached the end of the sacrifice before the others, should attain the highest place among them all. Viṣṇu reached the end before the others, and he thus became the highest of the gods and, therefore, they say that Viṣṇu is the highest of the gods.[26]

Nārāyaṇa is a non-Vedic divinity,[27] first time mentioned in the *Śatapatha Brāhmaṇa.* There is a passage in the *ŚB* that Puruṣa Nārāyaṇa wanted to be the supreme and by performing the *Puruṣamedha Pañcharātra yajña* he became highest among men.[28]

Regarding the etymology of the word Nārāyaṇa, Bernett was of the view that it is a *gotra* name derived from *Nara,* analogous to Kaṇvāyana, Kātyāyana and other similar formations.[29] Jaiswal suggests that Nārāyaṇa is a deity of Dravidian origin, and the name was applied to the male deity who was supposed to lie or reside on waters.[30]

In the view of R.G. Bhandarkar the word Nārāyaṇa is similar to Nāḍāyana, means the resting place or the place to which Nāḍa or a collection of Nāḍas go. So, Nārāyaṇa means the resting or goal of Nara or a collection of Naras.[31]

Vāsudeva-Kṛṣṇa was a historical hero of Vṛṣṇi clan. The city of Dwārkā was founded by Vāsudeva-Kṛṣṇa which later submerged in the sea is now being excavated by S.R. Rao. Though the palace building has been found, yet there is no major break through by which we may prove the authenticity of Kṛṣṇa.

The reference of Śiva and Skanda is found in a *Sūtra* of Pāṇini. It says that the images of these gods were not to be sold.[32] In another passage names of Śiva are given.[33] The evidence of the worship of Śiva goes back to the Indus Valley Civilization. A seal unearthed at Mohenjodaro which bears a three-faced horned figure 'seated on a low Indian throne in a typical attitude of yoga, with legs bent double beneath him, heel to heel and toes turned downwards, to either side of the god are four animals, an elephant and a tiger on his proper right, a rhinoceros and a buffalo on his left. The figure is a prototype of the historic Śiva-Paśupati.[34]

The Śiva-Paśupati aspect of the god merged with the Vedic Rudra, who possesses two divergent traits one destructive and the other benevolent.[35]

This god occupies a subordinate position in the *Ṛgveda* as it is celebrated in only three entire hymns and in one conjointly with Soma, while his name occurs about 75 times.[36] In a passage of the *Ṛgveda,* Rudra is one of the several deities identified with Agni. He is also associated with storm, rain and lightening, and his main weapons are a bow and an arrow with which he killed the animate beings.[37]

Rudra is described in the *Ṛgveda*[38] as fierce and destructive like a terrible beast. He is besought not only to preserve from calamity but also to bestow blessings and produce welfare for man and beast. His healing powers are mentioned with special frequency. He carries in his hands choice remedies.[39] He is greatest physician of physicians, and by his auspicious remedies his worshippers hope to live a hundred winters. He is besought to remove sickness from his worshipper's offsprings and to be favourable to man and beast, that all in the village may be well-fed and free from disease. In this connection Rudra has two epithets *'jalaṣa'* perhaps 'healing' and *'jalaṣa-bheṣaja'*[40] possessing 'healing remedies'.[41]

From the time of the *Yajurveda* and the *Brāhmaṇas* Śiva started acquiring high position. In the *Yajurveda* the deity represents both the darker and benign powers of nature. His benevolent form is termed *'Śivatanuḥ'* and *Aghora* 'non-terrific' as opposed to his malignant form called *Ghora, Bhīma, Ugra* etc. meaning terrific and awe-inspiring.[42]

Śiva's personality shows two opposite traits at the same time. He is hailed as the lord of forests, hunters, and highway robbers and at the same time as the lord of soldiers, army and commander-in-chief. All sorts of fierce weapons and sharp missiles are associated with him. The constant epithet of Rudra as *Saṁhatṛ* or the destroyer of the universe can be traced from *Vājasaneyi Saṁhitā.* The seer prays to the deity to take pity on him and not to kill his father, mother and not to injure person dear to him, not to kill the people and other created beings of the world.[43]

In the Post-Vedic age *Paśupati* became a special appellation of this god. The other epithets of Him as *Kapardin, Nīlagrīva, Śiti-Kaṇṭha, Gaṇapati, Bhava, Śarva, Pinākin* and *Trayambaka* are also described in the *Vājasaneyi Saṁhitā* and the *Śatapatha Brāhmaṇa.*

The traits of His becoming the supreme lord can be cited from the epithets such as *Jagataṁ patiḥ* the lord of the universe, *Viśvarupebhyaḥ* who assumes all forms, *Bhagavāna,* the all powerful god, *Īśāna* etc.[44] Further the earliest reference of Śiva of being the creator, sustainer and destroyer of the comos is found in the *Śvetāśvatara Upaniṣad.*[45]

The worship of, Pārvatī in four forms Bhavānī, Śarvāṇī, Rudrāṇī and Mṛḍānī was prevalent in Pāṇini's times. In all the ancient civilizations woman, being the mother of the race, were held in high esteem. Each early civilization around the eastern end of Mediterranean had its traditional mother-goddess e.g. Isis in Egypt, Ashtart in Phoenicia, Cybele in Phrygia and Demeter in Greece. In each case she was originally the patroness of productivity.[46]

Later on as civilization progressed the matriarchal pattern gradually faded away and the father became the head of the family unit. Consequently there was a change in the concept of God and the fatherhood of God was established.[47]

Jhov and Kullī Valley sites in Baluchistān have furnished a number of terracotta figurines. It has been suggested that these figurines were connected with fertility and they are the earliest representation of the primitive Mother-goddess in India.[48]

A large number of ring-stones and female figurines discovered from the sites of Indus Valley prove the prevalence of the Mother-goddess cult in Mohenjodaro and Harappā. The great majority of these female figurines appear as 'a standing and almost nude female, wearing a band or girdle about her loins, with elaborate head-dress and collar, and occasionally with ornamental cheek cones and a long necklance.[49]

Goddesses occupy a very subordinate position in Vedic belief and worship. They played hardly any part as the rulers of the world.[50] The number of female deities and beneficient and evil spirits of all classes having separate hymns or part of hymns or incidently mentioned in the *Ṛgveda* is much more than thirty three.[51] In these more than thirty three goddesses Aditi, Uṣās, Vāk, Sarasvatī, Bhāratī, Ilā, Mahī, Rātri, Purandhi, Dhisana are held in esteem.[52] It is wellknown that the names like Ambikā, Durgā, Kālī etc. are not mentioned in the *Ṛgveda*. Such names appear in later Vedic period.[53] In *the Vājasaneyi Saṁhita*[54], *the Taittirīya Brāhmaṇa and the Śatapatha Brāhmaṇa,*[55] Ambikā is styled as Rudra's sister. In *Taittirīya Āraṇyaka* she is described as Rudra's consort.

There is no direct reference of Sun-worship during the period under review. But there are two *Sūtras*[56] in which Sun is mentioned alongwith the other members of solar pantheon, viz., Pūṣan, Divākara, Uṣās, Chandramas and Soma. The traces of Sun-worship can be found in Vedic times also.[57] Sūrya or the sun as the orb that is seen in the sky and not as an imaginary god of light, was a Vedic deity.[58] Ten entire hymns of the *Ṛgveda*[59] may be said to be devoted to the celebration of Sūrya specifically. In the *Atharvaveda*[60] he is called the 'lord of eyes' and he is far-seeing, all seeing is the sky of the whole world, beholds all beings and the good and bad deeds of mortals. In various passages Sūrya is conceived as a bird traversing space. Sūrya shines for all the world for men and gods. He dispels the darkness with his light.[61]

There is a slight reference to the worship of Kārttikeya in the *Aṣṭādhyāyī* where Pāṇini mentions the image of Śiva and Skanda should not be sold.[62] The *Ṛgveda*[63] does not mention Kārttikeya and his other well-known name such as Skanda and Kumāra. Though the word *Kumāra* occurs seventeen times in the *Ṛgveda* yet it is often used as a form or an aspect of Agni. The occurrence of the words *Kumāra* and *Agni* in collation with each other may have afforded some basis for the mythology of Kārttikeya the son of Agni in later times. Moreover, the word *Guha* which has become an epithet of Kārttikeya in later times was first used for Agni in the *Ṛgveda*.

The *Śatapatha Brāhmaṇa*[64] clearly mentions *Kumāra* as the ninth form of Agni or Rudra.

The notion of Commander-in-Chief of the army of gods for Skanda Kārttikeya has been taken from Agni, as Agni is associated with army in the *Ṛgveda* as well as in the *Śatapatha Brāhmaṇa.*[65] The army is not only associated with Agni but also with Rudra. In the *Śatapatha Brāhmaṇa*[66] Rudra-Agni is stated as the golden-armed leader of army and lord of directions.

In the *Chhāndogya Upaniṣad*, which is most probably a pre-Buddhist work, the word Skanda occurs. Here Skanda is mentioned as another name of the Vedic seer

Sanatakumāra. The process of evolution of Skanda has rightly been analysed by Hopkins. He states "Skanda is a composite god. First there is Agni Kumāra the ever-youthful, with whom first Skanda was formally identified. On the other hand, as son of Agni Skanda was identified with all burning (fever) and other afflictions. The god who represented fire and affliction was naturally associated with the troops of afflicting beings grouped with Śiva and so became son of Śiva.[67]

The worship of the Mahārājās, the kings of Yakṣas, Gandharvas, Kumbhāṇḍas and Nāgas better known as Kubera, Dhṛtarāṣṭra, Virūḍaka and Virūpākṣa were prevalent in the age of Pāṇini.

The worship of Yakṣas like Śeval, Supari, Viśāla, Varuṇa and Arymā was also popular in Pāṇini's time. One more noble concept of this period was the deification of month, season, year and planet.

Megasthenes, as quoted by Arrian, mentions that Herakles (Kṛṣṇa) was the special object of worship of the Sourasenoi, an Indian tribe in whose land were the great cities of Methora and Kleisobora (Mathura and Kṛṣṇapur) and through which flowed river Iobares (Yamuna).[68] So it shows the popularity of Kṛṣṇa cult that even a foreigner mentions it.

The *Arthaśāstra* of Kauṭilya describes that in building a fort the apartments of gods such as Aparājitā (Durgā), Apratihata (Viṣṇu), Jayanta (Skanda), Vaijayant (Indra), Śiva, Vaiṣravaṇa, Aśvin (divine physicians), and abode of the goddess Madirā shall be situated.[69] The reference to Kārttikeya and Brahmā is also found in *Arthaśāstra*, but here they appear as guardian deities.[70]

In another passage the spies were advised to disguise as the ascetic worshippers of Saṁkarṣaṇa.[71] It is quite amazing that lesser famous gods like Aśvins are mentioned by Kauṭilya but not Sūrya.

The sculptures of Pārkham Yakṣa (now in the Mathurā Museum) and Dīdārganj Yakṣī (now in the Patnā Museum) are seen for the first time in Mauryan period, dated somewhere in c. 3rd and 2nd Century B.C.

This shows that the Yakṣa and Yakṣī as the cult deities held the status of supreme god and goddesses in Mauryan period.

c. 2nd Century B.C. to the Beginning of Christian Era

The Brahmanical cults breathed a fresh air during the reign of Śuṅgas in 2nd century B.C. as a revolt of Brahmanical system against the pro-Buddhist policy of the Mauryas. The *Mahābhāṣya* of Patañjali throws welcome light on this period.

By the time of Patañjali we find Vāsudeva and Baladeva associated with the Vṛṣṇis. He mentions the names such as Kṛṣṇa and Janārdana,[72] the synonyms of Vāsudeva, but also refers to the festive gatherings in the temples of Keśava (Vāsudeva) and Rāma (Balarāma). The references to the devotees of Vāsudeva (*Vāsudeva-bhaktas*), the staging of *Balibandha* connected with Viṣṇu and slaying of Kaṁsa by Kṛṣṇa.[73] are indicative of the devotion to the Lord gaining momentum who was addressed by different names.[74] The worship of *Chatur-vyūha* and *Pañcha-vīra* was also prevalent.

There are two references in the *Mahābhāṣya* which indicate the existence of a separate cult of the Śaivas. These refer to the devotees as *Śiva-bhāgavata* and *Śiva-Vaiśravaṇa.* Skanda and Viśākha were also respected by many people as the images of these gods and those of Śiva were the source of living to their keepers. *Liṅga* worship has not been formalized.[75]

The reverence to Sun and Moon is also found in the *Mahābhāṣya.*[76] Certain female deities, Lakṣmī (wife of Viṣṇu) and Suparṇī, are also mentioned. Lakṣmī, whose previous existence can be cited from the Vedas, was called Purandhi.[77] In the *Atharvaveda,* Sinīvalī is called the wife of Viṣṇu and sister of the gods.[78] The goddess Śrī and Lakṣmī were referred at the end of *Puruṣa sūkta* of *Yajurveda* where they are spoken of as two consorts of Nārāyaṇa Puruṣa.[79]

There is a story in the *Śatapatha Brāhmaṇa,*[80] where it is said that her beauty and resplendence made the gods envious and they wanted to kill her, but Prajāpati disuaded them from this act as she was a female and asked them to take away all her attributes sparing her life. Then Agni, Soma, Varuṇa, Indra, Bṛhaspati etc. took from her food, kingdom, universal sovereignty, noble rank, power, holy lusture, domination, wealth and beautiful form. By Prajāpati's advice she offered ten sacrificial dishes to the ten divinities and then everything was restored to her. According to Banerjea the inner significance of this story is that goddess embodies all the major things coveted by man.[81]

Lakṣmī and Śrī who at the beginning were two different divinities, tended to merge with each other in the Upaniṣdas.[82] But the *Śrī-sūkta*, a supplement to the *Ṛgveda* [83] is the earliest text which eulogises Śrī as a deity. And there is no difference between Śrī and Lakṣmī in the *Śrī-sūkta* because she is invoked by both these names.

The cults of lower divine-beings, Yakṣas and Nāgas, were also prevalent in Patañjali's time.

Amongst the epigraphic records of this period is the Besnagar (M.P.) pillar inscription (c. 2nd century B.C.), which was written in Prākrit influenced by Sanskrit language, mentions the setting up of the Garuḍa column (*Garuḍadhvaja*) of Vāsudeva, the god of gods (*devādeva*) by Heliodorous, a Bhāgavata, son of Dion and an inhabitant of Taxila who came as Greek ambassador from king Antialcidas to Kaśīputra king Bhāgabhadra.[84] This shows the influence of Vaiṣṇava cult was so powerful that a foreigner was also charmed by it.

A fragment of the shaft of another octagonal column from Besnagar (M.P.) found in a narrow street at Bhilsā, bears a Brāhmī inscription in one line recording the erection of the Garuḍa column of the excellent temple of Viṣṇu (Bhāgavata) by Gautamīputra, a *Bhāgavata.* As Garuḍa is considered the *Vāhana* of Viṣṇu, so these inscriptions are Vaiṣṇavite in character.[85]

The Punch-marked coins are the early indigenous currency which were put in circulation as early as the beginning of the fourth century B.C., if not earlier.[86] On these coins are punched the symbols like tree-within-railing, the wheel, lotus, rayed disc, the three-arched mountain with crescent, peacock and cock etc.

Different interpretations have been suggested about these symbols. Spooner opines that these are Buddhist in character. The so-called solar symbol stood for *dharma-chakra* and tree for *bodhi-tree.*[87] Later on he discarded his above view in favour of a second one and held that many of them were Zoroastrian in nature. Durga Prasad suggested that most of the symbols are tantrik in character. A.K. Coomaraswamy is of the view that the Punch-marked symbols show a definite stage in the development of Indian iconography.[88] J.N. Banerjea associated these symbol with Brahmanical cult deities. The tree-within-railing shows the representation of *Sthala-vṛkṣas* and *Chaitya-vṛkṣas,* the wheel, lotus, rayed disc are associated with Sun, the three-arched mountain with crescent moon is associated with Śiva, peacock and cock with Skanda. Accordingly these were the aniconic representations of the deities.[89] There are three stages regarding the depiction of deities on the coins-aniconic, theriomorphic and anthropomorphic. Punch-marked coins represent the aniconic stage.

A study of the local coins of this period (2nd century B.C.) also throw light on the prevailing faiths of the people. These coins are of two varieties—uninscribed and inscribed. The date of uninscribed coins ranges from c. 3rd century B.C. and c. 2nd century B.C. On the uninscribed coins of Ayodhyā, Kauśāmbī and Taxila we find the devices of flowers, *svastika,* tree-in-railing, mountain surmounted by crescent, *nandīpada,* dog, peacock etc.

A passage from the *Niddeśa* furnishes a curious record of the various religious systems and superstitions that prevailed during the fourth century B.C.[90] "The deity of the lay followers of the Ājīvakas is the Ājīvakas, of those of the Nighaṇṭhas is the Nighaṇṭhas, of those of the Jaṭilas is the Jaṭilas, of those of the Paribhājakas is the Paribhājakas, of those of the Avaruddhakas is the Avaruddhakas, and the deity of those who are devoted Puṇṇabhadda, Maṇibhadda, Aggi, Nāgas, Supannas, Yakkhas, Asuras, Gandhabbas, Mahārājās, Chanda, Suriya, Inda, Brahmā, Deva, Disā is the elephant, the horse, the cow, the dog, the crow, Vāsudeva, Baladeva, Puṇṇabhadda, Maṇibhada etc. respectively".[91] It may be summarised from above reference that if individual cults were not evolved around all these deities and animals, certainly they were objects of reverence for the people.

As an ancient practice divinities were first theriomorphically represented. Later on when these deities were conceived anthromorphically animals which symbolized them, were transformed into their vehicles (*vāhanas*). Thus the bull, which later on came to be regarded as Śiva's *vāhana* was at first used by the devotees as a symbol for Śiva.[92]

Bull on the coins of Ujjainī (*c.* 3rd and 2nd century B.C.) is identified as Śiva. Bull has also been represented on the tribal coins of ancient India. It appears on the coins of Arjunāyanas, Audumbaras, Yaudheyas, Mālavas, Śibis and Agras.[93]

A Śiva-linga like symbol has been represented on a pedestal placed between two trees inside railing. It is considered as the earliest representation of a *liṅga* on local coins of Ujjainī belonging to historical period.[94]

For the first time Śiva represented anthropomorphically on the Ujjainī coins and its environs belonging to the *c.* 3rd and 2nd century B.C. Śiva appears single-headed as well as three-headed on Ujjainī coins. His attributes include an object like a staff (*daṇḍa*) or spear (*śakti*) held usually in the right hand and an uncertain object the pouch or *kamaṇḍalu* in the left hand.[95]

The solar device 'a ball from which rays radiate' appear on the Mitra coins of the Pāñchālas. These coins belong approximately to the period between the *c.* 2nd century B.C. and end of the Ist century B.C.[96] Scholars, generally hold the view that the Sun god has not been represented anthropomorphically on any early indigenous coins. But V.C. Srivastava has discussed an uninscribed copper coin from Avantī belonging approximately to the period between *c.* 2nd century B.C. and 2nd century A.D. The obverse of the coin shows a human figure standing facing, clad in short-tailed coat and high *tiara, svastika* and taurine above, solar symbol composed of crescents and broad arrow-heads attached to central boss to the right and a standard surmounted by rayed Sun to the left. On the extreme left there is a tree. The reverse shows the Ujjainī symbol with an inner circle and dot in each orb.[97]

The figure of Lakṣmī as seated on lotus as well as holding a lotus in her hand appears on the uninscribed cast coins of Ujjainī belonging to the period between the *c.* 3rd and 2nd centuries B.C.[98]

The obverse of certain uninscribed copper of Ujjainī (*c.* 2nd century B.C.) depict two draped figures, identified by Allen as females, holding an uncertain object in raised right hand.[99] Below this motif appears a river with fishes in it. But J.N. Banerjea thinks that these two figures represent a male and a female and their dress and attitude are comparable with the Yakṣas and Yakṣīs figures from Bhilsā. Further the male figure on the coins wears the *graiveyaka* ornament so frequently worn by Yakṣa figures found at Mathurā and Gwālior. So the above device on the coins provides a comparatively early representation of the Yakṣa and Yakṣī couple.[100]

A few coins of Kāḍa depict the figure of snake alongwith Aśokan Brāhmī legend *Kāḍasa.*[101] According to J.N. Banerjea this refers to the descendants of the serpent called Kardu. Serpants in the shape of zig-zag and undulating lines have been represented on many early indigenous coins. Certain Punch-mark silver coins depict a thick wavy line, which[102] Allan takes to be the representation of a snake.[103] The double snake motif is represented on the coins of Ayodhyā.[104] The *liṅga* flanked by a snake is a very common symbol on the Pāñchāla coins.[105]

The most novel finding of this period was the six rectangular bronze coins of Agathocles, (c. 2nd century B.C.) found from Ai-Khanum on the borders of Russia and Afghānistān. Paul Benard had noted that the obverse and reverse of the coin shows two masculine personages, in Indian attires. They, according to Benard, wear *dhotī* covering the thighs upto just below the knees and half boots with curved sole ends. They also wear a kind of helmet on their heads. Their swords in a long sheath hang on a cross belt. One figure holds *chakra* and *maṇḍala*. The other figure carries a *mūsala* (pestle) and a *hala* (ploughshare). They are identified as Kṛṣṇa and Balarāma. The coins of Agathocles, therefore, prove that the Bhāgavata cult was popular among the Greeks who had settled in this country.[106]

The statues of cult deities are also found in art. The railings of Bharhut are decorated with the images of Viruḍako Yakho, Kupiro Yakho, Ajakālako Yakho, Gaṅgeya Yakho, Suchiloma and Supavaso Yakho.[107] These images are different in two aspects first, all have their hands in *Namaskāra-mudrā* and are dressed in a similar manner, secondly these stand on the vāhanas, which are altogether different for each Yakṣa.[108] The popular etymology of *Yakṣa* (Pali *Yakho*) offered by the Buddhist commentator is that to whom sacrifice is given for expiation or propitiation. It is the name of certain non-human being (amānuṣa) as spirits, ogres, dyrads, ghosts and spookes being half-deified and of great power as regards influencing people-party helping, partly hurting.[109] There is a famous story of Hāritī which shows the character of Yakṣa and Yakṣī. Hāritī was originally a Magadhan tutelary goddess. She was the wife of Pañchika and resided at Rājagṛha. She began to destroy the children of Rājagṛha by small- pox and so earned the name of Hāritī i.e. thief by which she is known in Buddhism. Metaphorically she is said to devour them and is represented as an ogress and it was an ogress that the Buddha encountered. The Buddha adopted the expedient of hiding her last born child (Piṅgala, who had been a human being in previous life, his birth as a Yakṣa being a penalty). She realized the pain she had been causing others and became a convert to Buddhism. But as she could no longer seek her accustomed food, the Buddha promised her that she shall receive regular offerings from pious Buddhists as patroness of children and fertility.[110] In Jain literature Yakṣa and Yakṣī appear as protectors of Jain Tīrthaṅkaras. Each Tīrthaṅkara has a Yakṣa and Yakṣī as attendant. They are called *Vyāntara* or gods of intermediate status and said to be dwelling in unoccupied houses, trees, forests or woods, ponds etc.

Another folk cult which is profusely depicted on the panels of Bharhut is that of a Nāgas. These demi-gods were represented guarding the gates of Bharhut stūpa. A Nāgarāja, named *Chakrāvaka* in the inscription, who like his companion doorkeeper is standing with his hands raised in adoration in an attitude which indicates his devotion to the Buddha. This Nāgarāja was in all probability a godling locally worshipped as his name is not known from elsewhere. He bears a human shape, but as if to remind his real nature, there is a five hooded snake crest surmounting his head. His feet are placed upon a rock in front of which we see a lake or pond full of lotus flowers enlivened by various aquatic animals.

On a bas-relief carved in the shape of a medallion at Bharhut shows a Nāgarāja accompanied by two *chaurī*-bearers. The Nāga is distinguished by usual five-hooded serpent crest.[111] Among the reliefs one decorating the so-called Prasenjit pillar on southern gate is remarkable. It shows the lord Buddha being worshipped by the Nāgarāja Elāpattra. Buddha is depicted by empty stone at the foot of a sacred tree. The Nāgarāja is depicted not less than three times. First, as a five-headed serpent emerged from lake. Next he appears in human form with a five-headed serpent crest and accompanied by two Nāgīs each wearing a snake emblem. For the third time the Nāga king is shown kneeling down in devout attitude at the side of the stone seat under the tree which indicates the Buddha's presence.[112]

From Bharhut we also find goddess Lakṣmī squatting with folded hands on a full-blown lotus springing from the *pūrṇa-ghaṭa.* On her either side an elephant standing on lotus is bathing her from a vessel held in its trunk. Lakkhi is the Pāli equivalent of Sanskrit Lakṣmī. She is also called Siri in Pāli (Sanskrit, Śrī). Sometimes both the names Siri and Lakkhi are mentioned together. However, to the Buddhists, Siri Lakkhi is the goddess of beauty and fortune.[113]. In Jain literature also she has an auspicious character. According to the *Kalpa-sūtras.* Śrī is one of the fourteen auspicious dreams of Triśalā, foretelling the birth of Mahāvīra.[114] In standing posture, goddess elaborately dressed stands on a full-blown lotus springing from the *pūrṇa-ghaṭa* and holds a lotus bud in her left hand.[115]

A standing image of a two-armed Balarāma, with a canopy of serpent hood over the head and snake coils carved at the back and sides of the body with distinguishing symbols a club (*mūsala*) in right hand and a plough (*hala*) in the left hailing from Mathurā, is now housed in the State Museum, Lucknow. The conspicuous turban, heavy ear-ring, the triangular folds of *dhotī* hanging between the legs and knotted girdle as well as frontal effect of the carving suggest that the statue belongs to Śuṅga period.[116]

The *stūpa* of Sāñchī is richly decorated with the cult-images of Gaja-Lakṣmī and of Nāgas.

Gaja-Lakṣmī is depicted in various forms on the panels of the Great *stūpa.* Generally she is shown in two forms, one sitting and other standing.

On the lower front panel of the northern *toraṇa* she is depicted as seated on a huge hemispherical lotus. Her folded left leg is kept on the lotus seat while the right folded leg is in *pralambapāda* posture. Her right hand holds a lotus flower while the left is placed in her lap. An elephant standing on her either side on a lotus is bathing her.[117] The Gaja-Lakṣmī panel in Buddhist art has become the matter of contention among scholars. Foucher is of the view that it is a scene of Nativity. The figure of Māyādevī holding the branch of sāla tree in the Lumbinī forest which bent low to come within her grasp to support her during delivery is called the Nativity scene. Others regard it as the purificatory bath of the new born Buddha. Buddhist scriptures describe the bath of new born Buddha by two nāgas, Nanda and Upananda.[118] But many scholars opine, which seems to be true, that it is neither a scene of Nativity nor of Buddha's first bath because of the absence of child and the presence of elephants instead of nāgas. Further in the Buddhist scriptures Lakkhi is considered as a deity of fortune and the artists might have been influenced by then prevailing faiths.

The two reliefs at Sāñchī represent the Nāgarāja Muchilinda sheltering the Buddha.[119]

The figure of Sūrya in human form is depicted on the railing pillar of Bodh-gayā. The god has been depicted riding on a one wheeled (*ekachakra*) chariot drawn by four horses. He is attended on either side by a female figure shooting an arrow and are the earliest reliefs standing for Uṣā and Pratyuṣā personifying the two different aspects of dawn, driving away darkness. The demon of darkness appears to be personified by a male bust on either side of the relief.[120]

The Ghosundi (Rājasthān) stone inscription (c. 2nd half of the Ist century B.C.) of King Sarvatāta speaks of the construction of an enclosing stone-wall round the place of worship of Saṁkarṣaṇa and Vāsudeva in the Nārāyaṇa Vāṭikā by Bhāgavata Gājayāna, son of Parāśarī.[121] The Nānāghāṭa (Pune) Cave inscription (c. Ist century B.C.) of queen Nayanikā mentions the name of Prajāpati, Dharma, Indra, Saṁkarṣaṇa, Vāsudeva, Chandra, Sūrya and four Lokapālas.[122]

This shows the Vaiṣṇava cult which originated at Mathurā did not stagnate there but spread far and wide in the regions of present day, Madhya Pradesh, Rājasthān and Mahārāshṭra States, and thus started holding sway over whole India. It is curious that though we get some inscriptions referring to the Bhāgavata shrines of the pre-Christian and early post-Christian era but very few representation of the cult god Vāsudeva Viṣṇu are found on the coins of the same period. On the other hand though the numismatic portrayal of the other cult deity Śiva is so very elaborate, very few epigraphic references to Śaiva shrines of the contemporaneous periods are forthcoming.[123]

On the reverse of coins of Viṣṇu Mitra of Pāñchāla a deity holding uncertain object in either outstretched hand is considered as two-armed Viṣṇu by Allan. The loose end of the robe of the deity led Cunningham to describe the figure as four-armed while others have identified the figure as Vāsudeva. But figure seems to be the four-armed Viṣṇu. In his upper left hand the god holds a longish object downwards, most probably a *gadā*. In his upper right hand the deity holds an object that resembles a *śaṅkha* on specimen. The object held in the lower right hand of the deity is indistinct, but in all probability it is a lotus. The *śaṅkha, chakra, gadā* and *padma* are the commonest attributes of Viṣṇu. The coin belongs to the first century B.C.[124]

The coins of Mathurā rulers of two different families Mitra and Dattas comprising Gomitra,[125] Brahmāmitra,[126] Dṛdhamitra,[127] Sūryamitra,[128] Viṣṇumitra,[129] Puruṣadatta,[130] Uttamadatta,[131] Balabhūti,[132] Rāmadatta,[133] and Kāmadatta[134] depicted the device of Lakṣmī on their coins. Lakṣmī also appears on the coins of Kṣatrapa rulers of Mathurā viz. Śivadatta, Hagamasa, Rājuvula and Soḍāsa.[135] The Gaja-Lakṣmī motif often appars on local coins. The uninscribed coins of Kauśāmbī,[136] belonging to third century B.C. depict Lakṣmī standing on lotus and being anointed by two elephants. The latter stand also on lotuses. The seated figure of Gaja-Lakṣmī appears on the uninscribed coins to Ujjainī[137] belonging to the period between the third and second centry B.C. This motif also appears on the coins of Mathurā rulers, Rājuvula,[138] Soḍāsa[139] and Azilises.[140]

The figure of Yakṣa and Yakṣī has been depicted on the coins of Indo-Greek rulers. The reverse of certain coins of Agathocles depict a female figure with long pendants in her ears. Whitehead describes her as a dancing girl.[141] But her long non-human head indicates that she is Yakṣī Aśvamukhī.[142] The obverse of certain coins of Telephanos depict a male figure holding lotus stalk in each hand developing from his own serpent like legs. This figure may be identified as of a Yakṣa.[143]

The wavy lines probably representing serpent appear on the copper coins of Mūladeva,[144] Vāyudeva,[145] Viśākhadeva[146] and Dhanadeva[147] rulers of Ayodhyā. Nāga devices in the form of undulating lines also appear on the coins of the Kuṇindas,[148] Yaudheyas[149] and of Taxila.

The epics provided foundation for the existing cults which were elaborated by the Pūraṇic tradition. The *Rāmāyaṇa* is based on the story of Rāma who is considered as a eighth *avatāra* of Viṣṇu. There are passages in the *Rāmāyaṇa* pointing to this, but there is good reason to believe that they are spurious or interpolated,[150] because the story on the whole treated him as an ideal hero not as a god. We find his name in the passage of *mokṣadharma* section of *Śānti Parva* [151] and also in all the Pūraṇas. But his name is neither mentioned by Patañjali nor an early archaeological evidence has come to light. It is difficult to trace precisely when the cult of Rāma originated. The panels depicting the episodes from the *Rāmāyaṇa* are found in the Gupta period.

The epics certainly gave momentum to the existing Vaiṣṇava cult. The personalities of three individual gods Viṣṇu, Nārāyaṇa and Vāsudeva-Kṛṣṇa were finally merged with each other in the *Mahābhārata*. There is a passage in *Vana Parva*[152] which describes the condition of things at the time of dissolution of the universe. There was water everywhere and a child was lying on couch placed on the branch of *nyagrodha* tree. He opened his mouth and took in Mārkaṇḍeya, who roamed inside and saw the whole universe and struck with wonder. Then the child vomitted or threw him out, when he saw again the water alone. Mārkaṇḍeya then asked the child who he was then he said : Formally I gave to the waters the name of Naraḥ, and those were my resting place (*ayana*) and, therefore, I am Nārāyaṇa. And thus he went on to describe his greatness. Finally Mārkaṇḍeya, who narrates story, says to Yudhiṣṭhira that Janārdana is identical with Nārāyaṇa.[153]

The concept of Viṣṇu as supreme god who is omnipotent, omnipresent and omniscient also occurs in the *Mahābhārata*.[154]

The *Anuśāsana Parva* of the *Mahābhārata* consists of an eulogy called the thousand names of Viṣṇu (*Viṣṇusahasranāma*.)[155] The amount of popularity gained by the Viṣṇuism is indicated by this eulogy. In several other passages of the *Mahābhārata* the meaning or cannotation of variety of his names has been enumeratd. The meaning of his very common names Nārāyaṇa[156] and Viṣṇu[157] are also described.

The concept of Nara-Nārāyaṇa seems to be popular in epics since in the opening stanza of the different books obeisance is made to these two gods.[158] Nara and Nārāyaṇa are sometimes called Ṛṣis. In *Vana Parva* Janārdana is represented to have said to Arjun, "you are not different from me and I am not different from you there is no difference between us".[159]

In another verse of *Śānti Parva* the lord says to Arjuna that they have come on the earth to lessen the burden of the earth.[160] In the *Udyoga Parva*[161] it is said, "The two heroes, Vāsudeva and Arjuna who are great warriors, are the old gods Nara and Nārāyaṇa."[162]

In this manner there are a good many examples of the identification of Arjuna and Vāsudeva with Nara and Nārāyaṇa. And thus the old tradition about the two Ṛṣis, was brought into connection with Arjuna and Vāsudeva Kṛṣṇa of the *Bhagavadgītā*. It is related with the notion of incarnation. The word *avatāra* literally means 'descent' which pictures the divine spirits as descending from heaven to earth and taking up abode in human body or other material form[163] is significant contribution of the early Vaiṣṇava cult. The concept of *avatāra* is based on the verse of *Bhagavadgītā* where Kṛṣṇa says to Arjuna, "whenever the *dharma* (right) declines and the *adharma* (wrong) mounts he creates himself to establish the *dharma*."[164]

The passage of *mokṣadharma parva* of *Śānti Parva* mentions only six *avatāras* viz. the boar (varāha), the man-lion (Nṛsiṁha), the dwarf (Vāmana), Rāma of Bhṛgu race (Paraśurāma), Dāśarathi Rāma and that assumed for the destruction of Kaṁsa (Vāsudeva-Kṛṣṇa).[165] This passage is followed after a short interval by another in which ten incarnations are given adding swan (Haṁsa), tortoise (Kūrma) and fish (Matsya) in the beginning and Kalki at the end. This passage appears to have been interpolated when the number of *avatāras* became fixed at ten.[166] The Matsya, Kūrma and boar incarnations were earlier associated with Brahmā. The earliest account of Matsya incarnation is found in the *Śatapatha Brāhmaṇa*[167] which was afterwards regarded as an incarnation of Viṣṇu. In this passage a wonderful fish is described. It is not supposed to have been an incarnation of any of the gods. Later on, the *Mahābhārata* associated it with Brahmā and subsequently the Purāṇas described it as the first incarnation of Viṣṇu.

The legend about Kūrma incarnation shows that it is Brahmā and not Viṣṇu who assumed the form of a tortoise.[168] The *Śatapatha Brāhmaṇa*[169] refers to that story, "Having assumed the form of a tortoise, Prajāpati (Brahmā) created offspring. That which he created, he made", hence the word Kūrma. Kaśyapa means tortoise hence men say, "All creatures are descendants of Kaśyapa. This tortoise is the same as Āditya."[170] The boar incarnation is also related with Brahmā in the *Taittirīya*, and the *Śatapatha Brāhmaṇa*,[171] we are told that earth being immersed in the ocean, Brahmā, in the shape of a boar raised it on his tusk. The reason behind assigning the characteristics of one god to other is, as the worship of Brahmā became less popular whilst of Viṣṇu increased in its attraction the names, and works of the one deity appear to have been transferred to the other.[172] The growth of the concepts of *Chatur-vyūha* and *Pañcha-vīras* immensely contributed to the development of early Vaiṣṇavism.

Balarāma, the elder brother of Kṛṣṇa, is associated with Ananta (Śeṣa) in the *Mahābhārata*. The association of the pestle and the plough makes him a deity of the agriculturists.[173] The cult of Balarāma, which was one time more popular than the cult of Vāsudeva-Kṛṣṇa due to his association with the Nāgas and the agriculturists, later on it became completely subordinate to syncretistic divinity Nārāyaṇa-Vāsudeva. The dependence of Balarāma is referred to in the *Mahābhārata*. Balarāma admits frankly that he could not dare cast his eyes on world without the favour of Kṛṣṇa and so he followed and assisted Keśava in whatever he wished to achieve.[174]

Śrī is considered at first, the goddess of fertility, as Śrī *sūkta* calls her *Hariṇī*[175] a she-deer.[176] In the *Mahābhārata*, Śrī tells Indra that one of reasons behind leaving the Asuras is that they, now, do not look after their cattle but neglect by not providing pasture, grass and proper food.[177]

Once Śrī-Lakṣmī came to be accepted as the goddess of wealth and plenty, her cult was bound to attract all sections of people.[178]

The account of the origin of Śrī-Lakṣmi is given in the *Ādi Parva* of the *Mahābhārata* in the myth of churning of the ocean. Śrī clad in white garments came out of the sea along with moon (soma) wine (*surā*), the white steed (aśva), the jewel (kaustubha) and Dhanvantari (the physician) who carried the nector pot (*amṛta-ghaṭa*) in his hand.[179]

Before being constantly described as consort of Viṣṇu which is the latest feature of her legend in the *Mahābhārata*,[180] Śrī was associated with various gods, all of them well allied with her.[181] She is associated with Kubera, in whose palace she stayed. She is also described as staying with Indra[182] and said to have left Indra and joined Viṣṇu. In the *Mahābhārata* Śrī is often described as the wife of Nārāyaṇa-Viṣṇu or his incarnation Vāsudeva-Kṛṣṇa.[183] The reason behind leaving Indra may be the emergence of Viṣṇu cult as the successor of Indra.

The cult of Ekānaṁśā which was once more popular than that of Vāsudeva Kṛṣṇa lost her importance due to greater prominence given to the male gods. The story of her origin is given in the *Harivaṁśa*[184] which speaks about her as the daughter of Nanda and Yaśodā, an incarnation of Viṣṇu's power of illusion (Yoganidrā). When dashed against a stone by Kaṁsa rose in the sky and assuming her divine form and informed him of the birth of Kṛṣṇa. We are further told that girl did not die, she was brought up like a son among the Vṛṣṇis and was worshipped by them for having protected Kṛṣṇa.[185] Later on she is identified with Bhadrā or Subhadrā who is worshipped with Balarāma and Keśava at Purī temple in Orissā.[186]

The epics defined Śiva in Liṅga and human forms. He is said to be the creator and destroyer of the universe. It was Śiva who saved the cosmos from destruction in the episode of chruning of ocean by swallowing the *kālakūṭa* poison (also called *halāhala*) and became *Nīlakaṇṭha*.[187] The *Mahābhārata* furnishes good amount of information about Śaivism.

In *Droṇa Parva* of the *Mahābhārata* Śiva is hailed by Kṛṣṇa as the originator and destroyer of the world.[188] The thousand names of Śiva (*Śivasahasranāma* in *Anuśāsana Parva*)[189] speaks of his superiority over other cult deities. It is for the first time through the epic literature we find Śiva's association with dance and music. In the *Mahābhārata* Śiva is described not only as dance-crazy, an eternal dancer and dancer *par excellence*[190] but also sings and plays different kind of musical instruments with equal dexterity.[191] It is related to Naṭarāja aspect of Śiva which is vividly described in the subsequent literature and art.

The story of Dakṣa's sacrifice in which Pārvatī immolated herself was a later development. Earlier the story was altogether different and shows Śiva as demanding his share in the sacrifice.

An interesting myth develop around Śiva having three eyes in the *Mahābhārata* when he had been engaged in austerities. Umā, attended by her companions and dressed in ascetic garb, came behind him and playfully put her hands over his eyes. The effect was tremendous. Suddenly the world became dark, lifeless and destitute of oblations. The gloom, however, suddenly dispelled. A great flame burst from Mahādeva's forehead, in which a third eye luminous as the Sun was formed, and thus earned the name *'Tryambaka*.[192]

The reference to the *liṅga* worship is first time found in the epics. The practice of worship of phallus was not only prevalent in India but in many ancient cultures a god with phallus was worshipped. Ancient Egypt has two Geb and Min (whom the Greeks knew as Priapus).[193] Many Liṅgas or Phalli found from Indus Valley prove that the people of Indus Valley worshipped the god of fertility in the form of liṅga. The reference also occurs in the *Ṛgveda*.[194] It seems Rudra was not revered by the Aryans in the form of a phalli as Indra is besought not to let the *śiśnadevaḥ* approach the sacrifice and he is said to have slain the *śiśnadevaḥ,*when he won the treasure of the hundred gated-fort. The phallus (Liṅga) became symbolic of Śiva's generative power in the post-Vedic literature.[195]

In the *Rāmāyaṇa* we found Rāma and Rāvaṇa worshipping Śiva in the form of a *liṅga*. The *Anuśāsana Parva* of the *Mahābhārata* also informs the worship of Śiva in the form of a *liṅga* as no other god is worshipped in this manner.[196]

Umā the consort of Śiva, is known as Pārvatī only in a few late passages of the Rāmāyaṇa and the *Mahābhārata*. The earliest reference to Umā occurs in the *Kena Upaniṣad*. It is mentioned that on one occasion Brahman conquered the enemies of the gods, but the gods took credit to themselves for the victory and proud of their achievements. Agni, Vāyu and Indra were sitting together, engaged in joyous conversation, when there appeared at some distance a spirit. Agni first went out to see what it was. The spirit asked him the nature and extent of his power and laid down a blade of grass, which he asked him to burn away. Agni was not able to do this and returned baffled. Then went Vāyu, who also was not able to blow away the blade of grass, afterwards went Indra, and at his approach the spirit disappeared. Indra was disappointed, but he saw a beautiful woman named Umā-Haimavatī and asked her who the spirit was, she said it was Brahman.[197] The commentators of this passage declare that Umā means knowledge. By this time she is not identified as wife of Śiva. But, by the time of the *Baudhāyana Gṛhyasūtra*, the position of Rudra's consort is well established and she is worshipped like the god himself.[198]

Her common synonyms are, Giriputrī, Girirājaputrī, Śailarājaputrī, Girijā, Nāgarājaputrī, Girīśā and Parvatarājakanyā. Pārvatī is unknown as Durgā in the epic literature except[199] in the *Harivaṁśa* [200] and two late hymns in the *Mahābhārata*, which also give many other famous names as Durgā-Nandā, Śivā, Kṛṣṇā, Mandāravāsinī, Kumārī, Āryā, Kālī, Kapālī, Sandhyā, Rātri, Bhadrakālī, Kṛṣṇā Mahākālī, Chaṇḍī, Tāriṇī, etc.[201] The *Mahābhārata* styled her as the sister of Vāsudeva Kṛṣṇa.[202] The two famous Durgā *stotras* of the *Mahābhārata* sung by Yudhiṣṭhira and Arjuna respectivley, and one from the *Harivaṁśa Purāṇa*, contain evidence as seeds for the growth of Śakti cult as a separate identity.

Another deity who held in esteem is Kārttikeya or Skanda. He is regarded as the son of Śiva and Pārvatī but in the *Rāmāyaṇa* Agni, the god of fire, and Gaṅgā are portrayed as Skanda's parents. [203] The *Vana Parva* [204] of the *Mahābhārata* also describes him as the son of Agni, and his true wife Svāhā, who had assumed the forms of the wives of six Ṛṣis, whom Agni loved. But here he is called the son of Śiva also, as

Agni is one of the forms of that god.[205] There are many other stories which awarded parenthood of Skanda to Śiva and Pārvatī. The purpose of his birth was to kill the demon Tāraka and he was appointed as the commander-in-Chief of the Army of the Devas for that purpose.[206]

The god Brahmā emerged with the coming up of the epics, who is referred by Kauṭilya as a guardian deity. The word B*rahman* does occur in the *Ṛgveda* but it does not stand for Brahmā as god.[207] In the Vedas the notion of the personality of Brahmā is shared by a number of deities like Prajāpati, Vāchaspati, Brahmaṇaspati, Brahman, Hiraṇyagarbha, Dhātā, Vidhātā etc. Later on Brahmā is identified with these personalities.[208] Brahmā has no important role to play in the *Rāmāyaṇa* except bestowing boons on Rāma and also extending his favours to Rāvaṇa and other demons.[209] Brahmā is regarded as the creator of the world. There are many stories regarding his birth. The account given in the *Śānti Parva* says that he was born from the lotus that sprang from the navel of Viṣṇu.[210]

Sarasvatī, a spouse of Brahmā, is a goddess of importance in the Vedas. She is celebrated as a river [211] and in the *Śatapatha Brāhmaṇa* as goddess [212] and also identified with Vāk,[213] is called the mother of the Vedas in the *Mahābhārata.*[214]

The god Sūrya enjoys a favourable status in the epics. In the *Rāmāyaṇa,* important characters such as Rāma, Lakṣmana and Sītā and some Ṛṣis, are referred to as invoking Saviṭr, the latter with their hands raised upwards and facing the rising Sun.[215] In the *Mahābhārata* the Sun-god is portrayed in antropomorphic form. We are told in *Sabhā Parva* [216] that in the *Kṛta Yuga* of old the exalted deity Āditya once came down from heaven in the world of men.[217]

The description of Sūrya given in the *Mahābhārata* says that he has seven green steeds yoked to his chariot, having one wheel. Aruṇa is represented as his charioteer. Yama and Manu are his sons. He has an attendant named Daṇḍa. His two daughters named Tāptī and Yamī are also mentioned.[218] The hundred and eight pious names of Sūrya are also given in this text.[219]

Though Gaṇeśa finds mention in the *Mahābhārata* but not as the son of Śiva and Pārvatī, but as a scribe to the sage Vyāsa for writing down the *Mahābhārata.*[220] He does not appear as an elephant-headed deity in the epics except in the *Mahābhārata* in the introduction which is considered as a late addition. And moreover, *Gaṇeśa,* the Lord of hosts, is an epithet of Śiva in the *Mahābhārata.*

The deities like Yakṣas and Nāgas are mentioned in the epics as semi-gods.

The stories regarding the origin of the Yakṣas are narrated in the epics. The *Ādi Parva* of the *Mahābhārata* tells us that the Yakṣas were born after Brahmā's birth from the *aṇḍā* of the *Virāṭa Puruṣa.*[221] In another passage of the same *Parva* the Yakṣas are said to be the progeny of the sage Pulastya. The palace of Kubera, the king of Yakṣas, is described in the *Mahābhārata.* It is said that earlier Lakṣmī was associated with Kubera but later on she was associated with Viṣṇu.

The Nāgas were the progeny of Kadru and Kaśyapa[222] and dwell in the beautiful underground city of Bhogavatī.[223] The sacrifice of Janamejaya, which he performed to take the revenge of the death of his father Parīkṣita by the serpent king Takṣaka. The episode of Kāliya-mardan in the *Harivaṁśa* indicates that the cult of Nāgas was superseded by the cult of Kṛṣṇa.

The Gandharvas and Kinnaras, who possessed human heads and horse's bodies, were the celestial musicians.[224] The number of Gandharvas is fixed as 27 in some *Yajus* texts and is even said to be 6333 in the *Atharvaveda.* [225] The evidence of the *Ṛgveda* is so scanty and vague that no definite idea as to its original character is possible to arrive at. Gandharva is often associated with Soma[226] in the *Ṛgveda.* Their connection with water made their association possible with the Apsarases[227], which dwell in the waters.[228]

c. Ist Century A.D. to 3rd Century A.D.

The advent of foreigners, the Greeks, the Śakas, the Pārthians and the Kuṣāṇas during the period under review did not effect the growth of religious cults, but as a result of their patronage to indigenous cults these grew more vigorously.

Many foreigner adopted the Indian cults due to certain reasons. Firstly, since the alien tribe wanted to settle down permanently, therefore, these adopted the culture and traditions of this country. Secondly they were personally impressed by the existing cults in India owing to superior appeal.

The *Nāṭya-śāstra* of Bharata invokes gods like Śiva, Brahmā, Viṣṇu, Indra[229], Sarasvatī, Lakṣmī, Siddhi, Medhā, Soma (Chandra), Sūrya, Marut, Lokapālas,[230] Rudra, Garuḍa, Nāgarāja, Samudra, Muni, Bhūtas, Piśāchas, Yakṣas, Asuras and Apsarās. In another passage author prayed to six-headed Kārttikeya.[231] This evidence from the *Nāṭya śāstra* proves the existence of various cults.

An inscription of the first century A. D. recovered from a well at Morā village, seven km. West of Mathurā city, records the setting up of the statues of the holy five heroes of the Vṛṣṇis in a stone temple built by a woman named Tośā. The images, made of stone were meant for worship and are said to have a glowing and exceedingly handsome appearance.[232] Lüder identified the five heroes as Baladeva, Akrūra, Anadhrsti, Sarana and Viduratha on the basis of Jaina sources.[233] But J. N. Banerjea with help of a passage in the *Vāyu Purāṇa* identifies them as Baladeva, Vāsudeva, Sāmba, Pradyumna and Aniruddha.[234]

The coins immensely help us to gauge the position of various cults. The coins of the Kuṣāṇas portray deities belonging to the pantheons of Greek, Brahmanical, Buddhist and Zoroastrian.[235]

The most popular Brahmanical deity during the Kuṣāṇa era was Śiva. He is depicted in aniconic, theriomorphic and anthropomorphic forms on the coins. His anthropomorphic form can be seen on the coins of all four principal Kuṣāṇa rulers viz. Wema Kadphises, Kaniṣka, Huviṣka and Vāsudeva[236]. It is surprising not to find Śiva's phallic representation on the Kuṣāṇā coins whereas the deity is shown with all his traditional attributes except the serpent. The first representation of Śiva in theriomorphic form i.e. humped-bull is found on the coins of Kadphises I. Wema Kadphises was a staunch devotee of Śiva, which is evident from his epithet *Mahiśvara* which stands for Maheśvara, probably meaning the devotee of Maheśvara (Śiva).[237]

The figure of Śiva has been used as common reverse device on the Wema Kadphises's coins with the exception of only one type of coin where we find only a Śavite emblem trident with battle-axe. This type assumes special importance since after Wema Śiva has not been represented in aniconic form on the Kuṣāṇa coins.

Śiva in human-form on these (Wema Kadphises) coins is two-armed. He is invariably shown as standing frontly, *abhaṅga* [238] with face turned to his left, wearing head-dress and drapery over shoulder, holding trident in right hand, before the bull right to left.[239] The coins of Gondophares also depict him in this manner. Sometimes he is depicted holding trident and battle-axe in his right hand.[240]

A unique coin of Wema on which Śiva with his head to left, holds trident in right hand, carries drapery over left arm hanging at back, flames rise from head and behind him stands an humped bull to right.[241]

Though on the coins of Kaniṣka deities of the other pantheons are also depicted yet Śiva continued to occupy important position. Śiva has been named as *Oesho* on the coins of Kaniṣka. This title was adopted as an appellation of Śiva by all the subsequent rulers.[242]

Śiva is usually depicted on coins of Kaniṣka as two or four-armed deity, standing to his left, nimbate, hair on top of head. The four-armed figure holds respectively a vase, a drum, a trident and a goat.[243] Sometimes goat is replaced by an antelope. Śiva invariably appears on Kaniṣka coins without his mount.

The iconic development of Śiva is further descernible on the coins of Huviṣka. Śiva can be seen on these coins in three forms namely one-faced, three-faced, and Śiva with Umā possessing two or four arms.

On the reverse of Huviṣka gold coins, Śiva is three-headed, nimbate, clad only in waist band, ithyphallic, has four arms and carried goat, wheel, trident and thunderbolt.[244]

The appearance of Śiva with three faces marks a significant development which portray him as Mahādeva, the great god, or probably represent three different aspects of Śiva as Creator, Preserver and Destroyer.[245]

On the reverse coins of Huviṣka, sometimes, we find two standing figures, male and female, facing each other. On right side the Indian god Śiva is shown nimbate, four-armed holding a deer and trident with two left hands, and a small drum and water vessel in his two right hands. On left the goddess Nānaia, is seen diademed and holding her peculiar symbol. To right OKPO to left NĀNO.[246]

On the coins of Vāsudeva Śiva is depicted as two-armed or four-armed having one or three faces. On the reverse of one of the gold coins Śiva is represented facing, having three faces and two arms hold wreath and trident standing before bull left to right.[247] This marks further development in iconography showing Śiva as three-faced and two-armed.

The pageant of gods, goddesses and mythical figures from almost all ancient pantheons on Kuṣāṇa coins is startling. Although Viṣṇu does not appear on any Kuṣāṇa coin available to us so far. But the evidence of a 'nicolo seal', struck during the period of Huviṣka proves that the Kuṣāṇa king accorded due respect to this Brahmanical god.[248] The above seal shows an alien chief, wearing the typical head-dress attributed to Huviṣka, standing in suppliant attitude before the four-armed Viṣṇu. Ghirshman found a combination of Viṣṇu, Śiva and Mihira in the representation.[249] But according to Cunningham and figure of deity depicts only Viṣṇu.[250]

A copper coin of Huviṣka, now in the Indian Museum,[251] has a legend which Smith reads as 'OOSNA' written by the side of the figure of a deity. On the basis of the legend the deity has been identified with Viṣṇu. But the reading of the legend seems to be doubtful, because the attributes of the deity as described by Smith from right, to left are thunderbolt, trident, water-vessel and wreath. None of these attributes have affinity with the emblems of Viṣṇu. Rather these attributes are found with Śiva as depicted on a large number of Kuṣāṇa coins.[252]

The reverse of unique stater of Huviṣka depicts a female figure with Śiva.[253] Rapson has read the accompanying legend as *Ommo.* This coin was first published by Cunningham, who identified the figure with goddess Nānā (or Nānaia). But the figure cannot represent Nānā because a peculiar sceptre, tiped with a horse head is usually seen in the hand of Nānā. But the goddess holds a different object which is most probably a flower.[254] Since she appears with Śiva and the legend describes her as OMMO, she may easily be identified with Umā, the consort of Śiva.[255]

On a copper coin of Huviṣka we find an archer standing to right holding a bow as long as himself with string inwards, accompanied by the legend in Brāhmi script as *Gaṇeso.*[256] The name Gaṇeśa generally denotes the elephant-headed god who is described in the Pūraṇic accounts as the son of Pārvatī. In *Bṛhat Saṁhitā* Gaṇeśa is described as elephant-faced, pot-bellied, holding a hatchet *(paraśu)* and a ball of sweet (modaka) and having one tooth. The present coin has no similarity in any respect with the above description. The word *Gaṇeśa* probably stands for Śiva as it denoted the deity as lord of Gaṇas, which in wider sense stands for Bhūtanātha, lord of all created beings. Thus coin of Huviṣka presented Śiva in rare and unique fashion.[257]

Sūrya is frequently depicted symbolically on early indigenous coins but we find only one coin from Avantī on which he is depicted anthropomorphically. The figure of the deity in human form have been found on the coins of Indo-Greeks and Kuṣāṇas.[258] These figures of the Sun-god are associated with non-Indian cults related to Greek and Zoroastrian religions called Helios and Mihira[259] respectively.

The figure of Helios riding a four-horsed chariot may be seen on the reverse of the coins of the Indo-Greek king Plato.[260] Helios is shown to right, radiating and clad in chiton and chlamys. The parallel of this figure can be found from Bodh-Gayā where Sun is riding in a chariot drawn by four horses. A bronze coin of Philoxenus shows on the obverse, Helios riding on a four-horsed chariot, clad in chiton, himation and boots, holding in his left hand a sceptre and extending his right arm.[261] According to Chattopadhyay in the pre-Christian epoch there existed two distinct solar cults, one Indian having the Vedic Sūrya as its supreme god and the other alien god Helios or Mihira, wearing characteristically foreign dress. The alien Solar cults, although mainly confined to the western Punjab region, yet it considerably succeeded in influencing the indigenous cult.[262] The figure of Helios as seen on the coins of Philoxenus served as a prototype of the figures of Helios or Mihira on the coins of Kaniṣka and Huviṣka.[263] The figure of Sun-god is found with Greek legends MIPO, MIOPO or MIYOPO but never Mihira.[264] On the gold coins of Kaniṣka the figure of Helios, is seen diademed, clad in chiton and himation, with a radiating disc behind head, right hand advanced and left placed on hip.[265] On the coins of Huviṣka Mihira is shown radiate, holds wreath and sceptre and sword at waist,[266] sometimes he is shown radiate, left hand holds spear, right rest on hip, sword at waist.[267]

The cult of Mother-goddess also became quite popular during the period under review. Nānā (Umā Or Ambikā) this name is found on Kuṣāṇa gold and copper coins in different forms viz. NĀṆĀ, NĀNAIA, NANAPAO, NĀNO etc.[268] She is depicted on the coins of Kaniṣka, Huviṣka and Vāsudeva.

On the coins of Kaniṣka she is represented as nimbate and diademed, head surmounted by crescent, holding sceptre (ending in forepart of horse) in left hand,[269] and a bowl in right hand. On the coins of Huviṣka deity faces to left, hold staff with animal protome in right hand and a bowl in the left hand.[270] The coins of Vāsudeva[271] depicts her similarly in the fashion as on the coins of Huviṣka. A novel depiction of Nānā has been seen on the coins of Huviṣka. The diety sits frontly on lion, face to right, nimbate, wears a helmet with a lunar crescent, holds staff with animal protome in right hand and hold indeterminate object[272]. This device became a matter of contention among scholars. Nānā was a Mesopotamian goddess[273], a daughter of moon[274] identified with Akkadian as well as Assyrian deity Ishtar. One of the conceptions of Ishtar was that of a mother goddess and lion was sacred to her. In ancient Mesopotamian glyptic arts and statury she appears often armed with arrows or a mace, carrying flowers or a sceptre standing on a lion, or lions, accompanied by the planet venus whose astrological forces she embodied.[275] Ishtar and Nānā were connected with Anahita, the Persian goddess of fertility and war. These were further identified with Iranian Aphrodite, the goddess of vegetation, meadow, fertility, marriage, love, prosperity of men and beast due to their lunar aspect.[276]

Nānā is further correlated with Umā or Pārvatī, a consort of Śiva.[277] This presumption is based on a gold medal or coin in the British Museum which displays on the obverse a female figure wearing a turreted crown, clad in a loose robe or chiton and holding a half-opened lotus in her right hand. The inscription refers her Aṁpā, the deity of Pakhalavadi or Puṣkarāvatī of ancient Gandhāra (north-west region of Pakistan). The expression may stand for Aṁpā or Aṁbā, a mother as well as Durgā, the consort of Śiva. The identification of the deity as the consort of Śiva is also supported by the appearance of a bull on the reverse of the medal as bull is considered to be the theriomporphic form of Śiva. As Śiva was highly revered in ancient Gandhāra, where Puṣkarāvatī was situated. So his consort Aṁbā would have been regarded as the presiding deity or the mother goddess of that area. Her connection with Puṣkarāvatī, the name literally means, the lotus city, is further emphasised by the lotus in her right hand.[278]

The connection of Aṁbā or Durgā with Umā is further gauged by the coins of Huviṣka. On one coin Oesho depicted on the proper right and Ommo on proper left and holding a lotus. On other few coins of the same ruler the female figure standing by the side by Oesho is referred to Nāno.[279] This numismatic evidence thus distinguishes Nānā as a consort of Śiva and identifies or at least associates her with Umā alias Aṁbā. It seems that the concept of divine maternity common to Aṁbā, Umā and Nānā led to the identification of each with others. The lion was associated with her in the time of Azes I or II (middle of Ist century B.C. to the end of first quarter of Ist century)[280] as on some of coins of Azes a female figure holding a lotus flower in the right, and besides her a lion is shown.[281]

On the coins of Kaniṣka, Huviṣka and Vāsudeva goddess Ardoksho (counterpart of Indian Lakṣmī) is represented in various ways.[282] On Kaṇiṣka's coin, she is represented as female figure to right, wearing modius and nimbate, clad in chiton and himation, holds cornucopiae.[283] Later on she is depicted as seated on a throne nimbate, facing, with her feet on a foot stool, holds wreath and cornucopiae.[284]

The coins of Huviṣka depicts her as female deity to right in Greek attire, holding cornucopiae in both hands.[285] On Vāsudeva's coins goddess is seated on throne holding cornucopiae.[286] Arodoksho or Ashishang was a Persian goddess, who brings heavenly wisdom to men as well as all sorts of desirable things-jewelled furniture, offspring, chariots, swift arrows, sturdy camels, boards of gold and silver and victory.[287] She corresponds to Lakṣmī, the Indian goddess of prosperity, success, beauty, radiance and glory, and also to the Greek goddess Tyche and Roman Fortuna.[288]

The only foreign ruler to depict Kārttikeya, under the names of Skanda, Kumāra, Viśākha and Mahāsena, is the Kuṣāṇa king Huviṣka.[289] Mahāsena, a form of Skanda, is shown nimbate and diademed clad in coat and chalmys, holding standard surmounted by bird in right hand and a sword in left hand.[290]

A pillar surmounted a figure of cock on the top is found from Lālā Bhagat of this period from Kānpur.[291] C. Sivaramamurti has placed this pillar in the Śuṅga Period.[292] This device (cock on top post) is also found on the coins of Ayodhyā rulers, Devamitra[293] and Vijaymitra.[294]

Skanda and Viśākha are shown standing face to face, nimbate, each wearing chalmys and necklace, and sword at waist. On other coin of Huviṣka, Skanda holds in right hand a standard surmounted by bird and Viśākha carries a spear in left hand.[295]

There is another depiction, Skanda and Viśākha stand as above between them Mahāsena is shown horned facing, nimbate, clad in chalmys, and sword near waist.[296]

The coins of Huviṣka, according to D. R. Bhandarkar, contain three or four figures corresponding to three or four different names of the god Skanda, Kumāra, Viśākha and Mahāsena (Skando-Komaro-Bizago-Maaceno). He also believes that Skanda, Kumāra, Viśākha and Mahāsena were four different gods and not one god. Kārttikeya is given seventeen names in the *Amarakośa*.[297] In the above mentioned coins, the words *Skando* and *Komaro* have been written together and that too side by side in one line, indicating thereby that they (Skando and Komaro) form the name of one and only one god, while Bizago and Maaceno written separately evidently stand for two other gods. Banerjea has, therefore, rightly suggested that they were only three gods (three aspects of the same god) viz. Skanda-Kumāra, Viśākha and Mahāsena. It further proves as detailed in the *Mahābhārata,* the merger of various god concepts of allied character which went in the composition of Skanda-Kārttikeya cults. It is thus evident that Skanda and Viśākha were considered to be two different divinities up to the time of the Kuṣāṇa king Huviṣka, who ruled in the first half of the second century A.D. But these different deities, having, independent existence on Huviṣka's coins, fused into one sometimes after the rule of Huviṣka.[298] It is supported by a passage in the *Mahāmayūrī.*[299]

The anthropomorphic representation of Kārttikeya appears on the coins of Yaudheyas. The god appears poly-cephalous on one unique silver[300] and certain copper coins.[301] The obverse of these coins shows Kārttikeya, six-headed (Ṣaḍānana) but two-armed, standing holding a long spear *(śakti)* in right hand with left resting on his hip. The date assigned to these coins is 2nd century A.D. It has been suggested that the Yaudheyas introduced a new iconographic trait which was not popular with the contemporary sculptors and artists by representing Kārttikeya as six-headed on their coins. Early sculptures from Mathurā belonging to the Kuṣāṇa period show plain two-armed and single headed Kārttikeya. On Yaudheyas coins the six heads of Kārttikeya have been arranged in two rows with three heads in a row. Vertically seen the heads have been placed one upon the other. All the six heads have matted locks (*jaṭā*). The device of substituting more heads on top was known to Indian sculptors from the Mathurā region during the second century A.D.[302]

Another variety of copper coins of Yaudheyas, influenced by Kuṣāṇa type and style, belonging to the third and fourth centuries A.D., bear on the obverse the figure of Kārttikeya standing accompanied by his peacock on left. The god holds a spear in his right hand while the left rests on his hip.[303]

c. 3rd Century A.D. to 6th Century A.D.

The age of Guptas, as remarked by R. N. Dandekar, was not an age of renaissance but of the efflorescence of Hindu religion and culture.[304] Though the Gupta rulers were the patrons of Vaiṣṇava cult and styled themselves as *paramabhāgavatas* yet they did not cast off their eyes from other existing cults. The Brahmanical cults, which were evoluting from ancient times, reached to their zenith. The final shape was given by the Purāṇic Hinduism which flourished during the classical period of Indian history. At present there are 18 Purāṇas divided among the three main cult deities-Brahmā, Viṣṇu and Maheśa. Each deity is conferred with 6 Purāṇas on their personal *guṇas* (*rajas, sattva* and *tamas*).

Viṣṇu became the most popular deity of this period and in the *Viṣṇu Purāṇa,* he is designated as 'Creator, Preserver and Destroyer' of the *universe.*[305] The *Amarakośa* of Amarasiṁha gives a long list of 46 names of *Viṣṇu.*[306] The *Bṛhat Saṁhitā* of Varāhamihira mentions the iconometry of the *Viṣṇu image.*[307]

The popularity of Bhāgavatism, now synonymous with Vaiṣṇavism, is further attested by numerous inscriptions found from every nook and corner of India.[308] The Mehraulī Iron Pillar inscription of Chandragupta II states that lofty standard (i.e. Iron pillar) of the divine Viṣṇu was set up on the hill called *Viṣṇupāda.*[309]

The Udaigiri cave inscriptions of Chandragupta II dated c 401 A.D., which is written on the upper part of a smoothed and countersunk panel above two figures (one of the four armed god Viṣṇu, attended by his two wives, and the other twelve-armed goddess one of the forms of Lakṣmī, the consort of Viṣṇu).[310]

The Junāgarh rock inscription of Skandagupta inscribed in 455-56 and 457-58 A.D. records the construction of a temple of Chakṛabhṛt (i.e. Viṣṇu).[311] The Bhītarī inscription of Skandagupta dated 455-467 A.D. speaks of the installation of the image of Śarīngīn (i.e. Viṣṇu).[312] The Gadhwā inscription of the time of Skandagupta of 467-68 A.D. records the insallation of an image of Anatasvāmin Viṣṇu and a grant of some land at a village belonging to the same god under the name of Chitrakūṭasvāmin.[313] The Eran inscription of Buddhagupta of 484 A.D. refers of the erection of a *dhvajastambha* dedicated to Janārdana by Mātṛviṣṇu and Dhanyaviṣṇu.[314]

The Gaṅgādhar inscription of the time of Viśvavarman, records the erection of a temple of Viṣṇu by Mayūrarakṣaka, (a minister of Viśvavarman).[315]

Thus, it is evidently clear that the cult of Viṣṇu had become fairly popular in the age of the Guptas under several names such as Chakrabhṛt, Śāringīn, Anatasvāmin, Chitrakūṭasvāmin etc.[316]

Viṣṇu had also become a favourite device on the Gupta coins and depicted in theriomorphic and anthropomorphic forms.

As far as his theriomorphic representation is concerned, Viṣṇu appears to have the form of Garuḍa. Garuḍa is seen on the Standard[317] and the Kacha[318] type of coins of Samudragupta and the Archer Type coins of all the Imperial Gupta monarchs. On these coins Garuḍa is shown as a plumb bird with outspread wings and placed on the top of the column, which is accordingly called *Garuḍadhvaja*.[319] On the reverse of the silver coins of Chandragupta II the Garuḍa has been depicted in the form of a full-fledged bird with outspread wings.[320] A peculiar change in the iconography of the Garuḍa is marked in the copper issues of Chandragupta II showing hybrid form with human face and arms (adorned with bracelets) but its body is that of a bird having outspread wings.[321]

On the obverse of a copper coin of Chandragupta II Viṣṇu is depicted as *Chakra* or wheel which is an attribute of Viṣṇu.[322] Viṣṇu is depicted as a Chakra-Puruṣa on the obverse of the Chakra-Vikrama type of gold coins of Chandragupta II. The coin shows a deity standing within a double rimmed wheel which is oval in shape and goes round the entire body of the deity above the knees. The deity has a crown wears a *dhotī,* and is adorned with necklace and wristlets in hands and holds a mace *(gadā)* in the left hand.[323]

The idea of incarnation *(avatāra)* became established and popular through the composition of the Purāṇas during the Gupta period. The contradictory views regarding the number of *avatāras* found in the *Pūraṇas* may be regional variations or a matter of family tradition of the composer. A verse of the *Bhagavadgītā* refers to innumerable incarnations.[324]

The *Vāyu Pūraṇa* gives the description of the ten *avatāras.* They are Haṁsa, Yajña, Nṛsiṁha, Veda Vyāsa, Vāsudeva-Kṛṣṇa and Kalki.[325] The *Matsya Purāṇa* also gives a table of ten *avatāras.* They are Dattātreya, Māndhātā, Jamadagni, Dāśarathi Rāma, Veda Vyāsa, Buddha and Kalki.[326]

The Purāṇas delineated the causes of descent of god on earth through the stories. Matsya (fish), came when the earth has overwhelmed by a universal flood. Viṣṇu took the form of a fish, who first warned Manu of the impending danger and then carried him, his family and the seven great sages (Ṛṣis) in a ship fastended to a horn on his head. Viṣṇu also saved the Vedas from the flood.

Kūrma (Tortoise) : Many precious treasures including *amṛta* were lost in the flood. Viṣṇu took the shape of a great tortoise and on his back gods placed the Mount Mandāra and twining the divine snake Vāsuki around the mountain churned the ocean. From the churned ocean emerged the *amṛta* and other precious treasures including Lakṣmī.

Varāha (Boar) : A demon, Hiraṇyākṣa cast the earth once more into the depths of the cosmic ocean. Viṣṇu took the form of an enormous boar, killed the demon and raised the earth on his tusk.[327]

Kālidāsa also mentions the Varāha incarnation in the *Raghuvaṁśa*.[328] No other *avatāra* of Viṣṇu seems to have been glorified during the regime of the Guptas as prominently as the Varāha-*avatāra.*

The Eran inscription of Toramāṇa and Dhanyaviṣṇu hails Viṣṇu in the form of Boar.[329] Moreover Cave No. 4 at Udaigiri is dedicated to this god and two colossal image of Vārāha have come to light from Eran.

Nṛsiṁha : the demon Hiraṇyakśipu obtained a boon from Brahmā that he could not be killed either in day or night, by god, man and beast. Thus being saved he teased men including his pious son Prahalāda. When Prahalāda called Viṣṇu for help who appeared before him in the form of a half-man and half-lion when it was neither day or night and killed the demon.[330]

This incarnation of Viṣṇu seems to be favourite in Gupta society.

The 'Lion-trampler Type' coins of Kumāragupta contain a legend *Nṛsiṁha* as it were incarnate, the lion like Mahendra, is ever victorious.[331]

Vāmana (Dwarf) : A demon named Bali gained supernatural powers through asceticism and became a fear for the gods. Viṣṇu appeared before him and asked as a boon as much space he could cover in three strides. When the boon was granted the god became a giant, and in two strides covered earth, heaven and middle air. Somehow he refrained from taking third stride and left the infernal regions to the demon.[332]

In the *Meghadūta* Kālidāsa has referred to this *avatāra* of Viṣṇu[333].

Paraśurāma (Rāma with an axe) : Viṣṇu took the human form and became the son of a brāhmaṇa Ṛṣi Jamadagni. When Jamadagni robbed by Kārtavīrya, Parśurāma killed the latter. The sons of Kārtavīrya in their turn killed Jamadagni. This enraged Paraśurāma and he destroyed the Kṣatriya race for twenty-one times in succession.[334]

The incarnation of Paraśurāma is cited by Kālidāsa in the Meghadūta.[335]

Rāma : the hero of the *Rāmāyaṇa* was the prince of Ayodhya. Viṣṇu incarnates himself in this form to save the humanity from the oppressions of the demon Rāvaṇa.

The story of Rāma and his lineage is beautifully delineated in the *Raghuvaṁśa.* The *Pratimānāṭakam* and the *Abhiṣekanāṭakam* of Bhāsa are based on the episodes of the Rāmāyaṇa.

Kṛṣṇa : the most popular and important incarnation of Viṣṇu, saved the world from the clutches of Kaṁsa. The whole fifth book (*khaṇḍa*) of the *Viṣṇu Purāṇa* contains a detailed biography of cowherd Kṛṣṇa in which the same adventures are described which we find in the *Harivaṁśa.*[336] The enchanting stories of the childhood of Kṛṣṇa are also beautifully captured by Bhāsa in his play the *Bālacharita.* His other play the *Dūtavākya* deals with the episode of the *Mahābhārata.*

A very striking reference to Kṛṣṇa is made in the Bhitarī pillar inscription of Skandagupta. Describing in a picturesque manner, Skandagupta encounter with the Huṇas, after his victory over Puṣyamitra, the inscription hails, "who, when (his) father had attained the skies, conquered (his) enemies by the strength of (his) arm, and established again the ruined fortunes of (his) lineage, and betook himself to (his) mother, whose eyes were full of tears from joy, just as Kṛṣṇa, when he had slain (his) enemies, betook himself to (his mother) Devakī.[337]

Buddha : the founder of Buddhism is also considered the incarnation of Viṣṇu, who descended on earth to preach the world the notion of Ahiṁsā.

Kalki : is yet to be born. At the end of this dark age Viṣṇu will appear in the form of a man mounted on a white horse with a flaming sword in his hand. He will judge the wicked, reward the good and restore the age of gold.[338]

The rationalist interpretation of these *avatāras* can be given in the words of R. N. Dandekar. In the beginning there was water everywhere and to suit this condition of the world, the first incarnation of Viṣṇu was in the form of a fish. Then when part of water transformed into land, the second incarnation of Viṣṇu appeared as a tortoise which could move easily both on land and in water. The later stages of evolution-namely, the animal life in the forests, the life of wild humanity, (Primitive man) the meagerly developed condition of warring cave man, the development of family life and domestic virtues and growth of complex social and political relations—are said to have been symbolically represented respectively by Varāha (boar), Nṛsiṁha, Vāmana (dwarf), Paraśurāma (axe-man), Rāma and Kṛṣṇa.[339]

Lakṣmī, the goddess of fortune, is held in high esteem in Gupta era. It is in this period with the coming of the *Purāṇas* she was clearly and exclusively associated with *Viṣṇu.*[340] And a passage from the *Viṣṇu Purāṇa* shows this union. "As the lord of worlds, the god of gods Janārdana descends amongst mankind in various shapes, so does his consort Śrī. Thus, when Hari was born a dwarf, the son of Aditi Lakṣmī appeared from the lotus as Padmā, or Kamalā, when He was born as Rāma (Paraśurāma) of the race of Bhṛgu, she was Dhariṇī, when He was Rāghava (Rāmachandra), She was Sītā, and when He was Kṛṣṇa she was Rukmini. In the other descents of Viṣṇu she was his associate. If He takes a celestial form, she appears as divine, if a mortal, she becomes a mortal too, transforming her own person agreeably to whatever character it pleases Viṣṇu to assume."[341]

The *Amarakośa* gives synonymous of her names[342] and Kālidasā describes her in the *Raghuvaṁśa* as sitting on lotus and caressing the feet of Lord Viṣṇu.[343]

The popularity of Lakṣmī can be further gauged through the inscriptions and coin-devices of this period on which she is depicted abundantly. The Udaigiri cave inscription of Chandragupta II of 401 A.D., is written over two figures including one four-armed god Viṣṇu attended by his two wives and a twelve-armed goddess Lakṣmī.[344] The Junāgarh rock inscription of Skandagupta refers to Śrī-Lakṣmī with Viṣṇu, the latter being the permanent abode of the former.[345] The Gwālior stone inscription of the time of Mihirkula speaks of Viṣṇu as one who bears the goddess Śrī on his breast.[346] The Sārnāth inscription of Prakaṭāditya [347] and the Aphsad inscription of Ādityasena also speaks of Śrī as the wife of Vāsudeva.[348]

Lakṣmī on several types of coins of Samudragupta viz. 'Standard Type'[349], 'Archer Type'[350], can be seen holding a cornucopiae in her left hand and a noose in right hand.

As far as the representation of Lakṣmī is concerned minute change occur on the 'Battle-Axe Type' [351] and 'Lyrist Type' coins. Here, she is shown holding a noose in right hand and a cornucopiae or lotus bud in left hand.[352] Further, on the reverse of the Kacha Type she holds a flower in the right hand and a cornucopiae in the left hand.[353]

Lakṣmī appears on several types of coins of Chandragupta II. On the 'Archer Type' of coins the goddess is seen seated on a throne[354] as well as on lotus, holding a noose in right hand and a lotus in her left hand.[355] On one specimen the goddess of wealth can be seen scattering out gold coins by her right hand.[356] Another specimen shows a peculiar conical object above the right hand of the goddess. It is most probably a conch-shell.[357] On several specimen Lakṣmī is seen holding a noose in right hand and a lotus in left hand which is resting on the thigh.[358] On the reverse of "Chhatra Type" of coins of Chandragupta II Lakṣmī appears walking and usually holding a noose in right hand and lotus in left hand.[359] Lakṣmī is seen on the reverse of 'Couch Type' either holding a noose and a lotus in her right and left hands respectively[360] or with her right hand opened out and empty and holding a lotus in her left hand.[361] On the reverse of 'Horseman Type' of coins Lakṣmī appears holding a noose in her right hand and lotus in left hand.[362] On 'Chakravikrama Type' she is depicted standing on lotus with her right hand bent and its forefinger apparently pointing at something, her left hand is slightly bent and holding a lotus with a long stalk having a bud.[363] The figure of Lakṣmī appears on at least five different varieties on coins of Kumāra gupta I[364] On the reverse of the 'Archer Type' Lakṣmī holds flower in right hand and left hand resting empty on thigh.[365] "Apratigha Type' shows her left hand bent up and holding a lotus.[366] Lakṣmī can be seen on the 'Horseman Type' resting her left hand on waist and holding a lotus with long stalk, right hand holding a bunch of grapes to feed the peacock in her front.[367] On the reverse of 'Elephant Type' she is depicted standing, her right hand is bent up and holds a lotus creeper and left hand rests on waist holding a cornucopiae.[368] The 'Archer type'[369], the 'King and Lakṣmī Type'[370] and the Chhatra Type'[371] depicts her almost in a same manner holding a noose in her outstretched right hand and lotus in the left which rests on her knee.

The cult of Trimūrti, the Divine triad, which became popular in the later part of Hinduism, is mentioned in the *Purāṇas.*[372] The concept of Trimūrti is not a new one as in the Vedas, also, triad is formed by Agni, Sūrya and Indra. The Purāṇic concept is new in the sense that it accorded special duties and privileges to each god. Brahmā to create, Viṣṇu to preserve and Śiva to destroy. In the view of R.N. Dandekar, the Hindu triad represents an attempt to bring about a religious synthesis between Vaiṣṇavism and Śaivism on the one hand and between these two popular religious movements and Brahmanism on the other.[373]

Śiva was not quite popular among Gupta rulers yet it made a remarkable position in the society. It is impossible to give a connected account of the life of this deity. His career was not clearly defined like an *avatāra* of Viṣṇu, of which we have a history of his birth, life and death. Though he often appeared on earth in human form and frequently dwelt at his favourite city Vārāṇasī or Kāśī but his heavenly home was at Kailāsa or Himalāyas.[374]

Many stories regarding the birth of Śiva occurs in the Purāṇas. In the *Viṣṇu Purāṇa* we are told that in the beginning of the *kalpa* while Brahmā was meditating upon the birth of a son like himself a child, deep blue in colour, appeared on his lap and began running about crying aloud. The child asked Brahmā to give him a name. Though Brahmā told him that his name was Rudra and asked him not to cry, he cried seven times more. Then Brahmā gave him another seven names and the total eight names, eight *mūrtis* , wives and children were allotted. Bhava, Śarva, Īśāna, Paśupati, Bhīma, Ugra and Maheśvara were his additional seven names.[375]

Basically all these myths and stories of the *Purāṇas* have been created to propagate the cults among the masses.

The concept of Śiva as 'originator, preserver and destroyer' of the world firmly established with the *Purāṇas.* This made him the supreme godhead. The proof of this can be cited from the *Vāyu Purāṇa* where Brahmā and Viṣṇu are introduced as propitiating Mahādeva and receiving boons from his favours.[376] The *Amarakośa* refers to 48 names of Śiva.[377] Kālidāsa wrote the *Kumārasaṁbhavam* during this period discussing the marriage of Śiva and Pārvatī and the birth of their son Kārttikeya.

The Archaeological sources of this period also prove that the cult of Śiva occupied a high rank in the Gupta society. The Udaigiri cave inscription of Chandragupta II is Śaiva in character. The object of it is to record the excavation of the cave as a temple of the god Śiva, under the name of Śaṁbhu, by the orders of Vīrasena Saba, minister of Chandragupta II.[378] The Karmanda inscription (437 A.D.) mentions that Pṛthvīsena, the son of Śikharasvāmin, who was *mantrī* and afterwards *mahābalādhikṛta* of Kumāragupta I, constructed a temple of Śiva in order to commemorate his own name.[379] The cultic form of Śiva appears on the coins of Kuṣāṇa kings, but this is never the case with Gupta coins. It is quite strange that we do not find the figure of Śiva on any known Gupta issue.[380] The bull which is the mount of Śiva appears on the reverse of some silver issues of Skandagupta.[381]

The theriomorphic representation of Śiva in the form of *liṅga* was held in high esteem during this age and references of it occur abundantly in the Purāṇic literature. In the *Vāyu* and the *Brahmāṇḍa Purāṇa* the *liṇga* is used as a symbol of Śiva.[382]

The superiority of *liṅga* worship over the cult of Brahmā and Viṣṇu is described in the *Vāyu Purāṇa* through the pillar of flames.[383]

The form of Ardhanārīśvara seems to be quite well-known in the Gupta society. As Kālidāsa mentions this form of god in the *Kumārasaṁbhavam*[384] and the *Raghuvaṁśa*.[385]

The confrontation of two cults Vaiṣṇava and Śaiva was solved by devising a syncristic image of Hari-Hara which meant that each of them is one-half of the highest god, or the original form of God is said to be composed of two halves known individually as Śiva and Viṣṇu.[386]

The cult of Pārvatī, the goddess of earth, became famous in Gupta period. She was worshipped under various names and forms—Umā the gracious, Ambikā the mother, Satī the good wife, Gaurī shining the golden, Durgā, the unapproachable. Whatever name be given to Pārvatī she was the Śakti, the materialised energy of the god Śiva.[387] The Śakti is hailed in *Devī-Mahātmya* of the *Mārkaṇḍeya Purāṇa* in 12 cantos, consisting 700 verses in chapters 81 to 93.[388] Basically *Devī-Mahātmya* describes Devī Umā's victories over the demons Mahiṣāsura, Śuṁbha, Niśuṁbha and Raktabīja. In the concluding portion of the *Devī-Mahātmya*, the Devī assures the gods by granting them the boon that she will always became incarnate and deliver the world whenever it is oppressed by the demons.[389] Here we find the germs of *avatāra*-hood based on the tracts of Vaiṣṇavism. It seems that the worshipper of Śakti intended to make the Devī omnipresent and omnipotent.

The *Matsya Purāṇa* for the first time gives a complete list of 108 names of the goddess with specification of her association with particular holy places.[390]

The *Amarakośa* provides 21 names of the goddess.[391] The inscription and coins of this period also throw light on the privileged position of the goddess in the society. The

Gaṅgādhar stone inscription of Viśvavarman of 480 A.D. records that Mayūrarakṣaka, a minister of Viśvavarman, built a temple of divine mothers.[392] On the coins of Chandragupta II[393] and Kumāragupta I[394] goddess is represented seated on a lion.

Kārttikeya, the god of war and Commander-in-chief of the armies of the gods, though called the younger son of Śiva and Pārvatī, according to most of the Purāṇic legends is their son only in the sense that they formed him,[395] remain popular in this period. Later the *Skanda Purāṇa* is also devoted to him. The stories and myths related to him are on the same lines in the *Purāṇas* as in the epics. An enchanting narration of the story of birth of Kārttikeya has been given by Kālidāsa in the *Kumārasaṁbhavam,* where Pārvatī as the daughter of Himavān married to Śiva and brought forth Kumāra, who finally vanquished Tāraka demon.[396] The *Amarakośa* gives a list of 17 names of Kārttikeya.[397] The names of a few Gupta rulers (Kumāra gupta and Skandagupta) were based on the name of the deity. The Bilsād pillar inscription of Kumāragupta I, dated 415 A.D., speaks of the construction of a temple of Kārttikeya.[398] Kārttikeya is also depicted in theriomorphic[399] and anthropomorphic[400] forms on Gupta coins.

Gaṇeśa, lord of Gaṇas, for the first time in the *Purāṇas* is regarded as the elder son of Śiva and Pārvatī. According to the *Matsya Purāṇa,* Pārvatī herself got originated Gaṇeśa through bath oil and other secret substances. The *Amarakośa* mentions eight famous names of Gaṇeśa.[401] In this period we do not come across any inscription or coin mentioning Gaṇeśa, but in sculptural art for the first time he can be seen at Bhūmarā and Bhītargaon.[402]

Brahmā, embodiment of the *rajas guṇa* became a great god in the *Purāṇas.* There are many myths in the *Purāṇas* regarding the origin of the Brahmā, the father of the universe. According to some he is Svayaṁbhu, who is born at his will and no other cause is responsible for his birth.[403] The *Viṣṇu Purāṇa* holds a view that Brahmā originated from an egg.[404] The *Amarakośa* gives a list of his names.[405] We do not find an independent archaeological evidence of the worship of Brahmā.

Sarasvatī as a consort of Brahmā became an established fact during this period. According to the *Matsya Purāṇa* Sarasvatī was born out of the half portion of Brahmā's body as his daughter.[406] Because of her relationship with Brahmā and her identification with Vāk, Sarasvatī is considered as the mother of the Vedas. Thus she became the goddess of wisdom, eloquence[407] and fine arts especially of music and rhetoric.[408]

In the Gupta period, Sarasvatī is said to be represented on the reverse of the 'Lyrist Type' of Samudragupta's gold coins. The goddess is nimbate seated to left on a wicker stool, wearing a loose robe and holding a fillet in her outstreched right hand and cornucopiae in the left.[409] Though she has not been given her specific symbol in her own hand, the *Vīṇā* depicted on the obverse is taken to identify her with Sarasvatī the goddess of music.[410] Sarasvatī, is represented on the reverse of one of the 'Rājalīlā

Type' of coins of Samāchāradeva (550-557 A.D.) a predecessor of Śaśāṅka of Gauda. The goddess is shown standing on a lotus. Her left hand rests on a lotus with bent stalk by her right hand she draws up another lotus, below it is a goose (haṁsa) with upstreched neck trying to snatch a lotus leaf.[411] The presence of swan has led to identify her as the goddess Sarasvatī.

The literary and archaeological sources of this period prove that the cult of Sūrya was highly respected in this period. The *Purāṇas* like the *Matsya* prescribe the worship of the four gods e.g. Brahmā, Sūrya, Viṣṇu and Śiva without any sectarian bias. The most popular solar legend which is described in almost all the *Purāṇas* with slight difference is that of Sāmba. Sāmba, a son of Kṛṣṇa by his queen Jāmbavatī, was cursed by his father to become a leper. He was advised by Nārada to worship the Sun-god in this connection.[412]

Varāhamihira saluted the Sun god in the beginning and concluding part of the *Bṛhat Saṁhitā* and glorified him as the procreator of the universe.[413] In the *Raghuvaṁśa* of Kālidāsa Sūrya is hailed as a destroyer of sin and darkness.[414] The Indor Copper plate inscription of Skandagupta of the date 466 A.D. records the donation of a gift by one Devaviṣṇu for perpetually lighting a lamp in the temple of Sūrya.[415] The famous Mandsor inscription dated 437 A.D. and 473 A.D. reports that a guild of silk-weavers, who had migrated to Daśapur, built a temple of Sun-god at that place in 437 A.D. It further reports that 'under several kings a part of the temple collapsed and the temple was again repaired by the same guild in 473 A.D.[416]

The Gwālior inscription of Mihirakula also refers to the Sun-temple built by Mātṛcheta on the mountain called Gopa.[417]

The celestial rivers Gaṅgā and Yamunā were highly revered in their anthropomorphic forms by the Guptas. It seems that a cult around these goddesses was gaining ground. In the secular literature they were highly praised by Kālidāsa. The *Kumārasaṁbhavam* [418] and the *Raghuvaṁśa* [419] give an enchanting description of their journey from heaven to the earth. The Allahabad Pillar inscription of Samudragupta also describes this journey of Gaṅgā.[420] The names Bhagīrathī,[421] Jāhnavī[422] and Mandākinī[423] also occur in the inscriptions of the Gupta period. They were also portrayed on the Gupta coins.[424]

The Yakṣas rank as secondary deities and have much to reflect the assimilation and suppression by the higher cult deities as is evident from the *Purāṇas* in their mythological narration. It is possible to gather an idea of their cult during this period from the incidental references which are abundant but scattered in literature.[425] The hero of the *Meghadūta* is a Yakṣa, who is banished from Kailāsa for dereliction of duty away from his consort and his home,[426] suffers from the pangs of love and finds his deliverence through the cloud (Megha) and sends his message to his beloved.[427]

The Gandharvas, according to the *Viṣṇu Purāṇa* were the sons of Brahmā. In another place the same Purāṇa makes them the offsprings of Kaśyapa and Ariṣṭa and, therefore, grand children of Brahmā.[428] The position of Gandharvas, Kinnaras and Apasarases remain same as in the epics. They are the celestial musicians and dancers in the court of Indra. Their main work is to sing, dance and play music. Kālidāsa has described these demi-gods especially at many verses in the Meghadūta.[429]

The worship of trees and plants has been continuing since the pre-historic times. Evidence of tree-worship during the period under review is not lacking. The sacred *Aśvattha (Vaṭa) Nyagrodha* (Pīpala) trees were associated with Viṣṇu.[430] In the *Bhagavadgitā* Kṛṣṇa while enumerating his *Vibhūtis* refers to *Aśvattha* as the superior one among the trees.[431] *Vaṭa* tree, because of its longevity and nature of drooping roots from the branches, is considered immortal. And Nārāyaṇa sucking his toe (a symbol of eternity) is represented as lying on a *Vaṭa* (Banyan) leaf.[432] The *bilva* or bel (wood-apple) with its triple leaf, is specially dedicated to Śiva. Its leaves are laid on the *Liṅga* to cool the furious deity.[433] The plant of Tulsī is also held sacred because of its association with Viṣṇu.

The development of cult around the *āyudhas* of deities, styled as Āyudha-Puruṣas, was a novel contribution of this period, had become quite popular. The various weapons and emblems held by the gods and goddesses were personified on the basis of their gender as males, females or eunuches.[434] On the obverse of 'Chakravikrama type' of coin of Chandragupta II we find the representation of Chakrapuruṣa.[435] The triśula Puruṣa (emblems of Śiva) has been found standing with Śiva in a sculpture from Allahabad belonging to the period under review.[436]

References

1. Agrawala V.S., Bhakti Cult in Ancient India, *The Bhakti Cult and Indian Geography*, p. 11.
2. *Vedic Index*, 4.3.13, 5.70.4, 7.61.5
3. Bhardwaj, O.P., *Ancient Kurukshetra : Studies in Historical and Cultural Geography*, p. 122.
4. *Jaiminiya Brāhamṇa*, 3.203, 3.351,
5. Coomaraswamy, A. K., *Yakṣas*, p. 5.
6. Bhardwaj, O. P., *Ancient Kurukshetra : Studies in Historical and Cultural Geography*, p. 121
7. Vogel, J. Ph., *Indian Serpent Lore or Nāgas in Hindu Legend and Art*, p. 6.
8. *Vājasaneyi Saṁhitā*, 13.6.
9. Macdonell, A, *Vedic Mythology, p. 153.*
10. *Taittirīya Brāhamaṇa, 3.1.3.6.*
11. Ram Gopal, *India of Vedic Kalpasūr as*, p. 469.
12. *Ṛgveda, 7.34.23, 6.49.14.*
13. *Ibid*, 1.122.3

14. Macdonell, A., *Vedic Mythology*, p. 154.
15. Marshall, John, *Mohenjodaro and the Indus Civilization*, p. 65.
16. Macdonell, *A*, *Vedic Mythology*, p. 154.
17. *Aṣṭādhyāyī*, 4.3.98.
18. Bhandarkar, R.G., *Vaiṣṇavism, Śaivism* and Minor Religious Systems, p. 48.
19. Agrawala, V.S., *India as known to Pāṇini*, p. 350.
20. Macdonell, A., *A Vedic Reader for Students*, p. 30.
21. Macdonell, A., *Vedic Mythology*, pp. 37-38.
22. Dandekar, R.N., *Vedic Mythological Tracts*, pp. 74-75.
23. Basu, Jogiraj, *India of the Age of Brāhmaṇas*, p. 182.
24. *Ś.B.*, 1, 7, 2, 2.
25. *Ibid*, 14, 1.1.
26. Bhandarkar, R. G., *Vaiṣṇavism, Śaivism and Minor Religious Systems*, p. 47
27. Jaiswal, Suvira, *The Origin and Development of Vaiṣṇavism*, p. 32, See also Gavin Flood, *An Introduction to Hinduism*, p. 120.
28. *Śatapatha Brāhmaṇa*, ed. by Weber, 13.6.1.
29. Jaiswal, S., *The Origin and Development of Vaiṣṇavism*, p. 33.
30. *Ibid.*, p. 33.
31. Bhandarkar, R. G., *Vaiṣṇavism, Śaivism and Minor Religious Systems*, p. 42.
32. जीविकार्थे चापण्ये।

    Aṣṭādhyāyī, 5. 3.99.
33. इन्द्रवरुणभवशर्वरुद्रमृड।

    Aṣṭādhyāyī 4.1.49.
34. Marshall, John, *Mohenjodaro and the Indus Civilization*, p. 52.
35. Singh, S. B., *Brahmanical Icons in Northern India*, p. 2.
36. Macdonell, A., *Vedic Mythology*, p. 74.
37. *Ṛgveda*, 2.33.3, 7.46.3., 2.33.9., 2.33.10.
38. *Ibid.*, 1.114.7, 6.28.7
39. *Ibid*, 2.33.12, 7.46.3
40. *Ibid* 1.43.4
41. Macdonell, A., *Vedic Mythology*, p. 76.
42. Basu, Jogiraj, *India in the age of Brāhmaṇas*, p. 196.
43. *Ibid*, p. 196
44. *Ibid.*, pp. 197-201.
45. *Śvetāśvatara Upaniṣad*, 3, 2-4,; 3, 6,; 3, 7; 310-11;

    Gavin Flood, *An Introduction to Hinduism*, p. 153.

46. *Encyclopaedia of Religion,* ed. by Vergilius Ferm, p. 509.
47. Rajeshwari, D.R., *Śakti Iconography,* p. Intro. XV.
48. *Ibid.*, pp. 2-3.
49. Marshall, J., *Mohenjodaro and the Indus Civilization,* p. 42.
50. Macdonell, A., *Vedic Mythology,* p 124.
51. Chaudhuri, N. M., Mother-goddess conception in the Vedic literature, *Indian Culture,* Vol. VIII, 1941, p. 66.
52. *Ṛgveda,* 10.127.1, 10.125.1, 5.42.12.
53. Rajeshwari, D. R., *Śakti Iconography,* p. 5.
54. Vājasaneyi Saṁhitā, 3.58.
55. अम्बिका ह वै नामास्य स्वसा। *ŚB* 2.6.9.
56. असूर्यललाटयो: दृशितपो:।

    Aṣṭādhyāyi, 3.2.36.
57. राजसूयसूर्यमृषोद्यरूच्यकुप्यकृष्टपाच्याव्यथ्या:।

    Aṣṭādhyāyi, 3.1.114.
58. Bhandarkar, R. G., *Vaiṣṇavism, Śaivism and Minor Religious System,* p. 215.
59. *Ṛgveda,* 1.115.1; 1.50.7; 7.60.2; 6.51.2;10.177.1; 10.37.4
60. Atharvaveda, 13.1.45.
61. Macdonell, A., *Vedic Mythology,* pp. 30-31.
62. जीविकार्थे चापण्ये।
63. *Aṣṭādhyāyi,.* 5.3.99 *Ṛgveda,* 5.2.1.
64. कुमारो नवम: सैवाग्रेस्त्रिवृत्ता।

    ŚB, 6, 1, 3, 18
65. *Ibid.,* 5.3, 1, 1.
66. सेनान्ये दिशां च पतये नम डइत्येष एव हिरण्यबाहु:

    सेनानीरष दिशां पतिस्तद्यत्किं।

    ŚB, 9, 1, 1, 18.
67. Hopkins, *Epic Mythology,* p. 229.
68. Mc Crindle, *Ancient India as described by Megasthenes and Arrian,* p. 201 cit. Banerjea, J. N., *DHI,* p. 77
69. अपराजिताप्रतिहतजयन्तवैजयन्त कोष्ठकान्

    शिववैश्रवणाश्विश्रीमदिरागृहं च पुरमध्ये कारयेत्।

    Kauṭilya's *Arthaśāstra* ed. by R. Shamasastry, Book II, Ch. IV.
70. ब्राह्मैन्द्रयाम्यसैनापत्यानि द्वाराणि।

    Kauṭilya's *Arthaśāstra* ed. by R. Shamasastry, Book II, Ch. IV.

71. सङ्कर्षण दैवतीयोगो वा मुण्डजटिलव्यञ्जनः प्रहवणकर्मणा।

Arthaśāstra, Book XIII, Ch. III.

72. Cf. Puri, B. N , *India in the time of Patañjali,* p. 184.
73. कंस वधमाचष्टे कंसं घातयति बलिवंधमाचष्टे बलिं बन्धमति। *Mahābhāṣya, Vārtika,* 6.
74. Cf. Puri, B. N., *loc. cit.,* p. 184.
75. *Ibid.,* p. 188.
76. सूर्यचन्द्रस्थ।

Mahābhāṣya, 1.3.25.

77. Rajeshwari, D. K., *Śakti Iconography,* p. 16.
78. Macdonell, A., *Vedic Mythology,* p. 125.
79. Rajeshwari, D. R., *Śakti Iconography,* p. 16.
80. Śatapatha Brāhmaṇa, XI. 4.1
81. *DHI,* p. 371.
82. Gonda, J., The *Origin of Early Viṣṇuism,* p. 214.
83. *Ṛgveda,* Khilya, 6
84. Liider, H., *Appendix to El and Record of the ASI, A List of Brāhmi Inscriptions.* Vol. X, No. 669, See Also Sircar. D. C., *Select Inscriptions.* Vol. I. No. 2, pp. 88-89.
85. A.S.I. Annual Report 1913-14 Pt. II, p. 190, Puri, B. N., *India in the time of Patañjali.* p. 185.
86. Chattopadhyay, B., *Coins and Icons; A Study of Myths and Symbols in Indian Numismatic Art,* p. 8.
87. Agrawal, Bhanu, and Rai, Subhas, *The Punch-marked Coins.* p. 154.
88. Chattopadhyay, B., *op. cit.,* pp. 24-27.
89. Banerjea, J.N., *DHI.,* p. 109.
90. *Ibid.,* p. 76. However, Jaiswal opines, the date of Niddeśa passage is Ist Century B. C. (Jaiswal, S., *The Origin and Development of Vaiṣṇavism,* p. 75).
91. Bhandarkar, R.G., *Vaiṣṇavism, Śaivism and Minor Religious Systems.* p. 3.
92. Shastry, Ajay Mitra, Religious Study of the Symbols on the local coins of Central India, *Seminar Papers on the Local Coins of Northern India* (c. 300 B.C. to 300 A.D.), No. 2, 1968, p. 71.
93. Allan, *Catalogue of the Coins of Ancient India,* p. 243, Pl. XXXVI. 15, See also Mahalingam, T. V., *Seminar Papers on the Local Coins of Northern India,* (c. 300 B.C. to 300 A.D.), No. 2, 1968, p. 56.
95. Allan, John, *Catalogue of the Coins of Ancient India,* p. 249, Pls, XXXVIII. 15, Pl. XXXVIII. 17, p. 245., Pl. XXXVIII. 1.
96. Chakraborty, Swati, *Socio-Religious and Cultural Study of the Ancient Indian Coins.* p. 117.
97. Srivastava, V. C., *Sun-Worship in Ancient India,* pp. 287-89.
98. Chakraborty, Swati, *loc. cit.,* pp. 153-54.

99. Allan, *Catalogue of Coins of Ancient India*, p. 257, Pl. XXXVI, 1-3.
100. Banerjea, J. N., *DHI*, p. 151.
101. Cunningham, A., *Coins of Ancient India*, p. 62, Pl. II and III, No. 121 and 122.
102. Banerjea, J. N., *DHI*, p. 151.
103. Allan, *loc. cit.*, p. Intra. XXIX Pls X. 5, IX. 9.
104. *Ibid.*, p. 130 Pls. 6. XVI-11, XVI-13, XVI-14.
105. *Ibid.*, pp. 192-204, Pl. XXVII. 8-10 etc.
106. Chaudhary, K., Dionysos of Indo-Greek Coins—A Study, *JNSI*, Vol. XLV, 1983, p. 125.
107. Banerjea, J. N., *DHI*, p. 342.
108. Harle, J. C., *The Art and Architecture of Indian Sub-Continent*, p. 29.
109. Sharma, J. P., *Jaina-Yakṣa*, p. 44.
110. Coomaraswamy, AK., Yakṣas, p. 9.
111. Vogel, J. Ph., *Indian Serpent Lore or Nāgas in Hindu Legend and Art*, p. 39.
112. Vogel, *op. cit.* p. 39.
113. Haldhar, J. R., *Early Buddhist Mythology*, p. 106.
114. Singh, O. P., *Iconography of Gaja-Lakṣmī*, pp. 17-18.
115. *Ibid.*, p. 28.
116. Puri, B. N., *India in the Time of Patañjali*, pp. 249-250.
117. Zimmer, Heinrich, *The Art of Indian Asia*, Vol. II, Pl. VII.
118. Singh, O. P. *Iconography of Gaja-Lakṣmi*, p. 53.
119. Vogel, J. Ph., *op. cit.*, p. 40.
120. Puri, B. N., *loc. cit.*, p. 250.
121. Liider, H., *Appendix to Epigraphica Indica and ASI, A List of Brāhmi Inscriptions*, Vol. V, No. 6.
122. Sircar, D. C., *SI*, No. 82, p. 192.
123. Banerjea, J. N., *DHI*, p. 128.
124. Allan, *Catalogue of the Coins of Ancient India*, p. 202, Pl. XXIX. 6.
125. *Ibid.*, p. 170, Pls. XXV. 1-2, XLV. 1.
126. *Ibid.*, p. 173, Pl. XXV, 12.14. See also.
Cunningham, A., *Coins of Ancient India*, Pl, VIII. 12.
127. *Allan, loc, cit.*, p. 174, Pl. XLIII. 16.
128. *Ibid.*, p. 174, Pl. XXV. 17-21.
129. *Ibid.*, p. 175, Pl. XXV. 15-16.
130. *Ibid.*, p. 176, Pl. XXIV. 1-4.
131. *Ibid.*, p. 177, Pl. XXIV. 15-17.
132. Cunningham, A., *loc. cit.*, p. 87, Pl. VIII. Fig. 8.
133. *Ibid.*, p. 88, Pl. VIII, Fig. 11.

134. Allan, *op. cit.*, p. 182, Pl. XXIV. 8.
135. Banerjea, J. N., *DHI*, p. 111, See also *Allan*, p. 183, Pl. XXV, 26., p. 183, XXVI, 1-4, p. 185, Pl. XXVI 12, 190, Pl. xxvi 16.
136. Allan, *Catalogue of the Coins of Ancient India*, p. 149, Pl. XX. 15.
137. *Ibid.*, p. 256, Pl. XXXVI. 4-5.
138. *Ibid.*, p. 256, Pl. XXXVI. 4-5.
139. Ibid., p. 256, Pl. XXXVI. 4-5.
140. Whitehead, *Catalogue of the Coins in Punjab Museum*, Lahore, p. 173, Pl. XIII.
141. *Ibid.*, p. 17, Pl. II.
142. Banerjea, J.N., *DHI*, p. 111.
143. Chakraborty, *Swati, Socio-Religious and Cultural Study of the Ancient Indian*Coins, p. 172.
144. Cunningham, A., *Coins of Ancient India*, p. 92, Pl. IX, Fig. 4.
145. *Ibid.*, p. 92, Pl. IX, Fig. 5
146. *Ibid.*, p. 92, Pl. IX, Fig. 5.
147. *Ibid.*, p. 92, IX, Fig. 7.
148. Smith, V. A., *Coins of Ancient India, Catalogue of the Coins in the Indian Museum, Calcutta*, Vol. 1, p. 167.
149. Cunningham, *loc. cit.*, p. 78, Pl. VI, fig. 14.
150. Bhandarkar, R. G., *Vaiṣṇavism, Śaivism and Minor Religious Systems*, p. 65.
151. संधौ तू समनुप्राप्ते त्रेतायां द्वापरस्य च।

    रामो दाशरथिर्भूत्वा भविष्यामि जगत्पतिः।

    Ch. 326, Śloka 78.
152. Ch. 188, 189.
153. Bhandarkar, R. G., *Vaiṣṇavism, Śaivism and Minor Religious Systems*, p. 45.
154. गतिश्च सर्वभूतानां प्रजानां चापि भारत।

    व्याप्ता मे रोदसी पार्थ कान्तिश्चाभ्यधिका मम।

    Śānti *Parva, mokṣadharma parva*, Ch. 328, S. 37.
155. *Mahābhārata, Anuśāsana Parva*, Ch. 135, S. 14-120.
156. नारायणामयनं रव्यातमहमेकः सनातनः

    आपो नारा इति प्रोक्ता आपो वै नरसूनवः।

    अयनं मम तत्पूर्वमतो नारायणो ह्यहम्।

    Mahābhārta, Śānti *Parva, mokṣadharma parva*, Ch. 328, S. 35.
157. अधिभूतानि चान्तेऽहं तदिच्छंश्चास्मि भारत।

    क्रमणाच्चाप्यहं पार्थ विष्णुरित्यभिसंज्ञितः।

    Mahābhārata, loc. cit., Ch. 328, S. 38.

158. Bhandarkar, R. G., *op. cit.*, p. 46.
159. *Mahābhārata, Vana Parva*, Ch. 46, Ś 47.
160. त्वं चैवाहं च कौन्तेय नरनारायणौ स्मृतौ
भारावतरणार्थं हि प्रविष्टौ मानुषीं तनुम्।
Mahābhārata, Śānti Parva, mokṣadharma parva, Ch. 328, S. 33.
161. एव नारायणः कृष्णः फल्गुनस्तु नरः स्मृतः।
नारायणो नरश्चैव सत्वमेकं द्विधाकृतम्।
Mahābhārata, Udyoga Parva, Ch. 48, Ś. 20.
162. Bhandarkar, R. G., *op. cit.*, pp. 46-47.
163. Knappert, Jan., *Indian Mythology*, p. 43.
164. यदा यदा हि धर्मस्य ग्लानिर्भवति भारत।
अभ्युत्थानमधर्मस्य तदात्मानं सृजाम्यहम्।
परित्राणाय साधूनां विनाशाय च दुष्कृताम्।
धर्मसंस्थापनार्थाय संभवामि युगे-युगे।
Ch. 4, Ś. 7-8.
165. Ch. 326, Ślokas 72-82.
166. Bhandarkar, R. G., *Vaiṣṇavism, Śaivism and Minor Religious Systems*, pp. 58-59.
167. *Śatapatha Brāhmaṇa*, 1, 8, 1.
168. Wilkins, W. J., *Hindu Mythology*, p. 143.
169. ŚB, 7, 5, 1, 5.
170. Wilkins, *Hindu Mythology*, p. 144.
171. *ŚB*, 14, 1, 2, 11.
172. Wilkins, *Hindu Mythology*, p. 144.
173. Jaiswal, S., *The Origin and Development of Vaiṣṇavism*, p. 55.
174. *Ibid*, p 58.
175. हिरण्यवर्णां हरिणीं सुवर्णरजतंस्त्रजाम्।
Ṛgveda, Khilya 6, Ch. 2.
176. Gonda, *Aspects of Early Viṣṇuism*, p. 222
177. *Mahābhārata, Śānti Parva*, Ch. 221, S. 1-94.
178. Jaiswal, *loc. cit.*, p. 98.
179. श्रीरनन्तरमुत्पन्ना धृतात्पाण्डुरवासिनी।
सुरा देवीसमुत्पन्ना तुरगः पाण्डुरस्तथा।
Mahābhārāt, Ādi Parva, Ch. 16, S. 34-36.

180. Jaiswal, S., *op. cit.*, p. 105.

181. Gonda J., *op. cit.*, P. 223.

182. *Mahābhārata Śānti Parva*, Ch. 221, Ś. 80.

183. सा शचीव महेन्द्रेण श्री कृष्णेनेव संगता।

सुभद्रा युयुजे प्रीता पाण्डवेनार्जुनेन ह।

Mahābhārata Ādi Parva, Ch. 55, S. 34, Another one is also in *Ādi Parva*, Ch. 91, Ś. 6.

184. Ch. 4, Ś. 37-48.

185. एकानंशां योगकन्यां रक्षार्थं केशवस्य तु।

तां वै सर्वे सुमनसः पूजयन्ति स्म यादवाः।

Harivaṁśa, Viṣṇu Parva, Ch. 4, S. 47-48.

186. Jaiswal, *op. cit.*, p. 69.

187. Kramrisch, Stella, *The Presence of Śiva*, p. 148.

188. योगिनां च परमं ब्रह्म व्यक्तं ब्रह्मविदा निधिम्।

चराचरस्य स्रष्टारं प्रतिहर्तारमेव च।

Ch. 57, Ś. 42.

189. Ch. 17.

190. *Mahābhārata, Anuśāsana Parva*, Ch. 17, S, 49.

191. Sivaramamurti, C., *Naṭarāja in Art, Thought and Literature*, p. 74.

वैणवी पणवी ताली कालः कालकंटकटः।

Mahābhārata, Anuśāsana Parva, Ch. 17, S. 56.

192. Wilkins, *op. cit.*, p. 277.

193. Knappert, Jan., *Indian Mythology*, p. 151.

194. *Ṛgveda*, 7, 21, 5, 10, 99, 3.

195. Macdonell, A., *Vedic Mythology*. p. 155

196. हेतुभिर्वा किमन्यस्ते ईशः कारणकारणम्।

न शुश्रुम यदन्यस्य लिङ्गमभ्यर्च्यते सुरैः।

Ch. 14, Ś, 100-102.

197. Bhandarkar, *op. cit.*, p. 158.

198. Singh S. B., *Brahmanical Images of Northern India*, p. 146

199. Hopkins, *Epic Mythology*, p. 224.

200. विन्ध्यावासिनीं दुर्गन्धां रणदुर्गां रणप्रियाम्।

Ch. 106.

201. नमस्ते सिद्धसेनानि आर्य मन्दरवासिनी
कुलमारि कालि कापालि कपिले कृष्णपिङ्गले।
भद्रकालि नमस्तुभ्यं महाकालि नमाऽस्तुते।
चण्डि चण्डे नमस्तुभ्यं तारिणी वरवर्णिनि। *Bhiṣma Parva*, Ch. 23, Ś. 4-16.
202. वासुदेवस्य भगिनीं दिव्यमाल्य विभूषिताम्।
Virāṭa Parva, Ch. 6, Ś 4.
203. *Bālakāṇḍa, Sarga 37*
204. *Mahābhārata, Vana Parva*, Ch. 229.
205. Bhandarkar, R. G., *Vaiṣṇavism, Śaivism and Minor Religious Systems*, p. 214.
206. *Mahābhārata, Anuśāsana Parva*, Ch. 84.
Ibid., Śalya Parva, Ch. 43-45.
207. Mishra, Rajni, *Brahmā-worship, Tradition and Iconography*, p. 1.
208. बृहस्पतिर्वै देवानां ब्रह्मा।
ŚB, 1, 7,4,21.
209. Mishra, Rajni, *loc, cit.*, p. 10
210. ब्राह्मे रात्रिक्षये प्राप्ते तस्य ह्यमिततेजसः।
प्रासादत्प्रादुरभवत्पद्मं पद्मनिभेक्षण।
तत्र ब्रह्मा समभवत्स तस्यैव प्रसादजः।
Ch. 328, Ś. 15.
211. *Ṛgveda*, I. 164, 49, I. 88. 8, 2. 30.8, 2. 41, 16.
212. ŚB, 1.6.2.4., 4.2.5.22.
213. *Ibid*, 3.1.4.9.
214. Wilkins, *op. cit.*, 110.
215. Pandey, L. P., *Sun-worship in Ancient India*, p. 55.
216. पुरा देवयुगे राजन्नादित्यो भगवान्दिवः।
आगच्छन्मानुषं लोकं दिदृक्षर्विगतक्लमः।
Ch. 11, Ś. 2.
217. Pandey, L. P., *loc. cit.*, p. 60.
218. Pandey, L.P. *op.cit.* p. 60.
219. *Āraṇyaka Parva*, Ch. 3, Ś. 18.
220. Geity Alice, *Gaṇeśa*, p. 3.
221. Mani Vettam, *Purāṇic Encyclopaedia*, p. 893.
222. Hopkins, *Epic Mythology*, p. 23.
223. Basham, A. L., *The Wonder that was India*, p. 319.
224. *Ibid.*, p. 320.

225. *Atharva veda*, 11.5.2.
226. *Ṛg veda*, 9.83.4
227. *Ibid*, 10.123.5.
228. Macdonell, A, *Vedic Mythology*, pp. 136-137.
229. नमस्कृत्य महादेवं सर्वलोकोद्भवं भवम्।
     जगत्पितामंह चैव विष्णुमिन्द्रं गुहं तथा।
     Ch. III, Ś. 4.
230. सरस्वतीं च लक्ष्मीं च सिद्धिं मेधां धृतिं स्मृतिम्।
     सोमं सूर्य च मरूतो लोकपालांस्तथाश्विनौ।
     Ch. III, Ś. 5.
231. देवासेनापते स्कन्द भगवन् शङ्करप्रिय।
     बलिः प्रीतेन मनसा षण्मुख प्रतिगृह्यताम्।
     Ibid., Ś. 52.
232. Lüder, *op. cit.*, No. 14, See also Sircar, D.C., *SI*, Vol. I, No. 26 A, p. 122.
233. Jaiswal, S., *op. cit.*, p. 70.
234. Banerjea, J. N., *DHI.*, p. 94.
235. Chattopadhyay B., *The Age of the Kuṣāṇas*, p. 141.
236. Sharma, Savita and Tiwari, M. N., Śiva on Kuṣāṇa Coins, *JNSI*, Vol. XLV, 1983, p. 134.
237. *Ibid.* p., 135.
238. *Ibid.*, p. 136.
239. Gardner, Percy, *Coins of Greek and Scythic Kings of Bactria and India in British Museum*, p. 104, Pl. XXII, 9.
240. *Ibid.*, p. 124, pl. XXV. 8.
241. *Ibid.*, p. 124, Pl. XXV. 6
242. Sharma, Savita and Tiwari, M. N., Śiva on Kuṣāṇa Coins, *JNSI*, Vol. XLV, 1983, p. 136.
243. Gardner, Percy, *Coins of Greek and Scythic Kings of Bactria and India in British Museum*, p. 132, Pl. XXVI. 13.
244. *Ibid.*, p. 148, Pl. XXVIII. 16.
245. Sharma, Savita and Tiwari, M. N., *op. cit.*, p. 164.
246. Cunningham, A., *Coins of the Indo-Scythians, Śakas and Kusāṇas*, pp. 65-66.
247. Gardner, Percy, *op. cit.*, p. 159, Pl. XXIX. 10. While Gardner finds wreath in Śiva's hand, Whitehead, Smith and Cunningham *(Coins of Indo-Scythians, Śakas and Kuṣāṇas*, p. 71, Pl. XXIV. 3) consider it as a noose. (Chattopadhyay, B., *The Age of Kuṣāṇas*, p. 174).
248. Chakraborty, Swati, *Socio-Religious Cultural Study of Indian Coins*, p. 92.
249. Chattopadhyay, B., *The Age of Kuṣāṇas*, pp. 72-77.
250. Chakraborty, Swati, *loc. cit.*, p. 92.

251. Smith, *Coins of Ancient India, Catalogue of the Coins in Indian Museum*, Calcutta, p. 82, Pl. VII. 154.
252. Chattopadhyay, B., *loc. cit.*, pp. 176-177.
253. Cunningham, A., *op. cit.*, pp. 65-66, Pl. XXIII.1.
254. Chattopadhyay, B., *The Age of Kuṣāṇas*, p. 177.
255. Chakraborty, Swati, *loc.* cit., p. 170.
256. Smith, *op. cit.*, p. 81, Pl. XIII. 4.
257. Chattopadhyay, B., *loc. cit.*, p. 176.
258. Chakraborty, Swati, *loc. cit.*, p. 139.
259. Banerjea, J. N., *DHI*, p. 139.
260. Gardner, Percy, *op. cit.*, p. 20. Pl. VI. 11.
261. *Ibid.*, p. 57, Pl. XIII. 9.
262. Chakraborty, Swati, *loc. cit.*, p. 123.
263. Banerjea, J. N., *DHI*, p. 140.
264. Chattopadhyay, B., *The Age of Kuṣāṇas*, p. 151.
265. Gardner, *op. cit.*, p. 129, Pl. XXVI. 2.
266. Gardner, *op. cit.*, p. 141, Pl. XXVIII. 1.
267. *Ibid.*, p. 142, Pl. XXVIII. 4.
268. Chattopadhyay, B., *op. cit.*, p. 164.
269. Gardner, Percy, *op. cit.*, p. 129, Pl. XXVI. 3.
270. Rosenfield, John, M., *The Dynastic Arts of the Kuṣāṇas*, p. 83. No. 14.
271. Gardner, *op. cit.*, p. 159, pl. XXIX. 8.
272. Cunningham, *op. cit.*, p. 63, Pl. XXII. 19.
273. Mukherjee, B. N., *Nānā on Lion*, p. 11.
274. Rosenfield, *loc. cit.*, p. 85.
275. *Ibid.*, p. 85.
276. Mukherjee, *Nānā on Lion*, p. 11.
277. Rosenfield, *loc. cit.*, p. 88.
278. Mukherjee, B. N., *loc. cit*, pp. 13-14.
279. Rosenfield, *The Dynastic Arts of the Kuṣāṇas.*, p. 94, No. 19 a and b.
280. Mukherjee, B. N., *Nānā on Lion*, p. 15.
281. Gardner, Percy, *Coins of Greek and Scythic Kings of Bactria and India in British Museum*, p. 85, Pl. XIX. 5.
282. Chattopadhyay, *The Age of the Kuṣāṇas*, p. 167.
283. Gardner, *op. cit.*, p. 130, Pl. XXXVI. 6.
284. *Ibid.*, p. 133, Pl. XXVI. 19.
285. Gardner, *op. cit.*, p. 137, Pl. XXVII. 10.

286. Whitehead, *Catalogue of the Coins in Punjab Museum*, Lahore, Vol. 1, p. 210, Pl. XIX.
287. Rosenfield, *The Dynastic Arts of the Kuṣāṇās*, p. 74.
288. *Ibid.*, p. 199.
289. Chakraborty, Swati, *op. cit.*, p. 128.
290. Gardner, Percy, *op. cit.*, p. 138, Pl. XXVII. 16.
291. Joshi, N. P., *Catalogue of the Brahmanical Sculptures in the State Museum*. Lucknow, p. 45.
292. Sivaramamurti, C., *Sources of History Illuminated by Literature*, p. 12.
293. Smith, *op. cit.*, P. 178.
294. Allan, *op. cit.*, p. 138, Pl. XVII. 22.
295. Gardner, Percy, *op. cit.*, p. 149, PL. XXVIII. 22.
296. *Ibid.*, p. 150, Pl. XXVIII. 24.
297. *Ibid.*, p. 149, Pl. XXVIII.22.
298. Sinha, Kanchan, *Kārttikeya in Indian Art and Literature*, pp. 82-83.
299. रोहितके, कार्तिकेयः कुमारो लोकविश्रुतः

     Mahāmayūri, Ver. 21.
300. Allan, *op. cit.*, 270, Pl. XXXIX. 21.
301. Smith, *op. cit.*, p. 181, Pl. XXI-15.
302. Chakraborty, Swati, *Socio, Religious and Cultural Study of Ancient Indian Coins*. p. 135.
303. *Ibid.*, p. 136.
304. Dandekar, R. N., *The Age of the Guptas*, Select Writings IV, p. 69.
305. Winternitz, *A History of Sanskrit Literature* Vol. I, Part II, *Epic and Pūraṇas*, p. 477.
306. विष्णुर्नारायणः कृष्णो वैकुण्ठो विष्टरश्रवाः।

     दामोदरो हषीकेशः केशवो माधवः स्वभूः।

     दैत्यारिः पुण्डरीकाक्षो गोविन्दो गरूडध्वजः।

     पीताम्बरोडच्युतः शार्ङ्गी विष्वक्सेनो जनार्दनः।

     उपेन्द्र इन्द्रावरजश्चक्रपाणिश्र्चतुभुर्जः।

     पद्मनाभो मधुरिपुर्वासुदेवस्त्रिविक्रमः।

     देवकीनन्दनः शौरिः श्रीपतिः पुरूषोत्तमः।

     वनमाली बलिध्वंसी कंसारातिरधोक्षजः।

     Svarga Varga, Ś. 18-21.
307. *Bṛhat Saṁhitā*, L VIII, S. 31-35.
308. Raychaudhri, *Materials for the Study of Early History of Vaiṣṇava Sect*, pp. 102-03.
309. Fleet, *CII*, Vol. III, No. 32, Pl. XXIA, p. 139, Sircar, *SI*, Vol. I, No. 14, p. 283.

310. Fleet, *CII*, Vol. III, No. 3, Pl. 11B, pp. 21-22;
Sircar, *SI.* Vol. I, No. 10, p. 279.
311. Fleet, *loc. cit.*, No. 14, Pl. VIII, p. 56, Sircar, *loc. cit.* No. 25, p. 307.
312. *Ibid.*, No. 13, Pl. VII, p. 52. Sircar, *op. cit.* No. 28, p. 349.
313. Fleet, *op. cit.*, No. 66, Pl. XXXIXD, pp. 267-68.
314. *Ibid.*, No. 19, Pl. XII A, p. 88. Sircar, *op. cit.*, No. 35, p. 334.
315. *Ibid.*, Vol. III, No. 17, Pl. X, pp. 72-76.
316. Dandekar, R.N., *The Age of Guptas and Other Essays,* Select Writings IV, p. 79.
317. Altekar, A.S., *Coinage of Gupta Empire,* pp. 47-48, Pl. XX.3.
318. *Ibid.*, p. 87. pl. XX.11.
319. Mukherjee, Chhanda, *Gupta Numismatic Art,* p. 91.
320. Altekar, *CGE* p. 156, Pl. XVI. 8.
321. Mukherjee Chhanda, Garuḍa on coins and seals of the Imperial Guptas.
JNSI. XLVI. 1984, p. 96. Altekar, *loc. cit.*, p. 156, Pl. XVI. 8.
322. *Ibid.* p. 160, Pl. XVI. 8.
323. Altekar, *CGE,* pp. 145-46, Pl. XVIII. 14.
324. यदा यदा हि धर्मस्य ग्लानिर्भवति भारत।
अभ्युत्थानमधर्मस्य तदात्मानं सृजाम्यहम्।
परित्राणाय साधूनां विनाशाय च दुष्कृताम्।
धर्मसंस्थापनार्थाय संभवामि युगे-युगे।
Bhagavadgitā, Ch. 4, S. 7-8.
The list excludes Matsya, Kūrma and Varāha and includes in its place Yajña, Dattātreya and Veda Vyāsa.
325. Mishra, Indumati, *Pratimā-vijñāna,* p. 186.
326. *Ibid.*, p. 187.
327. Basham, A.L., *The Wonder that was India,* pp. 304-305.
328. तत्रेश्वरेण जगतां प्रलयादिवोर्वीम्।
Raghuvaṁśa, XIII, 77.
329. Fleet, *CII,* Vol. III, No. 36, Pl. XXIIA, p. 158.
330. Basham, A.L., *loc. cit.*, p. 305.
331. Altekar, *CGE,* p. 187, Variety A (Pl. XII, 6-3).
332. Basham, A.L., *loc. cit.*, p. 305.
333. तेनोदीची दिशमनुसरेस्तिर्यगायामशोभी।
श्यामः पादो बलिनियमनाभ्युद्यतस्येव विष्णोः। Ś. I. 60.
334. Basham, A.L., *op. cit.,* p. 305.

335. प्रालेयाद्रेरूपतटमतिक्रम्य तांस्तान्विशेषान्।
हंसद्वारं भृगुपतियशोवर्त्म यत्क्रौञ्चरन्ध्रम्॥
Ś. 1, 60.
336. Winternitz, *A History of Sanskrit Literature,* Vol. I, Part II, *Epics and Purāṇas,* p. 484.
337. Fleet, *CII,* Vol. III, No. 13, Pl. VII, p. 55.
338. Basham, A.L., *The Wonder that was India,* p. 309.
339. Dandekar, R. N., *The Age of the Guptas and other Essays,* Select Writings-IV, pp. 354-55.
340. Srivastava, M.C.P., *Mother-goddess in Indian Art, Archaeology and Literature,* p. 119.
341. Wilkins, *Hindu Mythology,* p. 128.
342. लक्ष्मी: पद्मालया पद्मा कमला श्रीर्हरिप्रिया।
इन्दिरा लोकमाता मा क्षीरोदतनया रमा।
भार्गवी लोकजननी क्षीरसागरकन्यका।
Ś. 1, 27
343. श्रिय: पद्मनिषण्णाया: क्षौमान्तरितमेखले।
अङ्के निक्षिप्तचरणमास्तीर्णकरपल्लवे।
Ś. X, 8.
344. Fleet, *CII,* Vol. III, No. 3, Pl. 11B, pp. 21-22.
345. *Ibid.*, No. 14, Pl. VIII, Line 1, p. 61.
346. *Ibid.*, No. 37, Pl. XXIII B, p. 161.
347. *Ibid.*, No. 79, Pl. XLIIIC; p. 284, Line 4.
348. *Ibid.*, No. 42, Pl. XXVII, p. 200 ff.
349. Altekar, *CGE,* p. 48, Pl. XXIII. 44.
350. *Ibid.*, p. 55
351. *Ibid.*, p. 59, Pl. XXIII. 47.
352. Ibid., p. 76, Pl. XXIII. 46.
353. *Ibid.*, p. 88, Pl. XXIII. 50.
354. *Ibid.*, p. 93, Pl. XXIII. 51.
355. *Ibid.*, p. 99, Pl. IV. 13.
356. Altekar, *CGE,* p. 94, Pl. IV. 8.
357. *Ibid.*, p. 101, Pl. V. 7.
358. *Ibid.*, p. 99, Pl. IV. 13.
359. *Ibid.*, p. 130, Pl. XXIII, 52.
360. *Ibid.*, p. 137, Pl. IX. 4.
361. *Ibid.*, p. 136, Pl. IX. 1.

362. Chakraborty, Swati, *Socio-Religious and Cultural Study of Ancient Indian Coins,* p. 164.
363. Altekar, *loc. cit,* p. 146, Pl. XVIII. 4.
364. Chakraborty, Swati, *loc. cit.,* p. 165.
365. Altekar, *loc. cit,* p. 172, Pl. X. 4.
366. *Ibid.,* p. 209, Pl. XXIV. 69.
367. *Ibid.,* p. 195, Pl. XXIV. 67.
368. *Ibid.,* p. 195, Pl. XXIV. 67.
369. *Ibid.,* p. 243, Pl. XIV. 8.
370. *Ibid.,* p. 247, Pl. XXVI. 24.
371. *Ibid.,* p. 247, Pl. XIV. 12.
372. Mathuothu, Kurian, *The Development of the Concept of Trimūrti in Hinduism,* p. 3.
373. Dandekar, R.N., *op. cit.,* p. 353.
374. Wilkins, *op. cit.,* p. 266.
375. Mani Vettam, *Purāṇic Encyclopaedia,* pp. 723-724.
376. Wilson, H. H., *Analysis of Purāṇas,* p. 149.
377. शम्भुरीशः पशुपतिः शिवः शूली महेश्वरः।

ईश्वरः शर्व ईशानः शङ्करश्चन्द्रशेखरः।

भूतेशः खण्डपरशुर्गिरीशो गिरिशो मृडः। मुत्युञ्जयः कृत्तिवासाः पिनाकी प्रथमाधिपः।

उग्रः कपर्दी श्रीकण्ठः शितिकण्ठः कपालभृत्। वामदेवो महादेवो विरुपाक्षस्त्रिलोचनः।

कृशानुरेताः सर्वज्ञो धूर्जटिर्नीललोहितः। हरः स्मरहरो भर्गस्त्र्यम्कबकस्त्रिपुरान्तकः।

गंङ्गाधरोडन्धकरिपुः क्रतुध्वंसी वृषध्वजः। व्योमकेशोऽभवो भीमः स्थाणू रुद्र उमापतिः।

Amarakośa, I, Ś, 30-34.

378. Fleet, CII, Vol. III, No. 6, Pl. IVA, pp. 34-35.
379. Sircar, SI, Vol. I, No. 11, p. 279.
380. Mukherjee, Chhanda, *Gupta Numismatic Art,* p. 93.
381. Altekar, *CGE,* Pl. XXV. 13, p. 252.
382. Pranabananda Jash, *History of Śaivism,* p. Intro. 9.
383. Kramrisch, Stella, *The Presence of Śiva,* p. 159.
384. तया तु तस्यार्धशरीरभाजा पश्चात्कृताः स्न्धिजनाशिषोऽपि।

Ś., vii, 28.

385. वागर्थाविव संपृक्तौ वागर्थप्रतिपत्तये।

जगतः पितरौ वन्दे पार्वतीपरमेश्वरौ।

Ś, I, 1.

386. Gonda, *Viṣṇuism and Śaivism,* pp. 108-109.
387. The Mythologies of the East, ed. by J. Hackin, *et. al.* p. 122.

388. Knappert Jan, *Indian Myhthology*, p. 80.
389. Bhattacharya, N. N., *The Indian Mother Goddess*, p. 120.
390. *Ibid.*, p. 120.
391. उमा कात्यायनी गौरी काली हैमवतीश्वरी ।
शिवा भवानी रूद्राणी शर्वाणी सर्वमङ्गला।
अपर्णा पार्वती दुर्गा मृडानी चाण्डिकाऽम्बिका।
आर्या दाक्षायणी चैव गिरिजा मेनकात्मजा।
Ś., I, 36-37.
392. Fleet, *op. cit.*, No. 17, Pl. X, p. 72.
393. Altekar, *CGE*, p. III, Pl. VI. 1, p. 112, Pl. VII. 10.
394. *Ibid.*, p. 187, Pl. XIII, p. 188, Pl. XII. 3, p. 189, Pl. XII. 6.
395. Wilkin, *Hindu Myhthology*, p. 334.
396. Navaratanam, R., *Kārttikeya, The Divine Child* (The Hindu Testament of Wisdom), p. 73.
397. कार्तिकेयो महासेनः शरजन्मा षडाननः।
पार्वतीनन्दनः स्कन्दः सेनानीरग्निभूर्गुहः।
बाहुलेयस्तारकजिद् विशाखः शिखिवाहनः।
षाण्मातुरः शक्तिधरः कुमारः कौञ्चदारणः ।
Ś., 1, 39-40.
398. Fleet, *op. cit.*, No. 10, Pl. V, p. 42, Sircar, *SI*, Vol. I, No.15, p. 285.
399. Altekar, *CGE*, p. 231, Pl. XVII, 22, p. 258, PL. XVIII. 19.
400. Wilkins, *Hindu Mythology*, pp. 323-327.
401. विनायको विघ्नराज-द्वैमातुर-गणाधिपाः।
अप्येकदन्त-हेरम्ब-लम्बोदर-गजाननाः।
Amarakośa, I, 38.
402. Geity, Alice, *Gaṇeśa, A Monograph on the Elephant-faced God*, pp. 25-26.
403. Misra, Rajni, *Brahmā-Worship*, p. 3.
404. Wilkins, *op. cit.*, p. 100.
405. ब्रह्माऽऽत्मभूः सुरज्येष्ठः परमेष्ठी पितामहः।
हिरण्यगर्भो लोकेशः स्वयंभूश्चतुराननः।
धाताऽब्जयोनिदुहिणो विरञ्चिः कमलासनः।
स्रष्टाः प्रजापतिर्वेधा विधाता विश्वसृड् विधिः।
नाभिजन्माण्डजः पूर्वो निधनः कमलोभ्दवः सदानन्दो रजोमूर्तिः सत्यको
हंसवाहनः।
Amarakośa, 1, 16-17.

406. Mishra, Rajni, *Brahmā-worship,* p. 3.
407. Wilkins, *op. cit.,* p. 110.
408. Mishra, Rajni, *loc. cit.,* p. 15.
409. Altekar, *CGE,* pp. 75-77, Pl. XXIII. 46.
410. Sahai, B., *Iconography of Minor Hindu and Buddhist Deities,* pp. 145-146.
411. Altekar, *CGE,* p. 328, Pl. XIVA. 7.
412. Pandey, L. P., *Sun-worship in Ancient India,* p. 132-136.
413. जयति जगतः प्रसूतिर्विश्वात्मा सहजभूषणं नभसः।
     द्रुतकनकसदृशदशशतमयूखमालार्चितः सविता।

     Bṛhat Saṁhitā I, 1.
414. दुरितं दर्शनेन ध्नंस्तत्त्वार्थेन नुंदस्तमः।
     प्रजाः स्वतन्त्रयांचक्रे शश्वत्सूर्य इवोदितः।

     Ch. 17, Ś 74.
415. Fleet, *CII,* Vol. III, No. 16, Pl. IX B. p. 68, Sircar, *SI,* Vol. I, No. 27, p. 318.
416. *Ibid.,* No. 18, Pl. XI, p. 79.
417. *Ibid.,* No. 37, Pl. XXIII, B., p. 161.
418. मूर्ते च गङ्गायमुने तदानीं सचामरे देवमसेविषाताम्।
     समुद्रगारूपविपर्यये़ऽपि संहसपाते इव लक्ष्यमाणे।

     Ch. VII, Ś. 42.
419. क्वचिच्च कृष्णोरगभूषणेव भस्माङ्गरागा तनुरीश्वरस्य।
     पश्यानवद्याङ्गि विभाति गंङ्गा भिन्न प्रवाहा यमुनातरङ्गैं।
     समुद्रपत्नयार्जलसंनिपाते पूतात्मनामात्र किलाभिषेकात्।
     तत्वावबोधेन विनाडपि भूयस्तनुत्यजो नास्ति शरीरबन्धः।

     ch., XII, 54-58.
420. Fleet, *CII,* Vol. III, No. I, Pl. I, P. 1 line 30.
421. *Ibid.,* No. 55, Pl. XXXIV. P. xI, Line 4.
422. *Ibid.,* No. 37, Pl. XXIII B, p. 169, Line 15.
423. *Ibid.,* No. 39, Pl. XXV, p. 184.
424. Altekar, *CGE,* p. 72, Pl. XXIII. 48, p. 192, Pl. XXIV, 62, p. 198, Pl. XXIV. 63.
425. Mishra, R. N., *Yaksha Cult and Iconography,* p. 31.
426. Krishnamachariar, M., *History of Classical Sanskrit Literature,* p. 359.
427. कश्चित्कान्ताविरहगुरूणा स्वाधिकारत्प्रमत्तः
     शापेनास्तङ्गमितमहिमा वर्षभोग्येण भुर्तः।
     यक्षश्चक्रे जनकतनयास्नानपुण्योदकेषु।
     स्निग्धच्छायातरूषु वसतिं रामगिर्याश्रमेषु।

     Meghadūta, i.i.

428. Wilkins, *Hindu Mythology,* p. 484.

429. प्रत्यहं रक्तकण्ठैरूद्गायद्भिर्धनपतियशः किन्नैरर्यत्र सार्धम्।

Meghadūta, ii, 10.

संरक्ताभिस्त्रिपुरविजयो गीयते किन्नरीभिः।

Meghadūta, i. 59.

430. Wilkins, *Hindu Mythology,* p. 329.

431. अश्वत्थः सर्ववृक्षाणां।

Bhagavad Gitā, 10, 26.

432. Thomas, P., *Epics, Myths and Legends of India, A Comparative Survey of HIndu, Buddhist and Jain,* p. 135.

433. Martin, E. Q., *The Gods of India,* p. 240.

434. Rao, TAG, *EHI,* Vol. I, Part I, p. 288.

435. Altekar, *CGE,* pp. 145-146, PIXVII. 14

436. Joshi, N. P., *Catalogue of Brahmanical Sculptures in the State Museum* Lucknow, p. 107, Figs. 34, 35.

Iconographic Forms in Ancient Texts

4

The emergence of *bhakti* led the devotees to have the images of their favourite deities with all beauty and decorations. It is desired that the image should be well proportionate, otherwise, it would be harmful to the worshipper. A beautiful image instantly strucks the mind of a meditator and helps in concentration (dhyāna). This kind of thought process to a great extent was responsible for producing the works dealing with the Śāstric iconographic forms.

A very interesting account of the practice of image-worship is given in the *Viṣṇudharmottara Pūraṇa.* King Vajra puts a question to the sage Mārkaṇḍeya, "What would obtain for him great happiness in this and other world?" Mārkaṇḍeya answers the question saying 'anyone desiring the best of the two worlds must worship gods. He further emphasizes that, "In the former three ages *kṛta, tretā* and *dvāpara* men were able to see a god directly but in the *kali* age men have lost that faculty and, therefore, they have to worship them (gods) in an image".[1]

The term *Icon* (Gr. *eikon*) means a figure representing a deity or a saint which is specially meant for worship.[2] This Greek word *eikon* has close parallel in such Indian terms as *archā, bera, vigraha* etc. which definitely denote sensible representations of particular deities or saints receiving the devout homage from their *bhaktas* or exclusive worshippers.[3]

The early works which contain references to Iconograpahy of the deities are the *Divyāvadāna,* the *Lalitavistara* assigned to the centuries of Christian era. The *Bṛhat Saṁhitā* of Varāhamihira and a few Purāṇas—*the Matsya, the Agni* and the *Viṣṇudharmottara,* belong to the Gupta phase which deal with various forms of art e.g. music, dance, painting, sculpture and architecture. A long list of the deities, whose worship should be done for fulfilling of the desires is found in the *Divyāvadāna.* These are Indra, Brahmā, Hari, Śaṅkara, Rudra, Makradhvaja (Kāmadeva), Kārttikeya, Varuṇa, Kubera, Ārāma-devatā and Vana-devatā.[4] The *Lalitavistara* refers to the imges of Śiva, Skanda, Nārāyaṇa, Kubera, Chandra, Sūrya, Vaiśravaṇa, Śakra, Brahmā and the Lokapālas. It does not give the iconographic details of the deities.[5] It is for the first time that the *Bṛhat Saṁhitā* deals with the iconographic traits of various gods and goddesses.

Brahmā

The image of Prajāpati Brahmā must have four faces, a water vessel in his hand and be seated on a lotus.[6] These two names Prajāpati and Brahmā are used by Varāhamihira as synonymous.[7] The *Matsya Purāṇa* depicted that the image of Brahmā should be made with four heads, the complexion should be reddish, like the bed of the lotus, with four hands holding a *Kamaṇḍalu* and a staff in the left hands and sacrificial ladle *(sruvā)* in the right hand. He should be made riding on a swan or seated on a lotus. He should be represented as engaged in the work of creation, wearing white clothes, deer-skin and a sacred thread.[8]

The *Agni Purāṇa* like *the Matsya Purāṇa* holds the view that the icon of Brahmā is to be represented as possessing four hands and four faces, looking towards the four quarters and riding on the swan and his long beard and clotted hair reaching down the prodigious belly. In his right hands are the rosary and the sacrificial ladle, in his left hands a water-pot and a vessel to hold the sacrificial clarified butter, the goddess Sarasvatī and Sāvitrī should be made as respectively waiting on the right and left side.[9]

It is from the time of the Gupta era the practice of making images on śāstric injunctions was started and the consquence of this was the classical sculptures and painting of this period. The *Viṣṇudharmottara Purāṇa* not only gives the instructions for the making of images but also provides the symbolism of various weapons and attributes of the deities.

Adhyāya 44 of the *Viṣṇudharmottara Purāṇa* starts with a description of the divine trinity. Here, *Viṣṇu* is the supreme god because the *Viṣṇudharmottara* like the *Viṣṇu Purāṇa* is a work, which prescribes the worship of the supreme divinity under the name of Viṣṇu. The three *mūrtis* (forms) of Viṣṇu, called Brāhmī, Vaiṣṇavī and Raudrī, is the result of the *rājas, sattva* and *tamas guṇas*. The three guṇas respectively represent the functions of creation, preservation and destruction.[10]

The *Viṣṇudharmottara Purāṇa* (Chapter 46) also described Brāhmī Mūrti i.e. the image of Brahmā having four faces, four arms and matted hair *(Jaṭā)* on his head and wearing the skin of a black antelope as a garment. He sits in the *padmāsana* pose in a chariot drawn by seven swans. Each of his right arm is put in the palm of each of the left hand. In his right hands he carries a rosary and a *kamaṇḍalu*. He wears all kinds of ornaments. He possesses all auspicious marks and has a tranquil form and eyes closed in meditation.[11]

The four faces of Brahmā represent the four Vedas, the eastern *Ṛgveda*, the southern *Yajurveda*, the western *Sāmaveda* and northern *Atharvaveda*. His four arms represent the four directions. The whole universe comes out of water, therefore, Brahmā has a kamaṇḍalu in his hand, which contains water. The rosary, which he is counting, represents time. The *yajña,* personified by two types of ceremonies, *śukla* and *aśukla* (or *kṛṣṇa*) is represented by the antelope skin which Brahmā wears. The seven *lokas* are symbolized by seven swans dragging the chariot of Brahmā. He sits with his eyes closed in meditation for visualising the world. The herbs maintain the world, which are symbolized by the matted hair of Brahmā. The different branches of learning which enlighten the world, are signified by ornaments.[12]

Sarasvatī

Varāhamihira does not give any description about Sarasvatī. The *Matsya Purāṇa* also does not give a detailed account about the form of Sarasvatī, except that, it should be placed on the right side of Brahmā. According to the *Agni Purāṇa* the image of Sarasvatī should be made as holding a book, rosary and lute in the hands.[13] The *Viṣṇudharmottara Purāṇa,* (Chapter-64) describes the iconography of Sarasvatī. The goddess should have a face like that of the moon and stand evenly on her feet *(samapāda).* Decorated with all sorts of ornaments she should have four hands. Her right hands should hold a book and an *akṣamālā* and the left hand *Vaiṇavī* and *kamaṇḍalu.*[14] Her four hands represent the four Vedas and the book represents all *śāstras.* The kamaṇḍalu in her hand is supposed to contain the immortal essence of all the *śāstras* and the rosary symbolizes the *kāla* (time). The Vaiṇavī is achievement *(siddhi)* personified.[15]

Viṣṇu

The *Bṛhat Saṁhitā* is of the view that image of Viṣṇu may be represented as eight, four or two-armed. Viṣṇu should have the sign of *śrivatsa* on his chest and adorned with the *Kaustubha* gem. He should be yellowish green in complexion like a lin flower and clad in yellow garments, his face being placid, he wears *kuṇḍalas* and a *kirīṭa,* his neck, chest, shoulders and arms being full and fleshy.[16] In case of an eight-armed image, three of his right hands should hold a sword, a mace and an arrow, the fourth being in the *śāntidā pose,* the hands on the left should carry a bow, shield *(kheṭaka),* discus and conch.[17] If he is intended to be four-armed, his right hands show a mace and *śāntidā mudrā,* while on left ones carry a conch and a discus. Of two-armed image, the right hand should be shown in *śāntidā-mudrā* and the left one holding a conch-shell.[18]

The *Matsya Purāṇa* also describes that the image of Viṣṇu should be eight, four or two-armed. The image should have a canopy (crown) over the head, with neck like a conch, beautiful eyes, raised nose, ears like the shell of mother of pearl, be peaceful and serene in appearance.[19] If the image is eight-armed, it should hold a sword, a club and arrow and a lotus in the right hands; and a bow, a shield, a conch and a disc *(chakra)* in the left hands.[20] The image with four hands should hold a club and lotus in the right hands and a conch and a discus *(chakra)* in the left hands.[21]

The *Agni Purāṇa* says that the image of Viṣṇu should be decorated with ornaments and emblems. The chakra should be placed in the upper right hand, the lotus in the lower one on the right. The *śaṅkha* in the upper left hand and *gadā* in the lower one on the left. The images of Śrī and Puṣṭi carrying a lotus and a harp respectively in their hands, reach upto the thighs of the image of Vāsudeva. The image of two Vidyādharas holding garlands in their hands should be carved into the space occupied by the halo around the head of the principal image and the images of celestial elephants are to be made in the region of the halo.[22]

The *Viṣṇudharmottara Purāṇa*, (Adhyāya 44 and 47) gives a vivid description of the image of Viṣṇu. Viṣṇu should be represented as seated on Garuḍa, wearing celestial yellow garment with *kaustubha* brightening his bosom and with all sorts of ornaments. His complexion would be like that of a cloud laden with water. He has four faces and eight arms. The eastern face is called *Saumya* i.e. placid, southern *Nṛsiṁha* i.e. indicating *Nṛisiṁha*, western kapils and Northern Varāha. He wears *vanamālā*. He carries in his right hands an arrow, a rosary, a club and in his left hands hide, cloth and rainbow.[23]

In Chapter 60 of the *Viṣṇudharmottara Purāṇa*, the details of two-armed and one-faced Viṣṇu image is met with. In another Chapter 85 a visual account of Viṣṇu as Vāsudeva is given. Viṣṇu is represented as having one face and four arms. The colour and ornaments are same as described above. The neck should have auspicious lines and bracelets around the arms and is decorated by the *vanamālā*, has *kaustubha* on his bosom and *kirīṭa* on his head. His arms are long with hands formed into fists. The nails of his fingers are thin and reddish. The earth portrayed in the form of a woman should be placed between his feet. On his right side a full-blown lotus and a *gadā* as a goddess having beautiful eyes and thin middle should be depicted and on the other side a *śaṅkha* and *chakra* with hanging belly, decked with ornaments should be placed.[24]

The *Viṣṇudharmottara Purāṇa*, also describes the significance of Viṣṇu's attributes. His four faces represent strength *(bala)*, knowledge *(jñāna)*, sovereignty *(aiśvarya)* and energy *(śakti)*. The eight hands symbolise the four quarters and the intermediate directions, of the ornaments the *kaustubha* signifies pure knowledge. The world is bound together by the long variegated and dark *vanamālā*. *Avidyā*, which keeps the world going is his garments, Garuḍa represents the mind pervading the bodies of all creatures. His weapons śaṅkha stands for the sky, *chakra* for the air, *gadā* for the light and lotus, for the water.[25]

Incarnations of Viṣṇu

Varāhamihira refers to two manifestations of Viṣṇu i.e. Rāma and Buddha.

The *Bṛhat Saṁhitā* does not speak about the features of Rāma expect that it should be made 120 digits high. According to Varāhamihira, Buddha should be shown with his palm and soles marked with a lotus, a placid countenance, very short hair and seated on a lotus seat.[26]

The Purāṇas contain detailed description of the iconography of the incarnations of Viṣṇu. The Matsya and the *Agni Purāṇa* say that the images of the Matsya and Kūrma *avatāras* of Viṣṇu should be made in the form of a fish and of a turtle.[27] According to the *Matsya Purāṇa* lotus and club should be placed in the hands of Varāha, the teeth should be sharp and at the left elbow should be placed the world uplifted by the teeth from the Pātāla and which bears calmly everything on her. His teeth should be very sharp and face full of joy and wonder. The right foot should be placed on the turtle and left foot on the head of the Śeṣa. All round Him should be made the images of Lokapālas in praying postures.[28]

According to the *Agni Purāṇa*, Viṣṇu in his boar incarnation should be endowed with a human body and a boar face, carrying *gadā* and other weapons in his right hands and conchshell, Lakṣmī or a lotus flower in the left hands.[29] The detailed decription of the image of Varāha is given in the *Viṣṇudharmottara Purāṇa* (Chapter 79). Varāha may be represented with human body and face of a boar or in a simple boar form. He should be shown standing on the back of Śeṣa in *ālīḍha* pose.[30] Śeṣa should be made with four hands, with beautiful jewelled hoods, eyes representing wonder and engrossed in looking at the goddess Pṛthvī. In his two hands should be placed the plough and the club and his other two hands should be shown in *añjali* pose. In the left hand of Varāha should be placed Vasudharā in the form of a woman. The goddess with her two hands should be shown in salutatiton pose. Śaṅkha is depicted in the hand which holds the earth goddess. His other hands should carry *padma, chakra* and *gadā*. [31]

The *Agni Purāṇa* refers to Nṛsiṁha incarnation as having a lion's head on a human body with four hands, two hands holding *gadā* and *chakra* and the other two tearing open the entrails of *Hiraṇyakśipu* who should be shown as lying on the thighs of the god.[32] The *Viṣṇudharmottara Purāṇa*, is also of the opinion that the icon of lord Nṛsiṁha should be made as a face of lion and a body of man. He should have thick shoulders, waist and neck. The middle part of body and belly should be lean. The colour of his garment should be blue and decked with ornaments. His haloed face and mane should be surrounded with flames. He should be represented as tearing the bosom of Hiraṇyakśipu with his sharp nails.[33] Nṛsiṁha can be represented in another way also. He can be shown as sitting at ease on lion-seat. His two hands should be placed on the head of *gadā* and body should be surrounded with flames.[34]

According to the *Matsya Purāṇa* the image of Vāmana should be made with arms by the side of his legs raised upwards, holding a goblet in the left hand and a small umbrella in the right hand. The face of the lord should be extremely meek and appealing.[35]

The Agni Purāṇa holds the view that the figure of Paraśurāma may hold the bow and arrow, a sword and an axe.[36]

According to the *Matsya Purāṇa* the image of Rāma should be made of ten *talas*. No other details about the image of Rāma arc given.[37] The *Agni Purāna* mentions that the image of Rāma should be made carrying a bow and arrow, a sword and a *śaṅkha*.[38] In the *Viṣṇudharmottara Purāṇa*, however, description of the image of Rāma is not given.

According to the *Matsya Purāṇa* the image of Kṛṣṇa should hold a club in the left hand and the conch and disc (*chakra)* may be placed high or low.[39] The *Viṣṇudharmottara Purāṇa* says that Kṛṣṇa should be made with the usual colour of the blue lotus, carrying a chakra in his hand.[40]

According to the *Agni Purāṇa* the figure of Buddha should be made as calm, having long ears, white complexion, wearing a cloth and seated on a lotus with its petals upwards and as conferring favour and protection.[41]

The *Agni Purāṇa* describes that the image of *kalki* to be represented as a twice-born endowed with a bow and quiver and destroying the foreigners. He should be represented as seated on the horse and holding a sword, conch, disc and arrow.[42]

Varāhamihira lays down that Baladeva should be depicted with a ploughshare in his hand with eyes round and rolling owning to inebrity, adorned with one earring, having complexion being as white as a conch-shell, lotus stalk or the moon.[43] The *Matsya Purāṇa* does not give any account of the image of Balarāma. In the *Agni Purāṇa* (Chapter 49) the image of Balarāma is said to be represented having a plough, mace, club and lotus. The details of the iconography of Saṁkarṣaṇa and Balarāma is also given in the *Viṣṇudharmottara Purāṇa.* Saṁkarṣaṇa should look like Vāsudeva. His colour should be white and should wear blue dress. In the place of *gadā* and *chakra*, he should hold *mūsala* and *lāṅgala* respectively. The *mūsala* and *lāṅgala* should have the beautiful human forms with a slender waist. The figure which shows the deity, carrying a ploughshare and a pestle, who is of white colour and wears deep blue garments and *kuṇḍalas* in ears, eyes intoxicated with drinks, is called Balarāma.[44]

Ekānaṁśā

The iconometry and iconography of Ekānaṁśā is dealt by Varāhamihira in three couplets. It shows the cult of the goddess was quite popular in 6th century A.D. According to him the image of Ekānaṁśā should be made two, four or eight-armed. She should be placed between Baladeva and Kṛṣṇa (if she is intended to be shown two-armed) her left hand should rest on her hip, the right hand should carry a lotus. If she is to be represented four-armed, she should hold in her left hands a book and a lotus, one of her right hands being in *varada* pose and other holding a rosary. When she is represented with eight arms, her left hands should carry a *kamaṇḍalu,* a bow, a lotus and a book, while her right hands should hold an arrow, mirror or a rosary, the remaining one being shown in the *varada-mudrā.*[45] The *Viṣṇudharmottara Purāṇa* states that Ekānaṁśā should be placed between Balarāma and Kṛṣṇa, with her left hand on her waist and right holding a lotus.[46]

Sāmba

The *Bṛhat Saṁhitā* holds the opinion that the figure of Sāmba should hold a mace in his hand.[47] According to the *Viṣṇudharmottara Purāṇa* the image of Sāmba should be made carrying a club in his hand and handsome in appearance. The colour of his body should be like that of white lotus and should be depicted in red garments. On his either side should be placed two women carrying sword in their hands.[48]

Pradyumna

The *Bṛhat Saṁhitā* holds the view that the image of Pradyumna should be shown with a charming personality, and carrying a bow in his hand. His wife should also be installed carrying a sword and shield.[49] According to *Agni Purāṇa* Pradyumna is represented as having a mace resting on the navel or holding the bow and arrow.[50] In the opinion of the *Viṣṇudharmottara Purāṇa* Pradyumna should look like Vāsudeva. His colour should be dark like the sprouts of *dūrvā* and should hold *chāpa* (bow) and arrow in place of *chakra* and *gadā.* The bow and arrow should be shown in human forms.[51]

Aniruddha

According to the *Agni Purāṇa* Aniruddha is represented as having four-arms. The colour of Aniruddha's body according to the *Viṣṇudharmottara Purāṇa* should resemble like that of leaf of lotus and he should wear red garments. He should carry shield and sword.[52]

Lakṣmī

Varāhamihira does not refer to the image of Lakṣmī. But the *Matsya Purāṇa* says that the image of Lakṣmī should be made youthful in appearance, having thick cheeks, red lips, knitted brows and adorned with jewels and earrings. Her face should be round and body should be adorned with finely dressed garments, garlands and bracelets. A lotus flower should be shown in her left hand and wood apple in her right hand. And, further, the goddess should be depicted as seated on a lotus-bed, surrounded by the buzzing black bees, bathed by a couple of elephants with vases and prayed by Gandharvas and Guhyakas.[53] The four-armed Lakṣmī should hold the disc and conch in the right hand and the mace and a lotus in the left hand according to the *Agni Purāṇa.* [54] The *Viṣṇudharmottara Purāṇa* says when Lakṣmī is depicted with Lord Viṣṇu she should have two hands. She should hold lotus in her hand and be decked with all kinds of ornaments. Her colour should be white and wear a white garment.

When Lakṣmī is represented independently, she should have four hands and seated on a beautiful *siṁhāsana.* Her right hand should have a lotus flower with a big stalk touching the end of the armlet and her left hand should have a nector-pot and similarly other two hands should carry a *bilva* and a conch. Behind her back there should be a pair of elephants bending down the pots as if in the act of pouring. On her head should be made a charming lotus.[55]

The conch represents good luck, bilva the whole world and the lotus in her hands stands for wealth. The pair of elephants personifies the two *nidhis* viz. *Śaṅkha* and *Padma.*[56]

Śiva

Vārahamihira refers to Śiva's images in anthropomorphic and phallic forms. In anthropomorphic form Śiva has a crescent on his head, a bull for his ensign and a vertical third eye on his forehead, in his two hands he holds a trident and the bow called *Pināka.* [57] Varāhamihira further states that his half may consist of the half of the daughter of the mountain (Pārvatī).[58] This shows that the form of Ardhanārīśvara was also popular in six century A.D.

The *Matsya Purāṇa* also describes Śiva in two forms *i.e.* anthropomorphic and phallic form. The text says the Śiva arms should be like the trunk of an elephant, the thigh and ankles should be beautifully round, the hair should be straight, the eyes should be broad and extended. His image should be represented as wearing a tiger skin and a girdle of three strings should be made round the waist. The image should be decorated with garlands, necklaces, armlets and serpents. The cheeks should be fatty and earrings should be placed in the ears. The hands should be made long enough to reach the knees and the general appearance should be serene and peaceful. *Kheṭaka* (sword) should be placed in the left hand and an axe in his right hand. Trident, *śakti*, and staff should be placed in right and skull, snake and *khaṭvāṅga* in left hands.

Śiva in a dancing posture on his bull should have two hands with one he should be depicted as bestowing boons and with the other hand holding an armlet or *rudrākṣa.* Ten-armed dancing Śiva should wear an elephant skin.

His image representing the scene of the destruction of Tripurā should be made with sixteen or eight hands. When he is depicted as having eight arms, he should carry a conch, a *chakra*, club, bow and an arrow.

In Bhairava form Śiva should be shown as having an aquiline nose, sharp teeth and formidable in appearance.[59]

The image of Umā-Maheśvara should be made either having four hands or two hands. Śiva should be depicted as having the matted locks on the head and a crescent moon placed on it. He should have three eyes and hands resting on the shoulders of the goddess. He should be adorned with tiger skin and jewels of various kinds.

The goddess Umā should be represented as seated on the left side of the Lord. She should be shown having nice tresses of hair and decked with armlets and earrings, and looking at the face of the Lord.[60]

The *Agni Purāṇa* does not refer to the anthropomorphic representation of the Lord Śiva. But the *Viṣṇudharmottara* refers to Mahādeva, who should be made seated on a bull, having five faces. The faces should be placid-looking, except the southern one which should be fierce, wearing a garland of skulls and signifying the destruction of universe. All other faces, except for northern one, should have three eyes. The crescent moon should be placed on the matted locks of hair. The fifth face should be on the top of it. In such an image Vāsuki serves as his *yajñopavīta.* Mahādeva should be represented with ten arms. In his right hands should be placed rosary (*akṣamālā*), trident (*triśūla*) an arrow *(śara),* a staff *(daṇḍa)* and a lotus (*utpala*) and in the left hands a citron (*mātuluṅga*), a bow (*chāpa*), a mirror (*ādarśa*), a waterpot (*kamaṇḍalu*) and a skin (*charma).* The colour of the whole image should resemble the rays of moon.[61] So far as the iconography of Bhairava is concerned image should be made having round and tawny eyes, with a hanging belly, a terrible face on account of tusks, wide nostrils and a garland of *kapālas* (skulls), and adorned on all sides with ornaments in the form of snakes. He should be shown wearing an elephant skin as his upper garment. He should have many arms, huge and long like *sāla* trees, bearing all sorts of weapons as ornaments and possessed of sharp and beautiful nails.[62]

The iconographic traits of the Ardhanārīśvara or Gaurīśvara form of Śiva are given in the *Viṣṇudharmottara Purāṇa.* In this form Śiva should be made on the right side and Pārvatī (or Gaurī) on the left side. Śiva should be made as having one face, two eyes, four arms which consists of a rosary and a trident and wearing all ornaments. Pārvatī should hold in her hands a mirror and a blue lotus. This form signified the identity-in-difference of Prakṛti and Puruṣa.[63]

The symbolism of the emblems of Mahādeva is explained by the *Viṣṇudharmottara Purāṇa* in Chapter 48. The eastern face suggests Mahādeva. His three eyes represent the Sun, the Moon and the Fire. The terrible southern face is called Bhairava. The western face is called Nandīvaktra. The northern face is known as Umāvaktra and the fifth face should be known as Sadāśiva. All have three eyes except the face of Vāmadeva which has only two eyes. These represented the five principle elements of nature. The face of Mahādeva is the earth *(bhūmiḥ),*the Bhairava face is light *(tejas),* the Nandī face is the wind *(Vāyu)*, the Umā face is the waters *(apaḥ)*and the Sadāśiva face is the sky *(ākāśa)*. Two hands are allotted to each face. The ten arms represents ten directions (*diśās*). In the hands of Mahādeva, there should be a rosary (*akṣamālā*) and a *kamaṇḍalu*, in the hands of Sadāśiva the bow (*chapa)* and arrow (*bāna)* and staff (*daṇḍa*) and citron (*mātulaṅga*) in the hands of Bhairava.[64]

Of these the staff stand for death and *mātulaṅga* indicates the seed of the world. The three śūlas of the triśūla represents *sattva, rājas* and *tamas guṇas*. The mirror and lotus in the hands of Pārvatī indicate pure knowledge and detachment. The matted locks of Mahādeva represent the variegated Brahman. The digit of the moon on the face of Śiva represents his divine power and Vāsuki, the king of serpent, represents anger which subdues the three worlds. The tiger-skin represents the wide the variegated *tṛṣṇā* (desire). The bull is the divine four footed *dharma*.[65]

Hari-Hara

According to the *Matsya Purāṇa* the image of Hari-Hara should be made by dividing the image into two parts. The right half of the body should be assigned to Śiva and the left half to Viṣṇu. The right side of the body should be adorned with plaited hair and crescent, the right arm decorated with armlets of serpents, should be made in the posture of making a gift, the other one should be shown carrying a trident. His body should be depicted as wearing a tiger-skin, a serpent as sacred thread *(Yajñopavīta)* and the two feet adorned with jewels and serpents. The left half of the image should consist of Viṣṇu. His two arms should be decorated with jewels and armlets and carrying a conch and a discus (*chakra)*. A discus can be replaced by a club. He should be shown as wearing yellow garments studded with white gems and feet should be adorned with the ornaments and gems.[66]

The *Agni Purāṇa* is also of the opinion that the image of Hari-Hara should be divided into two halves. The right half of the image should have the features of Śiva and the left half should have those of Viṣṇu. The two right hands of Śiva should be represented as carrying a trident and a sword and other two hands of Viṣṇu should be depicted as holding a *gadā* and a *chakra*. The image of Pārvatī and Lakṣmī should be located on each side.[67]

Liṅga

Varāhamihira gives an account about the shape and proportions of the *liṅga*. The periphery of the round (upper most) portion of the *liṅga*, measured lengthwise, should be divided into three parts, the lowermost portion should be square, the middle one octagonal and above that circular. The square section must be placed in a hole dug out in the ground and the octagonal middle one into that cut in the pedestal, (only the circular section being visible), the pedestal on all the sides of the hole should be equal to the height of the visible (top most cylindrical) section. A *liṅga* lean and long, injured at the top was supposed to spell ruin to the country, town and its master respectively.[68]

The *Matsya Purāṇa* (Ch. 263) also provides information regarding the construction of *liṅga*. The size of the phallus should be according to the size of the temple or vice-versa. The phallus should be divided into three parts. The bottom part, called Brahmā should be square in shape. The middle part, which is accorded to Viṣṇu, should be octagonal and upper part which is of Śiva should be made round. The square part should be burried in the ground.[69]

According to the *Agni Purāṇa* the liṅga should be made of salt, ghee, cloth, wood, clay, gold and of gems. It should be constructed on a rectangular block of stone and divided into two parts (lengthwise), the lower part again being divided into eight parts and three parts of these divisions being left out, the remaining block formed by five parts should be divided breadthwise into three parts and the three gods should be assigned there. The square part assigned to Brahmā, octagonal to Viṣṇu and round part to Śiva.[70]

In the *Viṣṇudharmottara Purāṇa* (Ch. 74) also, details have been given regarding the phallic representation of Śiva. The upper portion of *liṅga* should be round and the portion below it eight-sided and further below four-sided. The round portion *i.e.* upper part of it should be made visible, the octgonal portion *i.e.* middle part should be inserted in the *piṇḍika* and the square portion *i.e.* bottom part in *brahmapiṭha*. The line on the top of the *liṅga* should be well rounded.[71]

Gaṇeśa

The *Bṛhat Saṁhitā* refers to the image of Gaṇeśa, who is the lord of the Pramatha, the hosts of Śiva. He should have the face of an elephant, with a single tusk, a bulging belly, a hatchet and a redish in his hand.[72]

The *Matsya Purāṇa* gives detailed iconographic features of Gaṇeśa. Accordingly he should be made as having the face of an elephant, three eyes, four arms, huge stomach, ears like those of an elephant and wearing a sacred thread. It further describes that he should be depicted as holding a large and long tusk and lotus with his right hand and a battle-axe and a ball of sweet with the left. He should be represented as riding on a mouse. Gaṇeśa is the owner of *riddhi* (Success and prosperity) and *buddhi* (intelligence).[73]

The *Agni Purāṇa* (Ch. 50) discusses the image of Gaṇeśa or Vināyaka. His image should have an elephant face with a big trunk and a human body with a big belly. He should be depicted as wearing a sacred thread and holding his own tusk which looked like an axe with right hand, and a ball of sweet *(modaka)* and lotus flower with the left.[74]

The *Viṣnudharmottara Purāṇa* agrees with the views of the *Matsya* and the *Agni Purāṇa* and states that the face of Gaṇeśa or Vināyaka should be of an elephant having four arms. A trident and a rosary should be depicted in his right hands and an axe and a vessel full of sweets in the left hands. No tusk should be shown on his left side. The vessel full of *modakas* should be on the tip of his fingers. He should have a drooping belly and stiff ears. He wears a tiger-skin as garment and a serpent as his sacred-thread. One foot should be on the foot-stool and the other should be on the seat.[75]

Skanda-Kārttikeya

The *Bṛhat Saṁhitā* has devoted only a half verse to the description of Skanda's iconography. It states that Skanda should look like a boy in appearance, carry a *śakti* (spear) and has a peacock for his ensign.[76] According to the *Matsya Purāṇa* the image of Kārttikeya should be made youthful in appearance like a newly risen Sun, holding a staff and a deer skin. He should have a peacock for his conveyance.[77] The image of Kārttikeya should be made having twelve, four or two-arms. If the image is intended to be twelve armed, the right hands should hold a javelin, a noose, a sword, an arrow and a trident, the lower most hand should be in the *varada* pose. In the left hands should be placed arrows, pointed ring-fingers, fists, other ornaments and a sword. The four-armed figure should be made holding a noose and a spear in the left hands and the right in *varada* and *abhaya-mudrā*. The two-armed image of Kārttikeya should have a śakti in his right hand and the left resting on the peacock.[78] The *Agni Purāṇa* clearly speaks that the image of Kumāra, also known as Śākha and Viśākha, should be sculptured as having a single face or as many as six faces.

Kārttikeya should be shown as youthful in appearance, having two arms and riding on a peacock. The images of his consorts, Sumukhī and Viḍālākṣī (cat-eyed), should be placed on his either side.[79]

The iconographic features of the image of Kumāra (Kārttikaya) are also given in the *Viṣṇudharmottara Purāṇa* (Ch. 71). Kumāra, also known as Skanda, Viśākha and Guha, has six faces. He is adorned with a tuft of hair. He wears a red garment and rides on a peacock. His right hands hold a cock and a bull and left the *vaijayantī* banner and a spear. Skanda, Viśākha and Guha should be made like Kumāra but they should be sculptured without having six-faces and do not ride on a peacock.[80]

Mātṛkās

Varāhamihira refers to Mātṛkās but is silent about their numbers. Originally these were seven which afterwards increased to eight, nine, twelve or even sixteen. The *Bṛhat Saṁhitā* does not state about their representation in art except that the Mothers should be shown with the emblems of the gods corresponding to their names.[81]

The iconographic features of the Mātṛkās are described in the *Matsya Purāṇa* (Ch. 261). The images of the different Mātṛkās should be made corresponding the forms of their respective lords.[82] The image of Brāhmī should be made as having four heads and four arms. She should be made as seated on a swan and holding a *kamaṇḍalu* and a rosary in her hands.

The image of Maheśvarī should resemble like Maheśvara. She should have matted hair, seated on a bull with a forehead adorned with a crescent moon. She should be shown having four hands and carrying a sword, skull, trident and a *khaṭvāṅga.*

The image of Kaumārī should be made after the form of Kārttikeya riding on a peacock, dressed in red, armed with a trident and a spear, decorated with armlets, garlands and holding a cock in her hand. The icon of Vaiṣṇavī should look like Viṣṇu. She should be depicted as seated on a throne and having a child. Her four hands should hold a conch, a *chakra,* a club and Garuḍa should be shown standing nearby her.

The image of Varāhī should be made riding on a buffalow, with a *chauri* over her head and carrying a club and a Chakra in her hands.

The image of Indrāṇī should resemble like Indra. She should be depicted as riding on an elephant, having many eyes, adorned with various divine ornamnets and of the colour of burnished gold. Her hands should be armed with a bolt, a club, a trident and a sword.

The image of Jogeśvarī should be made as having three eyes, a long tongue, hair standing on their ends, adorned with pieces of bones, having a set of ferocious teeth, slender waist, wearing a garland of skulls and head covered with flesh and blood. She should hold a head in the left hand and a *śakti* in the right hand. She should be depicted riding on a vulture or a crow, lean with a scanty stomach.

When Pārvatī assumes the form of Chāmuṇḍā she should be shown as wearing a tiger-skin and holding a bell in the hand.

The image of Kālikā should be represented as seated on an ass, holding a skull, undressed, adorned with red flowers and banners.

The image of Gaṇeśa should be placed near these Mātṛkās and the representation of Vīreśvara riding on a bull, having plaited hair had holding a *vinā* and trident in his hands should be depicted in front of the images of the Mātṛkās.[83]

The *Agni Purāṇa* (Ch. 50) mentions the images of Māṭṛkās. The four-faced Brāhmī should be represented as having fair complexion, rosary and a sacrificial ladle.

The Śakti of Śiva or Śaṅkari should be depicted as seated on a bull and holding a bow and arrow in the right hand and a *chakra* in the left.

The Śakti of Viṣṇu i.e. Vaiṣṇavī should be represented as holding a disc and conch in the right hands and a mace and lotus in the left hands.

The figure of Kaumārī should be made of red colour and riding on a peacock. Her two arms should be decorated with spears.

The image of Varāhī should be made as a maiden, mounted on a buffalo. She should have four hands. Her right hands should carry a conch, a *chakra* and left hands a mace and a lotus flower.

Aindrī should be shown as having thousand eyes and carrying a thunderbolt in the left hand.

Chāmuṇḍā should be sculptured as having made a foot-stool of the dead body of a man and possessed of three eyes sunk in their respective sockets and looking like a woman who has lost all flesh and has been reduced to skeleton. The hair on her head should be depicted as angrily standing erect and wearing a tiger-skin round her extremely emaciated body.[84]

The *Viṣṇudharmottara Purāṇa* is of the view that the mothers or māṭṛkās should have the emblems of the respective gods. All of them carry flesh and vessels full of blood. These are to be shown in dancing poses whose form is not described.[85]

Mahiṣāsuramardinī

According to the *Matsya Purāṇa* Pārvatī in her Durgā or Mahiṣāsuramardinī form should be depicted as having a discus, a trident, sharp pointed arrows, a spear and a sword, a bow, a noose, a goad, a bell, a battle-axe in the left hands. Below her image should be made the figure of the monster Mahiṣāsura with his severed head, holding a sword in one hand which is soaked in blood, ferocious at looking, tied in the noose, his bosom being pierced by the spear of the Devī and his intestines coming out. The conveyance of Goddess in the form of a lion should also be made. The right foot of the goddess should be placed on the back of the lion and the toe of the left foot should be made touching the body of Mahiṣāsura.[86]

The *Agni Purāṇa* is of the view that the goddess Chaṇḍikā or Mahiṣāsuramardinī should be represented as having twenty hands, ten on the right side and ten on the left.[87] She should hold the spear, sword, dart, disc, noose, club, *damaru,* spike in the left hands and one hand should be shown in the *abhaya-mudrā* and a snake, club, axe, goad, bow, bell, banner, mirror and iron mace should be placed in the right hands.[88] The buffalo should be sculptured below with its head entirely severed and the demon as issuing forth from its neck with rage and brandishing his sword in the air. The goddess is to be sculptured in a standing pose with her left foot on the shoulders of the demon. The image of the goddess should be made as possessing three eyes, fully armed and crushing the enemy of the gods.[89]

Sūrya

The *Bṛhat Saṁhitā* refers to the image of the Sun-god to be clad in Northerner's dress i.e. being covered from feet to the chest and carrying a lotus in each of his hands.[90] According to the *Matsya Purāṇa* the image of Sūrya should have beautiful eyes and be depicted as seated on a one-wheeled chariot drawn by seven horses. A red coloured crown should be placed on his head. He should be adorned with ornaments and two hands should be shown holding blue lotuses. His body should be covered with bodice. His feet should be made brilliant.[91] The figure of Daṇḍa and Piṅgala carrying sword in their hands should be placed on either side of *Sūrya*. The image of *Sūrya* should be surrounded by a number of divinities. The seven horses with long necks and well-decked and tied together with the string of serpents should be yoked to the chariot of the deity. Its reins should be properly held by Aruṇa, the charioteer.[92]

The *Agni Purāṇa* (Ch. 51) describes the icon of Sun should be depicted as riding in a chariot provided with a single wheel and drawn by seven horses. He should hold in his two hands the two celestial lotus flowers and the emblems of light and animation. On his right side stands his attendant Kuṇḍin holding in his hand a pen and an inkpot, symbolising the computation of the age.[93] Piṅgala, an attendant and gate-keeper of Sūrya should be placed on the left side with a mace in his hand. Sun-god should also have female attendants bearing *chaurīs* and the pale-looking consort by his side.[94]

In the *Viṣnudharmottara Purāṇa* (Ch. 67) a vivid description of the image of Sūrya is given. Sūrya should have a good form. The colour of his body should be red as vermillion. He should have moustache and dressed in northern style. He should be adorned with ornaments and wearing armour and girdle known as *Yaviyaṅga. Raśmis* in his right and left hands should be shown. They have the forms of a garland whose threads go up and full of all kinds of flowers. Daṇḍa, having an anthropomorphic form, should be placed on his left and Piṅgala of a deep tawny colour on his right. Both should be dressed in northern style. The remaining two-hands of Sūrya should be on the heads of these two (Daṇḍa and Piṅgala). Piṅgala carries a leaf and a pen in his hands. Daṇḍa has a shield and a trident *(śula)* in his hands. On the left side of the deity should be placed a banner having an emblem of lion. His four sons—Revanta, Yama, and two Manus should be placed on his two sides. His four wives—Rajanī, Ṛkśubhā, Chhāyā and Suvarchalā should also be placed on his two sides. He should be depicted seated on his one wheeled chariot with six spokes and drawn by seven horses. His charioteer Aruṇa is also sculptured. The seven horses signified the seven metres. They are Gāyatrī, Uṣṇik, Anuṣṭubha, Bṛhatī, Paṅkti, Triṣṭubha and Jagatī. With the rays in his hands he holds the entire universe. The lion on his banner represents *dharma* in person. His four wives Rajanī, Rkśubhā, Chhāyā and Suvarchalā representes the earth, the sky, the shadow and the lustre respectively. His colour is red because he is the source of all lustre and his limbs are concealed under unbearable lustre.[95]

Semi-divine Beings

According to the *Matsya Purāṇa* among the semi-divine beings the Nāgas should be made having the upper part of their body that of human being and serpent hoods on their heads and lower part should resemble like those of the natural serpents.[96]

In the opinion of the *Agni Purāṇa* the Kinnaras should be represented as holding lutes in their hands and the Vidyādharas as having garlands and moving in the sky.[97]

References

1. Shah, Priya Bala, *Viṣṇudharmottara Purāṇa*, Part II, pp. 1-2.
2. Banerjea, J. N., *DHI*, p. 1
3. *Ibid.*, p. 1.
4. शिववरुणकुबेरशक्रब्रह्मादीनायाचते आरामदेवतां वनदेवतां शृङ्गाटकदेवतां बलिप्रतिग्राहिकां देवताम्। *Divyāvadāna*, p. 1.
5. शिवस्कन्दनारायणकुबेरचन्द्रसूर्यवैश्रवणशक्रब्रह्मलोकपाल अथ प्रभृतयः प्रतिमहः। *Lalitavistara*, p. 184.
6. ब्रह्मा कमण्डलुकरश्चतुर्मुखः पङ्कजासनस्थश्च।
   Bṛhat Saṁhitā, Ch. 58, Sloka 41.
7. Bhat, Ramakrishna M., Varāhamihira's *Bṛhat Saṁhitā*, Part II, p. 358.
8. The *Matsya Mahā Purāṇam* Part II, p. 1127.
9. Gyani, S. D., *Agni Purāṇa—A Study*, p. 275.
10. Shah, Priya Bala, *Viṣṇudharmottara Purāṇa*, Part II, p. 138.
11. *Ibid.*, pp. 139-40.
12. *Ibid.*, pp. 140-41.
13. *Agni Purāṇa*, Part I, p. 133.
14. Shah, Priya Bala, *loc. cit.*, p. 154.
15. Ibid., pp. 140-141.
16. कार्योऽष्टभुजो भगवांश्चतुर्भजो द्विभुज एववा विष्णुः।
    श्रीवत्साङ्कितवक्षाः कौस्तुभमणिभूषितोरस्कः॥
    अलसीकुसुमश्यामः पीताम्बरनिवसनः प्रसन्नमुखः।
    कुण्डलकिरीटधारी पीनगलोरः स्थलांसभुजः॥
    Bṛhat Saṁhitā, Ch. 58, Śloka, 31-32.

17. Shastry, Ajay Mitra, *India as seen in the Bṛhat Saṁhitā of Varāhamihira,* p. 133.
18. *Ibid.*, p. 133.
19. *The Matsya Mahā Purāṇam,* p. 115.

    ....शङ्खचक्रधरशान्तं पद्महस्तंगदाधरम्।

    च्छत्राकारशिरस्तस्य कम्बुग्रीवं शुभेक्षणम्। तुङ्गनासंशुक्तिकर्ण प्रशान्तोरूभुजक्रमम्।

    Matsya Mahā Purāṇam, Ch. 258, Śloka 4-5.
20. *Ibid.*, p. 1115.
21. *Ibid.*, p. 1115.
22. Gyani, S. D., *Agni Purāṇa—A Study,* p. 274.
23. Shah, Priya Bala, *op. cit.* p. 141.
24. *Ibid.*, p. 142.
25. Ibid., p. 142.
26. Shastry, Ajay Mitra, *India as seen in the Bṛhat Saṁhitā of Varāhamihira,* p. 191.

    पद्माङ्कितकरचरणः प्रसन्नमूर्तिः सुनीचकेशश्च।

    पद्मासनोपविष्टः पितेव जगतो भवति बुद्धः॥

    Bṛhat Saṁhitā, Ch. 58, Śloka 44.
27. मत्स्यरूपं तथा मात्स्यं कूर्मं कूर्माकृतिं न्यसेत्।

    Matsya Mahā Purāṇam, Ch. 260, Śloka 38.
28. *Ibid.*, p. 1126.
29. Gyani, S.D., *Agni Purāṇa—A Study,* p 275.
30. Shah, Priya Bala, *op. cit.*, p 158.
31. *Ibid.*, p. 158.
32. Gyani, S. D., *loc. cit.*, p. 275.
33. Shah, Priya Bala, *op. cit.*, p. 157.
34. *Ibid.*, p. 157
35. *Matsya Mahā Purāṇam*, p. 1126
36. *The Agni Purāṇa*, Part I, p. 129.
37. *Matsya Mahā Purāṇam*, p. 1121.
38. *The Agni Purāṇa*, pp. 129-130.
39. *Matsya Mahā Purāṇam,* Part II, p. 116.

    कृष्णावतारे तु गदा वामहस्ते प्रशस्यते। यथेच्छया शङ्खचक्रेचोपरिष्टात् प्रकल्पयेत्।

    Matsya Mahā Purāṇam, Ch. 258. Sloka 10.
40. Shah, Priya Bala, *op. cit.*, p. 165.
41. *Agni Purāṇa*, Part I, p. 130.
42. *Ibid.*, p. 130.

42. *Ibid.*, p. 130.
43. Shastriy Ajay Mitra, *op. cit.*, p. 146.
बलदेवो हलपाणिर्मदविभ्रमलोचनश्च कर्तव्यः।
बिभ्रत्कुण्डलमेकं शङ्खेन्दुमृणालगौरतनुः।
Bṛhat Saṁhitā, Ch. 58, Śloka 36.
44. Shah, Priya Bala, *op. cit.*, p. 162.
45. Shastry, Ajay Mitra, *op. cit.* p. 158.
46. Shah, Priya Bala, *op. cit.*, p. 165.
47. Shastry, Ajay Mitra, *loc. cit.*, p. 148.
48. Shah, Priya Bala, *op. cit.*, p. 165.
49. Shastry, Ajay Mitra, *op. cit.*, p. 65.
50. *Agni Purāṇa*, Part I, p. 130.
51. Shah, Priya Bala, *op. cit.*, p. 162.
52. *Ibid.*, p. 162.
53. *Matsya Mahā Purāṇam*, Part II, p. 1133.
54. *Agni Purāṇa*, Part I, p. 133.
55. Shah, Priya Bala, *Viṣṇudharmottara Purāṇa*, Part II, Adhyāya 82, p. 154.
56. *Ibid.*, p. 155.
57. शम्भोः शिरसीन्दुकला वृषध्वजोऽक्षि च तृतीयमपि चोर्ध्वम्।
शूलं धनुः पिनाकं वामार्धे वा गिरिसुतार्धम्।
Bṛhat Saṁhitā, Ch. 58, Sloka 43.
58. Shastry, Ajay Mitra, *op. cit.*, p. 136.
59. *Matsya Mahā Purāṇam*, Part II, p. 1122.
60. The *Matsya Mahā Purāṇam*, Part II, p. 1124.
61. Shah, Priya Bala, *op. cit.*, pp. 143-44.
62. Shah, Priya Bala, *Viṣṇudharmottara Purāṇa* Part II, Ch. 59, p. 144.
63. *Ibid*, p. 144.
64. Shah, Priya Bala, *op. cit.*, pp. 144-45.
65. *Ibid.*, p. 145.
66. *Matsya Mahā Purāṇam*, Part II, p. 1125.
67. Gyani, S. D., *op. cit.*, p. 275.
68. Shastry, Ajay Mitra, *India as seen in the Bṛhat Saṁhitā of Varāhamihira*, pp. 136-37.
69. *The Matsya Mahā Purāṇam*, Part II, p. 1136.
70. *Agni Purāṇa* pp. 139-140.
71. Shah, Priya Bala, *Viṣṇudharmottara Purāṇa* , Part II, p. 161.
72. Bhat, Ramakrishna, M., *Varāhamihira's Bṛhat Saṁhitā*, Part II, p. 567.
73. *Matsya Mahā Purāṇam*, Part II, p. 1128.

74. *Agni Purāṇa*, p. 134.
75. Shah, Priya Bala, *op. cit.*, p. 152.
76. Shastry, Ajay Mitra, *op. cit.*, p. 152.
स्कन्दः कुमाररूपः शक्तिधरो बर्हिकेतुश्च।
Bṛhat Saṁhitā, Ch. 58, Śloka 41.
77. *Matsya Mahā Purāṇam*, Part II, p. 1127.
.... कार्तिकेयं प्रवक्ष्यामि तरुणादित्यसमप्रभम्।
.........दण्डकैश्चीरकैर्युक्तं मयूरवरवाहनम्।
Matsya Purāṇa, Ch. 260, Sloka 46.
78. *The Matsya Mahā Purāṇam*, p. 1127.
The Purāṇa does not describe whether the image of Kārttikeya should be one-faced or six-faced.
79. *Agni Purāṇa*, p. 134.
80. Shah, Priya Bala, *op. cit.*, p. 151.
81. Shastry, Ajay Mitra, *op. cit.*, 156.
मातृगणः कर्तव्यः स्वनामदेवानुरुपकृतचिन्हः।
Bṛhat Saṁhitā, 58, 56
82. *The Matsya Mahā Purāṇam*, Part II, p. 1131.
मातृणां लक्षणं वक्ष्ये यथावदनुपूर्वशः।
Matsya Purāṇa, 261, 24.
83. *Matsya Mahā Purāṇam*, Part II, pp. 1131-32.
84. Gyani, S.D., *Agni Purāṇa—A Study*, p. 277.
85. Shah, Priya Bala, *op. cit.*, p. 167.
86. *Matsya Mahā Purāṇam. Part II*, p. 1128.
87. Gyani, S.D., *op. cit.*, p. 276.
88. *Agni Purāṇa*, p. 132.
89. Gyani, S.D., *op. cit.*, p. 276.
90. Shastry, Ajay Mitra, *op. cit.*, p. 140.
91. वस्त्रयुग्मसमोपेतं चरणौ तेजसावृतौ।
Matsya Purāṇa, 261, 4
It is only in view of the *Matsya Purāṇa* that the feet of the Sun-god should be made while other texts consider it inauspicious.
92. *The Matsya Mahā Purāṇam*, p. 1129-30.
93. Gyani, S.D., *op. cit.*, p. 278.
94. *Agni Purāṇa*, Part I, p. 136.
95. Shah, Priya Bala, *op. cit.* pp. 146-50.
96. *Matsya Mahā Purāṇam*, p. 1133.
97. *Agni Purāṇa*, Part I, p. 137.

Iconography of the Brahmanical Deities

5

The icons are the inseparable part of the religious cults. Images provide a visual document of the religious and philosophical ideas. These were meant for understanding the ultimate aim of life i.e. Release (*mokṣa*) and thus art becomes one of the means of attaining this aim.[1] In a way it is quite surprising because art belongs to the world of *nāma* and *rūpa,* name and form, which is the realm of *kāma,* the creative desire, and *mokṣa* is the final extinction of desire, a state of existence which is beyond *nāma* and *rūpa.*[2] But a *bhakta* wants to remain in constant touch with his god, he cannot think of god as formless (*arūpa*) and nameless *(anāma),* because for him the *mokṣa* lies in seeing the beautiful face of God of his choice which can only be materialized through the icon or an image.

The propagators of cults and sects found art as a valuable, direct and effective means for popularising their myths and legends through symbols and images,[3] for drawing the attention of people. Moreover, the symbols, images and rituals proved helpful for the growth of the soul from its low and undeveloped state.[4]

No cult image in stone, prior to the Yakṣa and Yakṣi images of the Mauryan period is found. But the represenation of deities had begun in Indo-Pak subcontinent from the time of the Harappan Civilization (*c* 2500 B.C.). The figures have been identified with prototype 'Paśupati, mother-goddess, tree-spirit, nāgas etc.[5] in the extant art relics of that period. The allusion to the making of images have also been found in the *Ṛgveda.* The passage which is translated as "who will buy this Indra for ten cows".[6] The context indicates that there were permanent images of Indra made and sold for what was in probability an Indra festival.[7] A sūtra in the *Aṣṭādhyāyī*[8] refers to the sale of images of gods for livelihood.

But yet we are not certain about the material remains of the Vedic age.

VAIṢṆAVA IMAGES

The practice of making the images of Viṣṇu started in the late Mauryan or early Śuṅga period. Recently an inscribed image of Viṣṇu has been discovered from Malhār (District Bilāspur, Madhya Pradesh) (Pl. I).[9] This finding is epoch-making in two ways. Firstly, no image of Viṣṇu of pre-Kuṣāṇa period exists[10] and the earliest image of Viṣṇu found in Mathurā art belongs to first century A.D. Secondly, uptil now it is considered that the image of Balarāma was the earliest Brahmanical image discovered from Mathurā which belonged to c. 2nd century B.C.

It is four-handed life size image carved in the round, similar to the archaic Yakṣa statues. It stands erect (*samabhaṅga)*[11] on a stone pedestal. The upper part of the deity is bare. The lower part wears a garment, of palm leaves, indicating the *gopa-veśa* of Mathurā. Its head wearing a crown is much mutilated. One of the right hands hold a *chakra,* the rest two joined hands hold a conch, now disfigured due to later chiselling. There is a small sword attached to the waist on the left. The image is inscribed with one lined inscription in the Mauryan *Brāhmī* script of 2nd century B.C. on the mace which is very well preserved. It states that the image was made by a lady named Bharadvāja, the wife of Parṇadatta.[12]

Six rectangular bronze-coins of Agathocles have been reported from Ai-Khanum, on borders of Russia and Afghānistān. Paul Bernard has noted that the obverse and reverse of the coins show two masculine personages standing to front identically dressed in Indian attire. They wear Pagne (*dhotī*) covering the thighs upto just below the knees, 'chale' (*Uttarīya)* is attached to the shoulders (or where the arm bends) falling in front of the body upto the waist in deep curve showing bare chest and large earrings. And half boots with curved sole ends breathe with alien iconographic features. The shoes have only been prescribed in the image of Sūrya, when shown in *udīchya-veśa.* The helmet, with two floating ribbons, is surrounded by an immense transvernal 'aigrette'. Their swords in a long sheath hang on a cross belt. One figure holds *chakra* and *maṇḍala.* The other holds a *gadā* and a strange instrument.[13]

The identification of the figure having *chakra* and *gadā* on the coins of Agathocles is Vāsudeva-Kṛṣṇa which is supported by the *Harivaṁśa Purāṇa.*[14] The other figure according to A.K. Narain, carries definitely a *mūsala* and a *hala* should be *Balarāma.*[15] In the above figures of Kṛṣṇa and Balarāma the blending of Indian and Greek features is met with. These figures were represented by the Greek artists to suit the taste of the Greek population.

Kuṣāṇa Period

The Vaiṣṇava cult, which further developed during the Kuṣāṇa period, is also reflected in the proliferation of iconographic forms of its deities. During this period Viṣṇu is usually depicted as four-handed carrying a *gadā, chakra* and *kamaṇḍalu.*[16] One of the image of this variety, now in the Mathurā Museum, appears as a replica of Bodhisattva image only with a difference of two additional hands.[17] It is a figure of first century A.D. and before the discovery of Malhār Viṣṇu it was privileged as the earliest specimen of Viṣṇu. Viṣṇu is shown, here, holding a heavy mace and *chakra* in two additional hands. The normal two hands are exactly like those of Bodhisattva images the right in *abhaya-mudrā* [18] and the left holding a monk's bottle of long neck and conical bottom.[19]

A four-handed image of Viṣṇu of first century A.D. from Kaṅkālī Ṭīlā, Mathurā, now in the State Museum, shows the deity standing, having four hands, a *gadā* in his upper right hand, *chakra* in the corresponding left suspended below, and *Śaṅkha* in the normal left placed near the waist, and normal right hand is stretched forward with open palm pointing to the ground which is an unusual feature seen in the Kuṣāṇa Viṣṇu figures. The deity wears no crown but has curly hair. Small pendants are in his ears and bracelets in all the hands. A tight garland (*vanamālā*) consisting of flowers, buds and leaves is worn by him. A waist-band, the early form of *kaṭi-sūtra,* with both of its ends suspended on right thigh, is very clear. He wears a long *dhotī* in *sakachchha* style with one of its ends gathered together and allowed to remain hanging in between the legs. By the side of Viṣṇu's *gadā* there appears a kneeling male figure carrying some bowl-like object in his hands. The figure seems to wear a crown[20] and as such appears to be a devotee of elite class.

A bust of four-handed Viṣṇu of third century A.D. is preserved in the Mathurā Museum. The deity is shown wearing a crown and a *vanamālā.* His lower right hand is in *abhaya-mudrā* and upper right hand holds a *gadā.* His other hands upper left and lower left hold *Charka* and *Śaṅkha* respectively.

Two-handed images of Viṣṇu is rarely found in Kuṣāṇa period.[21] One example of this variety comes from Rupabas (Āgrā) and second from Mathurā,[22] and third reported from Rājasthān holding a mace and discus in hands.[23]

Virāṭarūpa

Eight-armed images of Viṣṇu of Kuṣāṇa period are also rare the two images of this type are now in the Mathurā Museum identified as *Virāṭarūpa* of Viṣṇu and another is housed in the state Museum, Lucknow.[24]

In one image from Mathurā Viṣṇu is shown having eight hands, of which four right hands which are preserved, three seem to carry the mount Govardhana, *pāśa* (Śakti) and *daṇḍa* and fourth one doubled at the elbow is stretched towards the breast and also holds an indistinct object.[25]

The second image shows Viṣṇu (Fig. 14) standing with his left foot bent and right firmly planted with identical attributes (like first image) in his right hands, in addition to a conch, in one of the extant left hands.[26]

The third image from Kosam, District Allahabad, now in the State Museum, Lucknow, is partly preserved. The proper right hand of the deity touches the chest. Another holds a group of arrows and the remaining two on the same side hold objects, which are now broken. He wears a crown, ear-pendant, torque, bracelets and armlets. Hands on the proper left side and portion below the waist are missing. The *ūrṇā* mark on the forehead deserves mention.[27]

Viṣṇu on Garuḍa

The image of Viṣṇu seated on Garuḍa has also come to light which is now in the Mathurā Museum. The figure is miniature in size. The deity is seen seated on the Garuḍa, who is in the bird form with its wings, wide spread. The image corresponds with the description found in the *Harivaṁśa Purāṇa.*[28]

Chatur-Vyūha Form

Viṣṇu is also depicted in *chatur-vyūha* form. One of this type of image, of third century A.D. discovered from the Sapta Sundarī well,[29] (Pl.II) is now housed in the Mathurā Museum. The central figure is of Viṣṇu carrying the usual attributes, a mace in his back right hand, while the front one is held in *abhaya mudrā.* In the front left hand he carries a conch, while the fourth hand is broken. Another badly mutilated figure is seen over the head of Vāsudeva above his back. Probably, there was another figure on the left shoulder of Viṣṇu, which is completely lost.[30]

Incarnations of Viṣṇu

Traditional ten incarnations of Viṣṇu does not seem to have gained ground during the Kuṣāṇa period although four forms were positively known. The *Harivaṁśa* major portion of which seems to be a composition of the Kuṣāṇa age, often refers to Varāha, Nṛsiṁha and Vāmana forms.[31] Till now only one image of Varāha of Kuṣāṇa period, hailing from Mathurā (Pl. III) is known to us. The image is four-armed but without a head flanked by four human beings. The deity is shown in *ālīḍha* pose. His two hands are in *katyavalambita-mudrā* and other two hands are raised above. Though the face of the image is broken yet a figure of woman identified with the Earth goddess can be seen there holding a lotus in her hand. The deity is adorned with a garland of flowers, bracelets, girdle, *dhotī* and a *śrīvatsa* sign.[32] The image of Hayagrīva has come to light from the Bharat Kala Bhawan, Vārāṇasī.[33] A figure of Nṛsiṁha of Kuṣāṇa period has been found from Kondamotu in South India, which is stylistically related to the Nagarjunakonda Sculptures. The main figure of Nṛsiṁha is flanked on the right side by two and on the left side by three figures. Nṛsiṁha is represented as a couchant lion with stout legs. The *śrīvatsa* mark appears prominently on his chest. At the level of the neck, the figure has two human hands holding mace and disc.[34] This figures seems to be made in accordance with the description of the *Harivaṁśa Purāṇa* having a face of beast and a body of a man.[35] Moreover, it seems that the depiction of the incarnations of Viṣṇu in art are based on the textual description of *the Harivaṁśa Purāṇa.*[36]

No figures attributed to the Kuṣāṇa period have yet been identified as those of Kṛṣṇa though Kṛṣṇa-līlā scenes have been found in sculptures and terracottas of this age.[37] A slab from Katra in Mathurā Museum, depicts a scene showing child Kṛṣṇa being carried in a basket by Vāsudeva crossing the flooded Yamunā in which crocodilies, tortoises, fish and a Nāga deity Śeṣa[38] are seen. On one slab from Mathurā Kṛṣṇa is shown fighting with the horse demon Keśina.[39]

According to some lists in the Purāṇas, Saṁkarṣaṇa has also been identified as one of the *avatāras* of Viṣṇu.[40] Balarāma's figures in Śuṅga and Kuṣāṇa art are mostly depicted as wearing a crown with three snake crests and only one earring generally in the left ear.[41] The earliest figure of Balarāma of second century B.C. from Mathurā is now in the Lucknow Museum. Balarāma is seen standing with a canopy of six serpent hoods and holding the *mūsala* in his right hand and *hala* in his left, both the *āyudhas* resting against his shoulders. He wears a very conspicious turban, heavy earrings in cloven ears, a torque with single cylindrical bead and double bracelet. The upper body is nude and lower is draped in a *dhoti* having creased arrangement with triangular fold and the girdle being similar to ancient Yakṣa statues of the Śuṅga period.[42] One more figure of Balarāma, of c. 2nd-3rd century A.D. from Mathurā now in the Lucknow Museum, is shown with right hand raised over his head with open palm. He wears a crown with triple crests and an earring in his right ear. As the corresponding portion of the stone is broken, it is difficult to say whether only one earring was provided in the complete piece, the latter being one of the chief characteristics of Balarāma.[43] The iconographic feature of this kind of image is detailed in the *Harivaṁśa Purāṇa.* Once Kṛṣṇa, Balarāma and Akrūra were going to Mathura in a Chariot, Akrūra wished to pay his homage to the Lord of the nāgas in the river Yamunā. Akrūra dived down into the world of snakes. In the middle he saw the lord of serpents with a thousand hoods. He carried a ploughshare and a pestle. He was adorned with one earring and intoxicated he slept.[44] It may be noted that the early images of Balarāma are exactly similar to the nāga images. The distinguishing point between them is the presence of *vanamālā* in the figures of Balarāma.[45]

Characteristics of Viṣṇu Image in Kuṣāṇa Period

The image of Viṣṇu is usually four-handed are starting from the upper right hands *gadā, chakra, śaṅkha* or water-vessel are shown (Fig. 15) in some cases clockwise. The normal right hand is seen in *abhaya* pose and raised to the shoulder.

Right palm of Viṣṇu shown in *abhaya-mudrā* is always plain and bears no auspicious marks as in the case of Buddha and Tīrthaṅkara figures.

Halo or *prabhā-maṇḍala* is absent throughout.

Viṣṇu figures are seen either with a cap-like tight head-gear or with a crown looking like a brimless top hat, often with circular medallions bearing floral pattern.

The deity is seen wearing *dhotī.*

The image of Viṣṇu is also seen wearing waist-band *(netra-sūtra)* with its end suspended on the right thigh.

The image is adorned with armlets, earrings, bracelets and necklace, but excluding the crown and earrings other ornaments are not always essential.

The figure is decked with *vanamālā* made of buds, leaves and a few flowers among which *kadamba* and *kamala* can be recognized.

Viṣṇu always appears wearing *yajñopavīta* (sacred-thread) (Fig. 16).

Gadā always appears in upper right hand of Viṣṇu. The weapon is shaped like a heavy club broad at the base and tapering towards the top and finally forming a grip.

In some figures Viṣṇu is shown holding a bottle-like object in his normal left hand placed near the hip.

Śaṅkha is usually held in normal left hand.[46]

Ūrṇā mark, which is found on the forehead of Buddha and Bodhisattva, can also be seen in the images of Viṣṇu.[47]

Transition Period

The death of Vāsudeva in c. 176 A.D. resulted in the disintegration of the Kuṣāṇa rule and there prevailed a disruption for more than a century till the Guptas came on the political scene of India in 319 AD. The art of the transition period (between the Kuṣāna and Gupta phase) is some times termed as Kuṣāṇo-Gupta art which shows the continuity of Kuṣānā features and beginning of the process of refinement. From this phase foreign features start vanishing, new ideals and new formulae start emerging.[48]

There is one image of Viṣṇu of this period in Mathurā Museum. The deity is shown as four-armed having Kuṣāṇa features, crown, light ornaments, half-closed eyes and serenity of countenance indicate the Gupta idiom.[49]

Gupta Period

The period between A.D. 320 to A.D. 600 [50] heralded a new epoch in Indian art. But it is only with the advent of third major Gupta ruler Chandragupta II a Gupta artistic style[51] i.e. devoid of foreign elements, totally indigenous came into vogue. It is not that Gupta or classical Indian art came abruptly and dominated the whole scene but it was the logical culmination of several centuries,[52] in which a significant role was played by the Kuṣāṇa art of Mathurā. Even Coomaraswamy also hold the same view that the Gupta style is derived from Mathurā Kuṣāṇa art.[53] It also assimilated regional styles that existed in the areas to which Gupta power spread in the fourth century.[54] The concept of beauty was now totally changed. And bidding farewell to the passionate addiction to wordly pleasures through the exposure of physical charm, the Gupta sculptor at Mathurā worked on a higher plane. Sensuous overtures were outdated and restrained giving way to spiritual ecstasy. Consequently the figures were lit with divine grace and bliss. But the most novel innovation of the art was a harmonious blend of physical form with inner feelings,[55] that (*blend*) can be observed in Viṣṇu image.

A bust of an image of Viṣṇu of 4th century A.D. now housed in the Barodā Museum has come to light from Bhinmal. He is clad in a dhotī and a scarf tied round his waist.[56] His lower right hand is in *Varada-mudrā,* the upper right holds a mace and the lower left hand holds a *śaṅkha* and the upper left hand is broken.

One more bust of Viṣṇu of this period has come to light from Bhīṭā. The figure is executed in the manner as mentioned above. Except the mace in upper right hand and *chakra* in upper left hand nothing is clearly visible in the extant image.

The four-handed image of Viṣṇu in Cave No. 6, Udaigiri standing in *samapāda* may be assigned to 402 A.D. The objects held in his front hands are no longer discernible. The lower right hand is placed on *gadādevī* and the lower left hand is on *chakra-puruṣa.* The deity wears the *kirīṭa mukuṭa* and a elaborate floral wreath around his shoulders which reaches up to his knees.[57] One more image of this type is carved in Cave No. 11 of Udaigiri but it is not in a good state of preservation.

The four-handed Viṣṇu from Kankali Ṭīlā, Mathurā, now in the State Museum Lucknow, is a beautiful specimen of Gupta Art. The figure is well-preserved above the knees except the two extra hands which are partly broken. The buff coloured image is assigned to fifth century A.D. The figure has a high crown, double stringed necklace, *muktā-yajñopavīta*, armlets with end shaped like the face of an alligator, bracelets and a long *vanamālā*, now partly preserved. In his elogated ear lobs are seen long coiled stalks of flowers. A part of his hair made in heavy curls are dangling on his shoulders. His crown with *kīrtimukha* emitting pearl strings in the centre is richly decorated with pearls and gems and floral patterns. Below the navel of the deity is the girdle string (*netra-sūtra*), slightly above the knees is seen the *uttarīya* arranged in narrow plaits ending in a looped knot appearing on the left thigh. The *dhotī* worn by the deity is apparently of transparent nature. Viṣṇu stands in *pralamba bāhu*[58] pose. He carries a conch, with its channel end upwards, in his normal left hand, a fruit, which has now mostly chipped off in the corresponding right. The non-existing extra hands are supposed to have held *gadā* and *chakra.* A big circular halo seen behind the head of the deity has floral patterns arranged in two concentric bands. The field in the centre is plain[59].

An outstanding Viṣṇu image of the Gupta period from Mathurā, now graces the galleries of the National Museum, New Delhi. The crown of the deity is more elaborate, below the surmounting lion head issuing pearls of festoons, are seen two alligator heads composed back supporting beaded strings. The central round rosette is replaced by an undercut scroll motif looking like a *vyālayakṣa*. The neck is marked by three auspicious lines and apart from the *ekāvalī*, is worn another necklace consisting of several beaded strings which are seen twisted towards the shoulders. The lion-cloth (*janghikā*) is tied by a belt. The figure probably wears cobra-shaped earrings (*nāgendrakuṇḍala*). The presence of serenity on the face is one of the most distinguishing characteristics of the Gupta age which has been infused well through the drooping eyes. This specimen is considered to be the best of all Viṣṇu figures from Mathurā[60].

A torso in the Mathurā Museum is yet another citation of quality products of Gupta art. The slimness of the body, light treatment of drapery and beautiful curls falling on the shoulders are indicative of fine craftmanship.[61]

A beautiful Viṣṇu head of fifth century discovered from Besnagar, now in Cleveland Museum, is attested by a simple *mukuṭa*, with its single lion's head and the trefoil pattern on its barely carved surface. The serene face, with its slightly pursed lips, has nothing in common with Udaigiri sculptures but harks back to the finest Mathurā tradition[62]. Besides this one image of Viṣṇu hails from Besnagar now beautifies the Gwālior Museum.

The colossal standing image of Viṣṇu[63] found from Eran, is stiff with plain body and wearing smooth transparent *dhotī, vanamālā* and a necklace.

The haloed image of Viṣṇu of mid fifth century[64] has come to light from Unchadih. It is now stored in the Allahabad Museum (Pl.IV). The lower right hand of deity is in *varada-mudrā* and the lower left hand holds a conch. The upper right hand is missing, while the upper left hand is placed on the head of the *chakra-puruṣa*. A novel feature of this image is the introduction of personified weapon of Viṣṇu i.e. *Āyudha-puruṣa*. Viṣṇu is also adorned with *vanamālā* hanging from the shoulders down to the knees.[65]

Another standing image of Viṣṇu of early or mid fifth century[66] from Jhusi (Pl. V.) is now in the Allahabad Museum. The upper right hand of the deity rests on the mace and the lower right is shown in *varada-mudrā*. In this image the upper left hand is placed on the *chakra* which rests on a small base and the lower left hand holds a conch with a fingers inside[67]. No such depiction has come to light from any other site.

An image of Viṣṇu from Mandasor is slightly clumsy execution of the deity and seems to be related to early phase. But the flattened depiction of the weapons and the stiff modelling of the main figure's leg suggest A.D. 510–520 as it's date as suggested by J.G. Williams.[68]

Seated Images

The seated images of Viṣṇu on Śeṣa were quite popular in South but not in the North India. One such type of image has come to light from the top of the doorway of the main sanctum of the Daśāvatara temple at Deogarh (Pl VI). Viṣṇu is shown seated on the coils of the seven hooded serpent. His lower left hand is placed on his knee and the upper one holds the conch, the lower right hand is in *abhaya-mudrā*, while the upper one holds the disc. His right leg hanging down is being shampooed by Lakṣmī who is sitting on the ground. To the right of the main figure there stands Nṛsiṁha and to the left Vāmana is seen *in añjali-mudrā*.[69]

Vaikuṇṭha Form

The other famous form of Viṣṇu is *Vaikuṇṭha* or Nṛsiṁha-Varāha-Viṣṇu. An image of fifth century A.D. of red sandstone from Mathurā is now preserved in the Boston Museum. It is seen with three heads and four arms. The right and left heads respectively are those of lion and boar. Elaborate head-dress, heavy earrings, armlets, necklace and a garland of flowers adorns the figure. The braided cord representing the sacred thread (*yajñopavīta*) is knotted with a flower below the left shoulder. The image is full and massive, having shoulders very broad and the waist slender. The arms above the elbow and the body from the waisț downwards are missing, and the features are damaged. A plain circular nimbus (*śiras-chakra*) is represented behind the head[70]. A terracotta image of Vaikuṇṭha Viṣṇu has also been found from Mathurā, is now housed in the Government Museum, Mathurā.

One more image of Vaikuṇṭha Viṣṇu is preserved in the Mathurā Museum (Pl.VII). In this image the central face is that of man, the right one is of a lion and left one is of boar. The arms of the image are broken. He is shown wearing *mukuṭa, yajñopavīta* and necklace.

Viśvarūpa Form

Sometimes *Vaikuṇṭha* image assumes the *Viśvarūpa* form. In such images the subordinate deities like the Lokapālas, Navagrahas etc. are shown in the aureole bordered by a series of images of Śiva in Rudra form.[71] Viṣṇu hailing from Bhankari district, Aligarh, now in the Mathurā Museum, projects his omnipresent and omnipotent aspects. The halo has the deities and the universe.[72]

The Viśvarūpa form of Viṣṇu has also come to light from Gaḍhwā (Pl.VIII) and Vārāṇasī.

Anantaśāyīn

Another variety of Viṣṇu in Gupta art is Anantaśāyīn. Kālidāsa has also referred to this form of Viṣṇu in the *Meghadūta*[73] and the *Raghuvaṁśa*[74]. This relief has come to light from Cave No. 6, Udaigiri in Madhya Pradesh (Pl.IX). The iconography is based upon the single textual source of the *Devī Mahātmya.*[75] The story is that lord Viṣṇu at the end of the *kalpa*, goes to sleep and the universe was converted into absolute ocean then two terrible Asuras named Madhu and Kaiṭabha, springing from the root of Viṣṇu's ear, sought to slay Brahmā. Brahmā, the prajāpati, stood on the lotus that grew from Viṣṇu's navel extolled (prayed) Viṣṇu's Sleep (*Yoganidrā*) the queen of universe. Viṣṇu subsequently wakened to kill the demons Madhu and Kaiṭabha.[76]

In the relief the subsidiary characters are enumerated from left to right, the goddess Tāmasī (Darkness, sleep), Brahmā on a lotus, the Garuḍa (latter not mentioned in the text), the personified *gadā, chakra* and *śaṅkha,* the kneeling sage Mārkaṇḍeya, as narrator and finally the two demons Madhu and Kaiṭabha. The four-armed Viṣṇu reclines upon the serpent Śeṣa.[77] The another most famous panel of Anantaśāyīn is depicted on the south face[78] of the temple of Daśāvatāra at Deogarh (Pl. X). This panel shows Viṣṇu, sleeping on the couch of the cosmic serpent Śeṣa. The goddess Lakṣmī is shampooing his right leg. Above is seen a row of divinities including Kārttikeya on peacock, Indra on elephant, Brahmā on lotus and Śiva-Pārvatī on Nandī. Below, a relief consisting of five male warriors and a female figure presumably shows four of the personified *Āyudhas* of Viṣṇu and two demons, Madhu and Kaiṭabha, in aggressive attitude.[79]

Anantaśāyīn panel is also found at Bhītargaon in U.P.[80] This panel is devoid of the deities and demons Madhu and Kaiṭabha.

Hari Form

There is yet another style in which, Viṣṇu is depicted, seated on Garuḍa and this form is called Hari.[81] On the north wall of Daśāvatāra temple, a panel (Pl. XI) has the scene of Gajendramokṣa in which the god is seated on the back of flying Garuḍa redemping the lord of elephants from the clutches of a giant serpent.[82]

The figure of Viṣṇu sitting on Garuḍa has also come to light from Vāmana temple Marhia.

Hari-Hara Form

Viṣṇu is also represented in Hari-Hara form. A detailed description of this form is given in the *Matsya Purāṇa,*[83] which became the main inspiration for carving out the images of Hari-Hara. The specimen of this type is preserved in the Patnā Museum in which right side represents Hara and left Hari. Śiva holds a trident and rosary. The end of the trident rests on the head of a squatting figure evidently representing the Triśūla Puruṣa. Viṣṇu holds the conch-shell in his lower right hand and the upper hand rests on the head of a figure, who is in all probability *Chakra-Puruṣa.*[84]

The image of Hari-Hara is also found from Kuṭārī now stored in the Allahabad Museum. (Pl. XII).

The temple at Bhītargaon was dedicated to Hari-Hara.[85]

Incarnations of Viṣṇu

During the Gupta period almost all of the incarnations of Viṣṇu were depicted in art. But on the whole Varāha, Nṛsiṁha and Kṛṣṇa appear to have been most famous and popular.

On a lintel of a gate from Pāwayā the churning of the Ocean of Milk a novel and impressive subject, is depicted. Probably indicates the second form of Viṣṇu in his Tortoise (Kūrma) *avatāra* supporting the churning.[86]

The scene of churning of the Ocean of Milk has also come to light from Cave No. 19, Udaigiri (Pl. XIII).

The incarnation of Viṣṇu as Trivikrama is not only depicted in art but also in literature.[87] The full depiction of the story of Trivikrama (Vāmana) *avatāra* is given on the lintel of a gate from Pāwayā (Pl. XIV). The centre of it bears the story of Viṣṇu's conquest of the presumptuous ruler Bali. At the left is Bali's sacrifice, accurately represented by a sacrificial platform. To the right, Bali raises his hand in the gesture of the omnipotent ruler (*chakravartī*), and his *guru* Śukra pours holy water upon the hands of Vāmana, who is Viṣṇu in disguise, granting the request for as much land as that dwarf could cover in three strides. The centre of the cross-bar shows giant form of Viṣṇu humbling Bali as he takes the three steps (Tri-vikrama). Eight arms of Viṣṇu that survive in this representation hold a garland, dagger, discus and bow.[88]

The image of Trivikrama Viṣṇu has also found from Mathurā is now in the Mathurā Museum (Pl. XV).

The figure of Vāmana is carved on a pillar from Rajaghāṭa dated to 478 A.D.[89] It is now housed in the Allahabad Museum (Pl. XVI). He is clad in *dhotī* and his untied hair hang upto shoulders. His hands are mutilated so it is not easy to discernible the objects which the figure was carrying originally.

The incarnation of Varāha seems to be quite popular during the Gupta period. In Cave No. 6 at Udaigiri the great boar (Mahā-Varāha) panel (Pl. XVII) is one of the largest as well as the earliest of great high-relief scenes depicting a divine event of mythological or cosmic significance. Viṣṇu, incarnated as the boar with a boar's head is raising the goddess earth (Bhū-devī) from the primeval waters.[90] The goddess Pṛthvī is suspended from the right tusk of the boar who supports her on his mighty left arm. The Mahāvarāha figure is extermely well built and wears a long garland, which in the Gupta period was called *kiñjakinī* and consisted of one thousand lotuses. The god is standing with his left foot on the cosmic serpent Ananta which provided support to all the actors in the drama during the great upheaval. By his side is the figure of Garuḍa with an eagle's head holding a serpent in its hands. There are four rows of the figures in the background representing gods and sages.

There are interesting scenes carved on the two sides of the god showing identical theme of the descent *(avatārs)* of the river-goddesses Gaṅgā and Yamunā from the heavens and their flowing into the sea. The relief carved on the left side of Varāha is better preserved. The river-goddesses are depicted both in their natural form first as two mighty streams taking their rise from heavenly world, shown here with divine dance and music, and on the earth they again appear in a human form i.e. Gaṅgā standing on *makara* and Yamunā on *kachchhapa* (tortoise), both holding in their right hand full vases.[91] There is no single textual version in which all the elements represented here are described. The closest source is the *Matsya Purāṇa.*[92] The allegory behind this scene is mentioned in historical perspective by some scholars, that earth should be considered as Rāmagupta's wife Dhruvsvāminī and Viṣṇu as Chandragupta II, who delivers her *(dhruvsvāminī)* from the clutches of his brother (Rāmagupta). Or the rivers Gaṅgā and Yamunā the two arteries of Madhyadesa, seems to have been adopted as the visible symbols *par excellence* of the homeland of the rising powers of the Guptas in the reign of Chandragupta II Vikramāditya.[93]

Two images of Varāha, one in half man and half animal form (Pl. XVIII) and other in the theriomorphic form, (Pl. XIX) have been found from Eran. J.C. Harle is of the opinion that the representation in the human form is the masterpiece of the Eran style and is one of the greatest of all Indian sculptures. This image is now in the Sāgar University[94] and dated between A.D. 470 and 485.[95] The head is larger than the Udaigiri relief and there is credible union between the human and animal parts. The stance is more stable both in itself and because of the strong vertical swang of drapery. The earth goddess is made purely dependent upon Varāha from whose tusk she hangs like a coat on a hook.[96]

The other great theriomorphic Varāha from Eran, executed close to A.D. 490 or in 510, is both the earliest and largest example of purely animal form of Viṣṇu as Varāha. The creature's body is invariably covered with rows of tiny figures like those on the ground of the Udaigiri panel. The sages are supposed to have taken refuge from the primeval waters among the bristles of the boar.[97] The theriomorphic style is referred to as an alternative to Man-boar in the *Viṣṇudharmottara Purāṇa*, although the text prescribes that the image be covered with demons.[98]

An image of Varāha from Kuṭārī now in the Allahabad Museum is quite interesting. It is carved on a square stone, which formed the part of a big pillar. It has four figures carved on it's four sides, one of which contains the image of Varāha with Vasudharā held on his left arm. Below his feet is seen the reclining serpent with human face, folding his hands in the *añjali-mudrā.* The left leg of the deity is placed on the serpent's chest and the other rests on the coils.[99]

The temple of Marhia was dedicated to Varāha. A panel depicting the deity has also come to light from the temple.

The other famous manifestation of Viṣṇu in Gupta period was Nṛsiṁha. Even a temple at Eran was dedicated to this God. On the door frame of the temple of Kumāra Math at Nachnā, dated to 5th century or later, has a depiction of Nṛsiṁha.[100] A peculiar image of Nṛsiṁha is represented in the Chaitya window of the famous Daśāvatāra temple at Deogarh (Pl. XX).

The god is seated on a full blown lotus in *ardhaprayaṅka* pose[101]. His upper right hand holds the mace, and the lower right, supported by his folded right knee holds the disc. The upper left hand holds the conch and lower left is placed on the thigh. The fierce face is supported by the thick locks of the mane spreading on the shoulders. The ornamental *mukuṭa* is an uncommon feature for the Nṛsiṁha image of the Gupta period. The sculptor has tried to create an impression of flames around his head in the form of a halo. To the left of the deity is a devotee in the *añjali-mudrā.*[102] There is one another distinctive image of Nṛsiṁha in Daśāvatāra temple. A panel projecting in the centre of the doorway has an image of Viṣṇu seated on a coiled serpent. To his right stands a small human figure with a lion's head, evidently Nṛsiṁha. It is four-handed with two of his hands in the *añjali-mudrā.*[103] Both types of images that are found in Daśāvatāra temple does not resemble with the textual representation of the image given in the *Matsya* or the *Viṣṇudharmottara Purāṇa* except the face of lion and body of a man. Nṛsiṁha images also hail from Udaigiri[104] and Eran.[105]

The image of Nṛsiṁha is also carved on the Rajaghāṭa pillar now housed in the Allahabad Museum. (Pl. XXI). The figure stands wearing *dhotī* and *vanāmalā.* The right hand of the deity is placed on the mace and the left hand is placed on the disc which is resting on a pedestal.

The figure of Nṛsiṁha (Pl. XXII) was also on the north wall of the temple of Marhia. The figure is shown here killing the demon Hiraṇyakaśipu, who is wrapped around one of the Man-lion's leg, a type which became popular later on.

Rāma, the seventh incarnation of Viṣṇu, is first time represented in the art of this period. Six *Rāmāyaṇa* scenes, datable to A.D. 500–510, have come to light from Nachnā. These include Sītā and Lakṣmaṇa hearing the golden deer calling out; Sītā rebukes Lakṣmaṇa for his unwillingness to leave; Lakṣmaṇa first ignores and finally he departs; Sītā is approached by Rāvaṇa disguised as a mendicant; Hanumāna approaching Rāma and Lakṣmaṇa at the behest of Sugrīva; Bālī and Sugrīva fight, while Rāma and Lakṣmaṇa watch, unable to distinguish them; Sugrīva is distinguished by a garland and Rāma shoots at Bālī, and Hanūmana is brought before Rāvaṇa in Laṅkā.[106] The Daśāvatāra temple at Deogarh also has panel reliefs representing the scenes of the *Rāmāyaṇa* (Pl. XXIII, XXIV, XXV). The chief episodes are—the redemption of Ahalyā, the pilgrimage of Rāma, Lakṣmaṇa and Sītā to the forest, their visit to the hermitage of the sage Agastya, and the mutilation of Śūrpaṇakhā by Lakṣmaṇa.[107]

Another famous theme of the Gupta period was Kṛṣṇa. It formed as one of the favourite subjects of decorating the walls of temple. The slabs discovered from Mandor of 4th c. A.D. (Pl. XXVI) have the youthful exploits of Kṛṣṇa. This include the following :

The overturning of the Cart-demon

The churning of butter.

The lifting of mountain Govardhana.

The killing of horse demon Keśina.

The killing of bull demon Ariṣṭa.

The release of two Yakṣa imprisoned in the twin *Arjuna* trees.

The taming of the serpent Kāliyā.

The killing of an ass demon Dhenukā.[108]

The episode of the killing of bull-demon Ariṣṭa and of horse demon Keśina is also found on door lintel at Pipariyā.[109] The panels of Daśāvatāra temple (Pls. XXVII, XXVIII) depicts the whole panorama of Kṛṣṇa life :

Devakī handing over the child to her husband.

Vāsudeva moving out to Gokula with the child.

Nanda and Yasodā holding Balarāma and Kṛṣṇa in their laps.

Kṛṣṇa kicking at the milk cart on which pots of milk have toppled over.

Kṛṣṇa seizing the demon Kaṁsa by the hair.

Kṛṣṇa lifting the Govardhana mountain.[110]

The image of Kṛṣṇa stealing butter is preserved in the Bharat Kala Bhawan, Vārāṇasī (Pl. XXIX).

The image of Kṛṣṇa as *Govardhanadhārī* is preserved in the Mathurā Museum[111] (Pl. XXX) and on one of the panel of Bhītargaon.[112] But the most colossal image of *Govardhanadhārī* hails from Vārāṇasī now in Bharat Kala Bhawan. The arms seems to be massive. The young Kṛṣṇa wears the typical pair of tiger claws (*Vyāghra-nakha*) on his necklace and a low crown and three locks of hair (*triśikhin*). The lower portion of the figure is covered in a *dhotī.*[113]

Nara-Nārāyaṇa is also considered as an incarnation of Arjuna and Kṛṣṇa. It seems that the Nara-Nārāyaṇa depicted on the Nāgarī gateway became the source and model for the Deogarh panel.[114]

The niche on the east side wall of Daśāvatāra temple represents the two sages

Nara and Nārāyaṇa (Pl. XXXI). Nara having two hands on the left and Nārāyaṇa having four hands to the right. They are shown to be sitting under a tree. Nara has his right hand in the *varada* and left hand in *abhaya-mudrā*. Nārāyaṇa holds the rosary and the lotus in his upper two hands and the *kamaṇḍalu* in his lower left hand. His lower right hand is in the *vyākhyāna-mudrā*.[115] There are flying Gardharvas in between the trees and Brahmā on the top. Lion and antelopes are seen below their pedestals[116] depicting the hermitage scene.

Characteristics of Viṣṇu Images

New features in the iconography of Viṣṇu images were introduced during the Gupta phase. The images were provided with a halo (*prabhāmaṇḍala*) sometimes richly carved with geometrical and floral designs. This feature was shared by other religions also. In the Kuṣāṇa art extra arms of Viṣṇu were normally shown as bifurcated from the arm-pits and raised above the shoulders (*udbāhu*). But during the Gupta age all the four arms have been shown suspended downwards (*pralamba-bāhu*).

The emblem of Viṣṇu, *gadā, śaṅkha* and *chakra*, continued. But the representation of a water-vessel seen in Kuṣāṇa sculptures is no more seen. The normal left hand holds *śaṅkha* in all cases but like the Kuṣāṇa figures the hand is not placed near the hip, but has slightly been protruded forward, and his right hand is often shown in *varada* or *abhaya-mudrā*.[117]

The tradition of adorning the Viṣṇu's bosom with the sign of *śrīvatsa* has not yet been started by the artists of Mathurā and Allahabad. It seems that the Besnagar school of art began this practice. Two Viṣṇu figures in the Gwālior Museum and one in the national Museum depicts *śrīvatsa* motif which is shown as a central pendent in the necklace of Viṣṇu.

The simple sacred-thread was replaced by the pearl sacred-thread (*mukṭa-yajñopavīta*).

The depiction of *vanamālā* became an inseparable feature of Viṣṇu images. Usually it is shown running round the back and rolling on the normal elbows reaching the legs below the knees and forming a long and loose loop. it looks like a heavy floral garland or sometimes a jewelled necklace.

The upper part of the body remained unclothed but lower part is decked with a *dhotī* of different types. One reaches upto the knees and is decorated with numerous light shrinks (*satavallika*) other covers only the thighs.

The waist-band now assumes the shape of a decorated rope like object representing *netra-sūtra* meaning a 'churning string'.

The novel innovation of this period was the anthropomorphic representation of the weapons named as *Āyudha Puruṣa* or *Āyudha-devī* according to their gender. The weapons in anthropormorphic form appear as miniature figures by the sides of Viṣṇu and on their heads often touched by the hands of the main figure.[118] A fine example of the *Chakra-Puruṣa* appears on the Chakravikrama type coins of Chandragupta II.[119]

ŚAIVA IMAGES

One of the oldest and also the most widely spread cult in India is that of Śiva.[120] And as far as the iconography of this deity is concerned it goes back to the Indus Valley Civilization where on one seal a three-faced horned deity is shown in a yogic posture and surrounded by four animals, an elephant and a tiger on his proper right, a rhinoceros and buffalo on his left. The figure is considered as a prototype of the historic Śiva-Paśupati.[121]

The depiction of Śiva in sculptural art began from the early Śuṅga period. Śiva was worshipped either in *Liṅga* form or in the anthropomorphic form, but very often the two forms were combined together in one way or other, and the earliest known icons used for Śiva's worship being of this very type.[122]

The *Liṅga* from Gudimallam in South India and another from Bhiṭā are known to be the earliest. Both of them have images of Śiva on them. At Gudimallam, a small village in Kalahasti taluk of Chittoor district,[123] exists one of the most important monuments of *c.* 2nd century B.C. or of pre-Kuṣāṇa Brahmanical art. The twany-brown coloured *liṅga* has a figure of Śiva (Pl. XXXII, Fig. 7), standing firmly on a crouching Yakṣa.[124] The two-armed deity holds a goat by its hind legs in the right hand and a globular vase of small size in the left hand. The battle-axe rests upon his left shoulder. The head of the figure has a covering resembling like a turban of plaited not matted hair. The face of the deity is arresting with its gently picked up eye brows, distinctly marked oblique open eye, sharp nose with well-marked nostrils, amply bulbous beautiful cheeks, well-defined chin and thick lower lip. The *ghaṭa-kuṇḍalas* in the ears, heavy and distended, hang down prominently. The deity is shown wearing *dhotī* and highly ornamental band (*aṅgadas*) on each of the upper arms as well as five-jewelled bracelets (*kaṅkanas*) of different patterns on the fore-arms. Round the neck is to be seen a *mālā* of rare workmanship and the image is devoid of *yajñopavīta.*[125]

A *pañcha-mukha Liṅga* of second century B.C., discovered from Bhiṭā in Allahabad district (Pl. XXXIII, Fig. 4.6), is now housed in the State Museum, Lucknow. The *Śiva-Liṅga* also has an inscription engraved in early *Brāhmī* characters. On, the top of the *Liṅga* there appears a figure of Śiva with two hands. Part of his head over the right cheeks has broken, but straight plaits of hair falling on the back, the two ear-ornaments-each shaped like double heavy rings and a tight collar are very clear. The right hand of the figure was raised to the shoulder in *abhaya* pose of which only a part of the palm, pointing finger and thumb now exist. The left hand which has been drawn up almost to the level of the chest, carries a water-pot with thick base. Heavy bracelets are to be seen in both the hands. A double line, running from the left shoulder to the right side, passes over the naval and looks like a sacred-thread (*yajñopavīta*). It may also suggest the border of scarf thrown over the left shoulder.

Below the hands of this figure appear two human heads. The one under the hand carrying vessel, represents terrific features such as pointed moustaches and two long teeth coming out of the lip ends. The head ornament, in this case, consists of double strings worn like a fillet decorated with three circular plaques, one in the centre and others over the two ears. A tight collar appears near the neck.

The next face with normal appearance has also got simple fillet, toplike ear-pendants and a narrow collar. On the back side as well appears two human faces. One next of face just above mentioned has a turban and proturding top-knot shaped like a small shell which clearly shows the *kapardin* aspects of Śiva. The fourth face has a shaven head without any earring or neck ornament.[126]

Kuṣāṇa Period

The *liṅgas* that are found in this period can be classified as—

(1) plain and

(2) *liṅgas* with figures of Śiva having a single or multiple faces.[127]

Plain Liṅgas

The Kuṣāṇa period is not only rich in the pursuit of making *Śiva-Liṅgas* in one style i.e. *liṅgas* with one or more faces but also produced plain *liṅgas* vigorously and in varied fashions.

The earliest *liṅga* is perhaps shown on slab from Mathurā, being worshipped by the winged animals.[128]

Śiva-liṅga of Ist c. A.D. discovered from Mathurā is now in the Lucknow Museum. It is shaped as a phallus. Around the upper most part runs a broad band, the two ends of which form a knot and are seen suspended. Purpose of this band is not clear, but it may be the earliest form of *brahmasūtra*, which later on became an inseparable part of the *Śiva liṅgas*. The *liṅga* has a rectangular tenon below intended to be inserted in the ground while fixing.[129]

Though the *liṅgas* are simply phallus-shaped yet sometimes these present new and interesting innovations. Double band running round the upper part of the shaft bearing varieties of decorations such as full blown lotus flower on cardinal points, or a string bearing a series of lotus petals, or one side of the shaft decorated with eight-petalled lotus. The base of the shaft, at times, has interesting features. Its side is decorated with leaves and flowers (Fig. 2), or show a lion, jar, a *Strī-mukha* and a

Gaṇa at its base. The latter example comes from Chaumā Bunḍpura (Fig. 3). Another Śiva linga from Mathurā (Fig. 11) shows only Gaṇas at base. The shaft of the Lucknow Museum *liṅga* shows a beautifully knotted band with its tassels hanging. In a few cases an inscription is also incised over them.[130]

Liṅga-with a Figure

A *Liṅga* with a four-armed figure of Śiva has come to light from Mathurā (Fig.8) which is placed in second or third century A.D. Whereabouts of this piece are not known at present.[131] Another linga from Mathurā (Fig. 9), now housed in the Philadelphia, depicts two-handed Śiva with turban on his head.[132]

Śiva-Liṅga with Face(s)

A fragment of Ist or 2nd Century A.D. from Mathurā now in the Lucknow Museum shows *liṅga* under a *pīpala* tree. The extreme left of the fragment shows an *eka-mukha liṅga* installed on a brick platform under a big *pīpala* tree. Tall shaft of the *liṅga* has a phallus-like top, to which the face with its hair made in a top-knot above, has been secured fit by means of a band. Near this platform stand two Yakṣa figures with their back towards the *liṅga*, as if returning after worshipping the deity. The one nearer to the platform is short-statured being, while the other one has a heavy face, corpulent body, full belly and short legs. The figure next to him is badly mutilated, but seems to be handing over a small box to the approaching Yakṣa. It also throws light on *liṅga* worship and the method of its installation during the Kuṣāṇa period.[133]

The *eka-mukha liṅga* of 2nd century A.D. from Mathurā, now in the Lucknow Museum (Fig. 12), shows one-faced Śiva with a third eye in horizontal form, pointed moustaches with ends turned upwards, elongated ear-lobs and matted locks of hair on the head. A double string runs round the forehead with a full blown flower in the middle serving as a crest. The head has been joined together with the shaft of the *liṅga* by means of a narrow band decorated with similar full blown flowers all round, of which three are still preserved.[134]

The stone *liṅga*, from Kauśāmbī (Pl. XXXIV), now in the Allahabad Museum, is four-faced. It is partly mutilated at the top, but there is sufficient evidence to show that it depicted some human figure or figures on one of its uppermost sides. Left hand and the left bent leg of one of the figures is still preserved. Like the Bhīṭā example the four heads were facing not the cardinal points but South-East, East-North, North-West and West-South respectively. The male faces represented Aghora, Uṣṇīṣa and the Yogī form, while the fourth one is that of a female.[135]

A four-faced *liṅga* (c. 2nd and 3rd century A.D.) has been found at Nandā (Fig. 10) near Ajmer in Rājasthān. The *liṅga* was profusely carved from top to bottom. It has a number of human figures in four parts, one upon the other, facing at cardinal points. The uppermost part presents seated Śiva in *ūrdhva-meḍhra* form with legs wide open.

The lowermost part of this *lings*, depicts a two armed Viṣṇu holding *chakra* and unblossomed lotus with stalk, which seems to be the representation of *gadā* because Viṣṇu holding a lotus is an unknown feature of Kuṣāṇa iconography.[136]

Anthropomorphic Śiva

The anthropomorphic representation of Śiva can be seen on the earliest tribal coins of Ujjainī, datable to c. 3rd–2nd century B.C.[137] Śiva is shown carrying a club in one hand and a water vessel in the other.[138] Śiva standing and holding a trident is seen on obverse of *Chhatvesvara* type of coins of Kuṇindas. These coins were issued in 2nd or 3rd century A.D.[139] The Śaka and Indo-Pārthian rulers[140] and Gondaphares[141] issued coins with the figures of Śiva in which deity is shown holding club and long spear and trident and palm branch respectively.[142]

The worship of Śiva gained popularity during the Kuṣāṇa period, different kinds of iconographic depictions were conceived by the artists of this period. The figure of Śiva can be seen having one-faced or three-faced[143] with two or four arms, holding various attributes such as wreath, thunderbolt, trident, water-vessel and *ḍamarū* on the coins of Kadphises,[144] Kaniṣka, [145] Huviṣka[146] and Vāsudeva.[147] Generally bull is shown standing behind Śiva on the coins of Kuṣāṇas.[148] On one of the coins of Huviṣka Śiva is depicted as standing with goddess Nānaia (Pārvāti). He is four-armed and holds a deer, trident and a small drum and water vessel, and Nānaia carries her peculiar symbol.[149]

The extant stone sculptures show three iconographic forms of Śiva which were popular during the Kuṣāṇa period. These include-Śiva alone or with Pārvatī or in syncretic form as Ardhanārīśvara or Hari-Hara.[150] The iconographic features of these forms are described here.

An independent image of Śiva of Kuṣāṇa period (Fig. 18) in standing form is preserved in the Mathurā Museum. The figure is badly damaged and remains only the lower part upto the knees and one hand. He is shown ithyphallic wearing a *dhotī* and a girdle round the waist and carrying a water-pot in his left hand.[151]

The depiction of Śiva and Pārvatī with Nandī is met in one sculpture of 2nd century A.D. and without Nandī of 3rd century A.D. is stored in the Government Museum, Mathurā.

The standing figure of Ardhanārīśvara (Fig. 19) is stored in the Government Museum, Mathurā. The upper part of the body is missing but extant portion showing only legs, the figures has been recognized as Ardhanārīśvara. The right half is of Śiva and left of Pārvatī. Śiva's side is shown ithyphallic and his *vāhana* Nandī also stands behind them.

The composite form of Viṣṇu and Śiva known as Hari-Hara is depicted in sculpture and on a gold coin of Huviṣka.[152] Śiva is seen facing, three-headed, nimbate, clad only in waist band, ithyphallic and has four hands with goat, wheel, trident and thunderbolt. *Triśūla, vajra,* and *chakra* are recognisable in the front left, back left and back right is not so very distinct.[153] The *chakra* is seen in one of the hands. The presence of *ūrdhvaliṅga* suggests it to be the proto-type of the composite image of Hari-Hara.[154]

A very uncommon form of Śiva, depicted on a railing pillar, has come to light from Mūsānagar (Kānpur). On one sides of the pillar (Fig. 20) two-armed and ithyphallic Śiva is shown standing in *abhaya-mudrā*. On his left side appears a standing lion and on his right side a *Kumbhodara Gaṇa*. On the other side of the pillar (Fig. 21) Siva is shown in *chatur-vyūha* form and seated on a throne in the *ūrdhva-meḍhra* pose. Two figures are seen coming out of his shoulders and one form behind his head. Here, the lion is shown sitting near the feet of Śiva.[155]

Characteristics of Śaiva Images

In the images of Śiva the third eye is shown horizontally although the depiction was not essential. The deity is sometimes shown having matted hair and *jaṭājūṭa*. The features such as Gaṅgā, snake normally associated with Śiva, were totally absent in this period. In the case of four-faced *liṅgas*, the faces represented different aspects of the deity.[156]

Gupta Period

The Gupta rulers gave impetus to Vaiṣṇavism but they did not cast off their eyes to other existing cults. This fact is proved by the inscription of Chandragupta II in Udaigiri cave. Vīrasena Saba (minister of Chandragupta II) came here, accompanied by the king in person who was seeking to conquer the whole world, out of devotion towards divine lord Śaṁbhu he caused the cave (now known as No. 7) to be made.[157] The temples at Khoh, Nachnā-Kuṭhāra and Bhūmarā, constructed during this period, were also dedicated to lord Śiva.

The representation of Śiva in *eka-mukha* or multifaced *liṅga* was a common feature of the Gupta era.

Eka-Mukha Liṅgas

The *eka-mukha liṅgas* of the period are known from Mathurā (c. 380 A.D.).[158] Udaigiri Cave No. 4 (c. 400 A.D.).[159] Barauni Khurd (District Datia)[160] and Khamhariā (c. 520–530 A.D.).[161] But the stone *liṅgas* from Khoh (Fig. 5) and Bhūmarā (Fig. 13) are most notable for beautiful carving and grandeur.

In Udaigiri Cave No. 4 the *liṅga* was installed in c. 400 A.D. Its round face has sharply defined features and a third eye is shown on the forehead. Its top-knot is held by ring from which hair strands fall down on either side in curls. It has a torque around neck, a typical Gupta ornament.[162]

A fifth century's finest example is a *Śiva-linga* with one face from Khoh (Pl. XXXV, Fig. 5), now in the Allahabad Museum,[163] which epitomizes the harmony of the mature Gupta style.[164] This *liṅga* is perpendicular on sides and rounded at its top. The face of Śiva is contemplative like a Mahāyogī. His *Jaṭājūta* appears to be a sort of crown, combed below and tied as hair-knot above. Disc-like ears have ring ornaments. A pearl necklace decorates his neck.[165]

The *eka-mukha liṅga* from Bhūmarā (Pl. XXXVI) strinkingly differs in facial type from Nachnā or Khoh versions not only in details of jewellery and head-dress but also in the introvert effect of slightly downcaste eyes beneath a horizontal brow.[166] The basic difference in jewellery is, seen in more elaborate torque round the neck, a *maṇimālā* near the line of hair on the forehead, and a *gavakṣa-chūḍamaṇi* ornament on the hair above. It is gigantic in size and represents the late fifth or early sixth century style.[167]

A *chatur-mukha liṅga* found near Lakhorbāgh and now in the compound of Pārvatī temple at Nachnā (Pl. XXXVII) was probably originally placed in this temple. This four-faced liṅga represents Śiva as Maheśvara, the heads corresponding on Sadyojāta (Earth), the feminine Vāmadeva (water) the angry Aghora (fire) and Tatpuruṣa (Air). The differentiation of the forms of Śiva is clear here and the association with the elements, while not textually documented until later Pūraṇic literature, is borne out by a few early images in which fifth head, appears holding aloft Sun and moon, the elements of the sky. The decor of the Nachnā linga is elaborate and carefully varied, the serpent thread through one of Aghora's ears gives a characteristic touch. A beautiful *chatur-mukha liṅga* of fifth century A.D. has also been found from Kosam (Pl. XXXVIII). This four-faced *liṅga* appears to have made on the iconographic injunctions described in the *Viṣṇudharmottara Purāṇa.*[168] One more *Chatur-mukha liṅga* of this period has come to light from Badoh-Patharī.

A *pañcha-mukha liṅga* of Gupta period is now preserved in the Mathurā Museum. The top part of it is broken and only four human heads emerging out of four shafts, carved from a single block, face the four directions. These heads are known as Tatpuruṣa, Aghora, Vāmadeva and Sadyojāta facing the East, South, West and Northern quarters respectively. Metaphysically these represent soul, material world, *buddhi* (intellect), Ahaṁkāra (ego) and the mind.[169]

Characteristics of the Mukha-Liṅgas

The style of depicting *mukha-Liṅgas* was quite different in Gupta period as compared to Kuṣāṇa phase.

The Kuṣāṇa band, which practically fixed the face with shaft, now disappeared.

The carving of *mukhas* became more expressive and attractive, as seen specially in the case of four-faced *liṅgas.*

Generally hair were tied in *uṣṇīṣa* in *Kuṣāṇa* period but in Gupta period head was decorated with different hair styles.

The third eye on the fore-head took a vertical shape.

The depiction of crescent moon, a new feature, was introduced in this period. But it is not seen in all the four-faced *liṅgas* of the period.

Another marked change was addition of *ekāvalī*, different kinds of necklaces and head ornaments.[170]

Anthropomorphic Form of Śiva

The anthropomorphic forms of Śiva in the Gupta period can be classified as :

Śiva as standing alone,

Ardhanārīśvara form,

Lakulīśa form,

Dancing Śiva,

Śiva-Pārvatī,

Rāvaṇa lifting Kailāśa,

Dakṣiṇa mūrti

Gajāsura vadha murtī

Kaṅkāla murtī

Śiva as Kirāta

Vīrabhadra form

Śiva with Triśūla-Puruṣa

Hari-Hara[171]

A figure of Śiva of 4th or 5th century A.D. from Lakhaneshwar Ḍīh, Balliā district, is in the State Museum, Lucknow is two-handed and carries a trident in his left hand. The right hand is in *varada*-pose. The deity has a vertical eye, a waist band, *graiveyaka* and an upper garment, which is to be seen running over the knees. The most usual feature of this figure is absence of the *jaṭā-jūṭa* on the head. Instead of it his hair has been parted from the middle and allowed to fall on the shoulders. The figure, though apparently half finished, gives an impression of well proportionate and robust personality.[172]

It seems that the Ardhanārīśvara form was quite popular in the Gupta period. It can be gauged by the fact that Kālidāsa begins the *Raghuvaṁśa* by offering prayer to Pārvatī and Paramveśara who remain inseparable like word and meaning.[173]

The Mathurā sculptors have produced two beautiful specimens of this theme. One (Pl. XXXIX) is a head in which male and female aspects have been nicely combined yet the distinguishing features are clearly discernible. The right side with matted hair and crescent is attributed to Śiva while the Pārvatī aspect is to be recognized through the beautifully arranged hairdo and round earring with a vertical string of pearl. The very look differentiates the masculine and feminine features. Śiva's eye-brow is drawn up and the female portion suggests sublimity.

The second is an exceptionally beautiful bust from Gosna, Mathurā. The right side with high matted hair (*jaṭā-jūṭa*) represents Śiva while the remaining half with tastefully decorated hair and tufts bedecked with flowers, large and heavy earrings is that of Pārvatī. The forhead bears a vertical third eye and an *ekāvalī* (pearled necklace) is worn round the neck. The beautiful lips, half-closed eyes and a subtle grace have further enhanced the attraction of composite features.[174]

Metaphysically it symbolises the union of the two great forces *Prakṛti* and *Puruṣa* or in the words of Kālidāsa inseparable like speech (*vāk*) and meaning (*artha*).[175]

Lakulīśa Form

Śiva holding a staff known as Lakulīśa is considered as an incarnation of Śiva-Maheśvara.[176] This depiction have been found from Mathurā. One octagonal pillar is of special significance. A dwarfish figure of nude Śiva with third eye carrying a shaft is carved on the base and the remaining portion of the pillar shows a big trident. It belongs to the c. 380 A.D.[177]

One more image of dwarfish Śiva in Lakulīśa form but without lakula is housed in the Govt. Museum, Mathurā (Pl. XL).

There is an architectural fragment in the Mathurā Museum which depicts Śiva seated cross-legged in preaching attitude (*vyākhyāna-mudrā*). He has an oval face, lotus-shaped eyes, elongated ears and slender waist. His eyes are half-closed in meditation. The head is covered with curly hair. He is ithyphallic and in the left arm holds a *lakula* or staff and right hand is in preaching attitude. A scarf (*yogapaṭṭa*) is fastened round his knees. In this fashion he assumes the position of a teacher or Āchārya and the two flanking attendants are his disciples.[178]

The figure of Lakulīśa from Tumain also represents the ithyphallic form of Śiva seated in *yogabandha*.[179]

The god from Nachnā (Pl. XLI) is seated cross-legged. His feet, resting on the pedestal and knees, tied with a flat band. His right fore-arm is broken off, the left hand holds an axe. He has a low ornamental crown, *ekāvalī* and *yajñopavīta*.[180]

The gateway of the temple at Nāgarī at its back in third panel from the right shows a seated figure with twisted locks in meditation, surrounded by four worshippers. Despite the lack of a club the figure appears to be the representation of Lakulīśa.[181]

Another figure of Lakulīśa of 5th century A.D. from Mathurā, now in the Lucknow Museum, shows Śiva seated on a lotus seat. The deity has curly locks on head, vertical third eye, elongated ear-lobes, sacred-thread and ithyphallic. His hands suggest the preaching pose but right one also holds a *mālā* and a big staff is seen on his left side.[182]

Naṭarāja

Śiva is also Naṭarāja, lord of dancers or king of actors,[183] who is supposed to be proficient in 108 modes of dancing as described by Bharata in his *Nāṭya-śāstra.*[184]

The temples of Nachnā, Bhūmarā, Tumain, Adbhar, Sirpur, Malhār and Raijim preserve representation of Naṭarāja.[185] But the earliest representation of Naṭarāja is known from Nachnā-Kuṭhāra,[186] (Pl. XLII) dated in early fifth century, now preserved in the National Museum, Delhi.[187] In the extant relic only upper portion of the bust remains viz. the head and arms adequately illustrate the action of the cosmic dance undertaken by the deity. The expression on the face of the deity bespeaks about great majesty and steadfast support to the titanic pulsations of the dance. The released energy is expressed through the upper two arms rhythmically thrown up and artistically framing the head, and also the pair of lower arms, one of which in puissant horizontal extension, is partially preserved. The fourth arm and the legs must have been portrayed in a manner to convey adequately the power and rhythm inherent in the performance. The twist of the bust towards the proper left is very significant feature making both the direction of the force and over all restrained exercise in the liberation. The ruffled matted hair or locks, the *chintāmaṇi* jewel on the head, the *ananta-valaya* on the arms and bangles on the wrists serve as happy items of decoration enhancing the general effect to the subject.[188]

The lintel from Sakhor bears in its centre a dancing Śiva with at least eight arms, a type which became vogue later in the sixth century in the western Deccan.[189] The image of Naṭarāja is also installed in the porch of the temple at Adbhar (Pl. XLIII) This figure is also eight-armed and one of its left arms is stretched across the chest and is static and stiff.[190]

Śiva and Pārvatī

The images of Śiva with his consort Pārvatī, also known as Umā-Maheśvara form, were fashioned in the Gupta age.

A figure of Śiva and Pārvatī of c. 459 century A.D. considered to belong to transition period from Kauśāmbī is now in the Indian Museum, Calcutta[191] (Pl. XLIV). It shows them standing. Śiva's hair is worn in smooth, bulging *jaṭā* or locks pulled up in a distinct sheath[192] and Pārvatī has a tastefully arranged hair do with wreaths and tufts on both sides. The most notable feature of the image is the presence of a horizontal third eye of Śiva.[193]

Another sculpture of Umā-Maheśvara form belongs to third or second quarter of fifth century.[194] It is in the Mathurā Museum which is carved on both sides. Śiva elegantly stands wearing matted hair, a tiger skin (*Vyāghra-ambara or Vyāghrajina*) as indicated by the paws marked on the suspending ends. He has third eye on the forehead and is ithyphallic. His vehicle *Nandī* wears a garland of skulls (*muṇḍa-mālā*). Pārvatī is seen on the left side of Śiva with a lily flower in her left hand which enhances the grace of the better half.[195]

The images of Umā-Maheśvara have also come to light from Tumain (now in the Gwālior Museum)[196] and Śaṅkaragarh.[197] A small niche cut into the natural rock of the Śaṅkaragarh hill bears a tiny delicately carved image of Śiva and Pārvatī of about c. 520 A.D. The figure of Śiva is ithyphallic and stands on left leg. The halo is plain and circular with a thin raised border. There is a crescent mark on the halo a little above the matted hair of the god. His right hand was perhaps in *abhaya-mudrā*. His left hand, which is drooped down parallel to the delineation of his body, holds a flask. Large *kuṇḍalas,* beaded necklace, *yajñopavīta*, bracelets short trousers are seen on his body. The figure of Pārvatī stands in *samapāda* pose.[198] Her right hand is damaged and left hand is dropped down with its palm broken off. A circular halo appears behind her head. The figure is seen with luxuriant hair, with a knot at the end, large *kuṇḍalas,* ring armlets, *muktāmekhalā, dhotī,* scarf going across the thighs and end in a luxuriant knot at the right side. Two ends of her *dhotī* are suspended from the waist-band. A zigzag vertical end of her *dhotī* runs between her thighs and legs and touches the ground level.[199] The image of Śiva-Pārvatī has also been stored in the Bharat Kala Bhawan, Vārāṇasī (Pl. XLV).

Rāvaṇānugraha-Mūrti

The earliest example of Rāvaṇānugraha[200] in a sculptural relief is preserved in the Mathurā Museum.[201] It depicts the episode of Rāvaṇa lifting the mountain Kailāsa on which Śiva and Pārvatī were sitting. The story behind this is that Rāvaṇa after defeating Kubera was passing through Kailāsa. His chariot was stopped by Nandīkeśvara an attendant of Śiva at Saravana.[202] On inquiry Rāvaṇa was informed that the area was prohibited as Śiva and Pārvatī were sporting. The angry demon of Laṅkā then started lifting the mountain in order to frighten Śiva and his retinue. Knowing the cause of disturbance Śiva pressed the mountain and Rāvaṇa with his foot. The load became unbearable and the mighty demon began to weep. As he wept he was called Rāvaṇa. He was relieved of the heavy burden Śiva was pleased after many prayers. The prowess of Rāvaṇa is shown through his strong physique, heavy head and terrific look. At the same time his anxiety is noticeable from the bulging face. Pārvatī clings to her husband who is seen in ithyphallic form and pressing Rāvaṇa with his right foot.[203]

The Rāvaṇānugrahamūrti is also delineated on the right doorjamb of Devarānī temple at Tala. The panel shows Śiva and Pārvatī seated on rocks with a running figure to one side, perhaps Rāvaṇa shaking Mt. Kailāsa.[204]

Dakṣiṇa Mūrti

A terracotta plaque of *c.* 5th and 6th century A.D. from Ahichchhatrā shows Śiva in Dakṣiṇa mūrti.[205] Being proficient in yoga, music and other science Śiva came to be known as Dakṣiṇa mūrti. According to another view, Daksiṇa mūrti form indicates that Śiva was seated facing the South when he instructed the ṛṣis in yoga and jñāna.[206]

Gajāsura-Vadha Mūrti

Gajāsura-Vadha Mūrti is also seen in this period on one of the badly mutilated panels on the southern wall of the Bhītargoan brick temple in Kānpur district (Uttar Pradesh).[207] The story of the destruction of an elephant *asura* by Śiva and his wearing the skin of elephant as his garment is found in the *Kūrma Purāṇa* while describing the liṅga named Krittivaseśvara in Kāśī. Sūta is said to have told that Śiva came out of this *liṅga*, when an Asura, who assumed the shape of an elephant, came near it to disturb the meditation of several Brāhmaṇas who had gathered round it. He killed the elephant and made its skin his upper garment.[208] But the *Varāha Purāṇa* gives a quite different account. The story is that when Śiva got ready to fight with Andhākasura after listening the complaint of devas, an Asura named Nīla, who had secrectly planned to kill Śiva. The asura came out in the meanwhile in the form of an elephant. Nandī came to know of this and informed Vīrabhadra and he took the shape of the lion (the natural enemy of the elephant) and attacked and killed the Nīla. The skin of this elephant was presented by Vīrabhadra to Śiva.[209]

Kaṅkāla Mūrti of Śiva

The depiction of Śiva as Kaṅkāla Mūrti began to be fashioned in this period. The subject has no precedent and later it became more characteristic of South India than of north.[210] The doorframe of Devarānī temple at Tala shows Śiva in penance for the sin of killing a *Brāhmaṇa.* There are different stories in the Purāṇas regarding the henious act of Śiva such as the cutting of fifth head of Brahmā. As it was a crime in all means so he (Śiva) has to undergo tapas for twelve years to get rid from the sin of *brahmahatyā.*

Śiva as Kirāta

One more new subject that was introduced in Śaiva iconography of this period was the depiction of Śiva as Kirāta. The doorway (*toraṇa*) of Nāgarī temple, of fifth century, delineated the story of the encounter between Arjuna and the *Kirāta* or hunter. In one panel Arjuna stands in one leg with arms raised in the pose of penance (*tapas*) presumably before Śiva. Next panel shows Arjuna confronting a boar, with Śiva and Pārvatī in the background in the form of a homely hunter and his wife. The arrows projecting from behind the boar must indicate that both Arjuna and the Kirāta have shot the animal. Next, in a broken panel, the two (Śiva and Arjuna) drew bows upon each other in jealousy, followed by a scene in which Arjuna, his supply of arrows exhausted, uses the end of his bow on the head of the Kirāta. The doorframe at Tala also represents Śiva in Kirāta *veśa*.[211]

Vīrabhadra

One of the best and perhaps the earliest representation of Vīrabhadra comes from Badoh (Pl. XLVI). He is depicted seated in *lalitāsana*, his right leg folded on a *chaukī* and left leg pendent resting on a foot pedestal below. The seat is three-legged with cushion on it. Vīrabhadra has a periwig like curly hair arranged in grades. His face is angry with open mouth and projecting third eye on forehead. He is ithyphailic and wears *ekāvalī, chhannavīra* waistband, earrings (one earring in the right ear and a large *kuṇḍala* in the left ear). He has mascular and powerful body and resting his hands on the knees.[212]

Triśūla-puruṣa

The various weapons and emblems such as *vajra, śakti, daṇḍa, khaḍga, pāśa, aṅkuśa, gadā, triśūla, padma, chakra* and *dhvaja* which are generally found in the hands of the images of Viṣṇu, Śiva and other gods are personified under the name of *Āyudha-Puruṣa* and are concretised as images.[213] The *āyudhas* of Śiva[214] and also of Viṣṇu began to be depicted in anthropomorphic form from Gupta era.

A fifth century Śiva and Triśūla-puruṣa figure (Pl. XLVII), discovered from Allahabad district, is now housed in the State Museum, Lucknow. It is depicted on a door-jamb and Śiva is shown standing in *bhikṣāṭana* pose. His hair has been tied in a knot over the head and further secured fit with a band decorated with three prominent skulls on it. Stray locks of his long hair seen suspended on his shoulders and dangling in front. In his left ear he has a *chakra-kuṇḍalas*, but in the right ear-lobe a coiled snake serves the purpose of the ear-ornament. His other ornaments are beaded necklace, armlets with crocodile-shaped ends, bracelets and a beaded *yajñopavīta*. Śiva is seen wearing short loin cloth of transparent nature. The figure has vertical eye on the forehead. In the left hand he holds a *bhikṣāpātra* full of alms. His folded right hand has been coiled round by his attendant. The attendant standing to the right of Śiva is dwarfish in nature, has a beautiful decorated hair, simple ornaments and *satavallika* (with hundred of shrinks) type of lower garment. The insignia, the trident, appearing on his head, makes it clear that the attendant figure is Triśūla-puruṣa.[215]

Hari-Hara

The combined image of Hari-Hara reflects an attempt at establishing peace and harmony between the Śaivas and Vaiṣṇvas. There is an image of Hari-Hara in the Mathurā Museum. The right half of which is rendered Śiva with matted hair, while the left half noticed with a crown is that of Viṣṇu.[216]

Characteristics of Śaiva Images

The characteristic features of Śaiva images of the Gupta period can be enumerated as the following :

The *dhotī* of Kuṣāṇa period is sometimes replaced by tiger-skin.

The dishelleved matted locks are now well-arranged in *jaṭā-jūta* or well combed hair gradually reach up to shoulder and fall on the back.

Third eye of Śiva is depicted vertically instead of horizontally.

Images of Śiva are sometimes shown having halo (*prabhā-maṇḍala*).

Śiva is sometimes decked with ornaments, including necklaces and beautiful fillet for head ornament.

In exceptional cases Śiva has been without any garment or only with a narrow *kakṣa-bandha.*

The appearance of crescent moon and skulls on the head of Śiva became the regular practice from the Gupta period.[217]

MOTHER GODDESSES

SARASVATĪ

Sarasvatī, the goddess of learning and fine arts, is held in high esteem by the Hindus, the Buddhist and the Jains. The Jains assigned her a specially honoured place in the hierarchy as the head of the Śruti-devatās and the Vidyādekis, while the Buddhists, regarded her as the consort of Mañjuśrī. In Hindu mythology she is associated with Brahmā both as his daughter and wife.[218]

The proto-type of the iconography of Sarasvatī may be traced from the Śuṅga period. The Yakṣī, carved on a railing pillar at Bharhut shown standing gracefully on an upright frontal position on a large full blown lotus, seen playing on a seven stringed instrument (*Vīṇā*), held up in front across her body may be referred to in this connection. She is youthful in appearance and decked with ornaments.[219]

A definite representation of Sarasvatī of Kuṣāṇa period discovered from Jaina site at Kaṅkālī Ṭīlā Mathurā (Pl. XLVIII) is now housed in the State Museum, Lucknow.[220] It shows, the goddess sitting squatted on a rectangular pedestal with knees up. Her head is broken and in her left hand she holds the sacred book which appears to be tied with a ribbon. The right hand, which was raised probably in the *abhaya-mudrā*, has been lost. The goddess wears a loose cloth round her loins and part of this cloth covers the shoulder. There is one bracelet on each of her wrist and part of the rosary (*akṣamālā*) is visible over the bracelet of the right hand. On either side of the main figure there is an attendant with hair beautifully dressed. The one, on the right of the goddess, wears a tunic and holds a jar (*kalaśa*) in her hand while the attendant on the left hand appears in foreign dress.[221]

This figure also bears a six-lined inscription[222] on the pedestal, probably belongs to the Śvetāmbara sect as her images are sometimes met with in the modern Jaina temples mostly of the Śvetāmbara sect. But old images like the present one are very rare. Sarasvatī is primarily a deity of the Hindu pantheon. In Hinduism worship of this goddess as presiding deity of learning and wisdom has been prevalent since early times, but it is surprising to note that the images of Sarasvatī in the Brahmanical art are hardly found before the Gupta period, when the image worship of this goddess had become popular. In the early and late mediaeval period beautifully carved and highly decorated images of Sarasvatī were made. The goddess is often represented as the attendant of Viṣṇu along with Lakṣmī and is depicted as playing on her *Vīṇā* and sometimes also holding the sacred book in one of her four hands. The occurrence of Sarasvatī figure in Jaina art need not surprise one. The goddess being the embodiment of learning and the presiding deity of music has been given a venerable position in the Jaina scripture and pantheon and hence she figures in the Jaina art as a symbol of knowledge and wisdom.[223]

Gupta Period

No independent sculpture of Sarasvatī of the Gupta period have been found. On the lyrist type gold coins of Samudragupta, nimbate goddess is seated to left on a wicker stool, wearing a loose robe, close fitting cap and jewellery and holding a fillet in her outstretched right hand and cornucopiae in the left. Though she has not been given her specific symbol in her hand, the *vīṇā* on the obverse is taken to identify her with Sarasvatī.[224] But this identification does not seem convincing.

Sarasvatī, is however, represented on the reverse of the Rājalīlā type of coins of Samācharadeva, a predecessor of Śaśāṅka of Gauda. The goddess is nimbate, standing on a lotus bed in *tribhaṅga* posture. Her left hand rests on a lotus with bent stalk, by her right hand she draws up another lotus with long stalk in front of her face (as if to smell it), below it, is a goose (*haṁsa*) with upstretched neck trying to snatch a lotus leaf in its front by its open beak.[225] The presence of goose can be taken to identify her Sarasvatī.

A Bhīṭā sealing showing a vase on a pedestal and legend *Sarasvatī* in Gupta characters appears to represent the river goddess Sarasvatī in a symbolic form. The vase is probably an aniconic representation of the same river goddess. It appears that earlier every river goddess represented by a *ghaṭa* symbol.

In course of time, rivers began to be represented as female figures and were provided with different *vāhanas* which served the purpose of label inscriptions. The sealing shows that even in the Gupta period the old methods of depicting the goddess by *ghaṭa* continued along with their anthropomorphic representation.[226]

LAKSMĪ :
Śuṅga Period

The depiction of Gaja-Lakṣmī or Śrī in Indian sculptural art started from Śuṅga period though her representation on tribal coins of Ujjainī[227] and Kauśāmbī[228] dates back to 3rd and 2nd century B.C. The goddess is shown standing (rarely seated) being bathed by two elephants.[229]

The goddess is not only depicted on the coins of Ayodhyā rulers[230] (Ist century B.C.) but also on the coins of alien rulers viz. Azilises,[231] Rājuvula[232] and Soḍāsa.[233] The Gaja-Lakṣmī device seems to be quite popular with the Indo-Greek rulers Pantaleon[234] and Agathocles.[235]

As far as the sculptural art is concerned, the motif of Gaja-Lakṣmī became popular with the artists of this period because she is vigorously and profusely depicted on the railings of the *stūpas* of Bharhut, Sāñchī, and Bodh-Gayā.

The 'Sirima-devatā' depicted on the railing of Bharhut (200 B.C.) is supposed to be the earliest representation of Lakṣmī in sculptural art.[236] The deity is shown, standing, wearing diaphanous costume and jewellery and holding a lotus flower in her right hand.[237]

The goddess is also represented in sitting or standing posture at Bharhut. In the case of former type, the goddess is seated on a full blown lotus springing from a *pūrnaghaṭa* in the pose of *yoga* and both of her hands are folded (*samputita*). On her either side an elephant, standing on lotus, is bathing her from a vessel held in its trunk. The full blown lotus on which the elephants stand, is also springing from the same *pūrṇaghaṭa*.

At another place goddess (Pl. XLIX) is shown standing and holding the stem of lotus bud in the left hand.[238]

The basic conception of the goddess remains practically the same at Sāñchī as at Bharhut. But in one panel of a railing post of *stupa*, No. 2, she is shown standing on a full-blossomed lotus with folded hands, while the two elephants, standing on lotuses are giving her bath from upturned jars held in their trunks.

The goddess is also depicted on the gateways of Sāñchī (Ist century B.C.). On the northern gateway she is shown standing on a fully blossomed lotus with holding a lotus-bud in right hand and left one a cloth. She is being anionted by two elephants standing on her either side on lotus flowers.

In another panel on the northern gateway Gaja-Lakṣmī is shown seated comfortably on the pericap of a full-blown lotus, with her left leg tucked up on the seat and the right one pendent and placed on another lotus of smaller size,[239] holding a lotus flower in her right hand while the left hand rests on the left thigh.

She is further depicted artistically on the eastern gateway. Here the goddess is shown seated-on full-blown lotus with the right leg folded and the left leg hanging downward. The elephant pouring down the water from two pitchers over the head of the goddess and the falling water looks like a tall crown.[240] She is further depicted in similar manner on Stupa No. 3.

On one rail medallion of Bodh-Gayā, Goddess is depicted with an elaborate hair do wearing *mauli*, standing on a lotus. She is adorned with kuṇḍalas, three-stringed necklace, two-stringed girdle and *nūpura* and *dhotī*. She holds a bud in her right hand while left one is on *kaṭi*. The elephant on her right side stands on the lotus while the elephant on her left is damaged. On the two sides are two buds and flowers with long stalk and on them stand both of the elephants. The latter holding the jar with their trunk are bathing the goddess.[241]

Gaja-Lakṣmī panel is also found from Kauśāmbī. The goddess is shown standing, holding lotus stalks in her both hands. The flowers of the same lotus stalks are supporting two elephants and they are sprinkling water by the jars held in their trunks.[242]

The scene of *abhiṣeka* of Lakṣmī of first century is also found on the doorway of the cave of the Ajantā Gumphā, Udaigiri, (Orīssā).[243]

Kuṣāṇa Period

In the sculptures of Kuṣāṇa period, Lakṣmī is represented as a two-armed female figure with lotus in her left hand, the right hand being held in *abhaya-mudrā*. Alternatively, she may have lotus in both of her hands. Two elephants sprinkling water over her head is also a common feature noticed in the Kuṣāṇa period.[244]

In one of the images of Lakṣmī from Kṛṣṇa Janmasthāna the deity is shown holding stalked lotus in left hand and right hand in *abhaya* posture.[245]

In another figure of Lakṣmī of 2nd century A.D. from Mathurā now preserved in the State Museum, Lucknow (Pl. L) the goddess is shown on a small slab, seated in the centre. In her left hand she holds a stalked lotus, while her right hand is raised in *abhaya-mudrā*. She wears ear-pendants, torque and necklace. Tips of her feet can be seen peeping out of the lower portion of a high stool, on which she sits. A canopy (a usual mark of Kuṣāṇa Period) is seen over her head. On her left there are two pot-bellied figures seen seated one over the other. Both of them hold in their left hand a purse like object, while their raised right hands have something like a garland. To the right of deity there are three standing figures with folded hands, obviously of worshippers, one of which is a female and the remaining two are of males.[246]

One another image of Lakṣmī of 2nd-3rd century A.D. from Mathurā is preserved in the State Museum, Lucknow. Lakṣmī is seated on a high seat with full-blown stalked lotus in her left hand. The right hand is raised in the *abhaya* pose. She wears an *ekāvalī* and other usual ornaments. On her right sits a corpulent male figure with a crested headgear to right. His right hand is in *abhaya*-pose, while an indistinct object is held in his left. On the corresponding left side is seated a female with her right hand raised to the shoulder in what appears to be *abhaya*-pose, while the left is held in a manner akin to the child carrying mothers.[247]

On one panel of first or early 2nd century A.D. from Jamālpur site (Mathurā), a figure of woman, probably representing abundance is seen standing on lotus flower springing from a globular jar.[248] This panel shows the representation of motherhood.[249]

In some figures from Mathurā Lakṣmī is seen with a stalked lotus in her left hand along with the child in cradle.[250]

Lakṣmī is also depicted with Kubera holding a child in her lap. In one panel from Manohāpurā mound (Mathurā) (Pl. LI), Lakṣmī is seen with Kubera and Hāritī on a stele with their feet fastened on pedestal. Lakṣmī is depicted as holding a stalked lotus[251] but without a child.[252]

The most important form of Lakṣmī is that of Śrī. One sculpture from Śitalā ghāṭī shows the canopied goddess is being anointed by elephants.[253]

One image of Gaja-Lakṣmī of 3rd century A.D. from Farrukhabad (U.P.), is now stored in the State Museum, Lucknow. The goddess is two-handed and stands in 'lotus forest' (*padma-vana*). She holds a long stalked lotus in her left hand which has been placed on *kaṭi*. Her right hand has been raised in *abhaya-mudrā*. [216] She has a canopy over her head. Her *uttarīya* is seen worn with a long loop in front. By the side of her head are seen two small elephants with jars in their trunks anointing the goddess. Lotus creepers with buds, leaves and flowers in the background stand for *padma-vana*, the favourite abode of goddess.[254]

Gupta Period

The goddess Lakṣmī seems to have been quite popular in the Gupta period. She is mentioned by Kālidāsa in the Raghuvaṁśa,[255] is depicted profusely on Gupta coins and also represented in plastic art.

A stone sculpture from Eran in Sāgar district (M.P.) belonging to the early Gupta period, shows the goddess as being anionted by a pair of elephants.[256]

A panel in the Gupta temple at Deogarh represents a typical Gaja-Lakṣmī seated in *padmāsana* [257] wearing curly hair with *jūḍa, kuṇḍalas, hāra, kaṅkaṇa, keyūra*, girdle and a fine drapery. She has two arms, holding a *padma-patra* in the left hand and the right is held in *abhaya-mudrā*. On either side, an elephant stands on a lotus, the stalk of which issue from the *āsana* of the goddess. The elephants carry an inverted jar, each in their trunk for consecrating the deity. The panel may be assigned to 5th or 6th century A.D. This figure of the deity tallies with the description of the *Viṣṇudharmottara Pūraṇa*.[258]

The image of Lakṣmī of 6th century A.D. is carved on a pillar discovered on one side (the other side has Durgā Siṁhavahinī) from Bhītarī, Ghāzīpur district, U.P., now housed in the State Museum, Lucknow. The goddess is shown standing in a *padma-vana*. Her hair have been arranged in a knot. She puts on small ringlets in the upper part of her ears and *chakra-kuṇḍalas* embossed with rosette patterns in the lower parts. *Chūḍā-mani, ekāvalī, Chhannavīra, aṅgada, kaṅkana, mekhalā* and *nūpura* are other ornaments. A ring in the small finger of each hand is a unique feature. The deity puts on an embroidered close fitting *sārī* reaching her ankles. A light scarf has been thrown over her arms, the left hem of which she holds in her hand. In her right hand she carries a fruit. Lakṣmī is flanked by a corpulent male figure on double lotus seat. They are Yakṣas often associated with the goddess and have sometimes been taken as *śaṅkha-nidhi* and *padma-nidhi*. The goddess is being anointed by two elephants carrying beautiful jars decorated with lotus patterns.[259]

Gaja-Lakṣmī is also depicted on the glyptic art of this period. The seals discovered from Basarh, Bhīṭā, Rajaghāṭa, Ahichchhatrā and Eran, the goddess is shown more or less in the same fashion i.e. standing on a lotus flower, holding a lotus stalk in her left hand and right hand raised in *abhaya* or *varada-mudrā*.[260] But on Bhīṭā seals she is found associated with Garuḍa—a new feature, enunciated in the iconography of this period.[261]

DURGĀ

An inscribed gold medal, now in the British Museum, London, shows that a female deity named Aṁpā or Aṁbā-denoting a mother Durgā or consort of Śiva who was the city goddess of Pakhalawadi or Puṣkalāvatī of ancient Gāndhāra region now in Pakistan.[262] On the obverse of the coins of Azes I a female deity, clad in himation, holds in raised right hand a flower, stands on lotus, besides her lion.[263]

It seems that the goddess with lion(s) Nānā probably influenced the iconography of Aṁbā by the end of the period of the group of Azes (I or II), who ruled from about 50 B.C. to 25 A.D.[264] By the time of Huviṣka Nānā was identified with Umā (or Aṁbā) as on one coin device the goddess is shown with nimbus, crescent and sceptre and seated on a lion.[265] She is also shown by the side of Oesho i.e., Śiva holding the cornucopiae apparently[266] in place of Umā's symbol the lotus flowei. And since Nānā might have received the horn of plenty from Tyche and through the concept of Umā or Aṁbā as the divinity in charge of fortune.[267]

These different syncretistic tendencies contributed to the growth of the concept of iconography of the goddess on lion which later on came to be styled as Durgā Siṁhavāhinī. The concept of Durgā with lion seem to have been conceived after Nānā's lion became associated with Aṁbā by the period of Azes (I or II) or Nānā herself was identified with Umā (or Aṁbā) by the time of Huviṣka.[268]

Kuṣāṇa Period

The depiction of Siṁhavāhinī Durgā began in sculptural art from Kuṣāṇa period at Mathurā. About half a dozen images of two, four or six-armed goddess either standing or sitting over her mount, the lion[269] fashioned by the Mathurā sculptors are now housed in the Government Museum, Mathurā.

One stone sculpture from Māṭ shows the lower part of a female as (the upper part mutilated), standing to front, wearing a diaphanous drapery and standing against a lion, couchant to left.[270]

The Statue made of red sandstone from Mathurā now in a private collection in the U.S.A. is quite important from the point of view of identification. The goddess is shown two-armed, standing to front on a lion couchant to right with face turning towards her. She holds a trident in her hand. Her half-raised right hand is in *abhaya-mudrā.*[271]

In one four-armed statue from the Government Museum, Mathurā, the goddess wears coiffeured hair or *jaṭā-jūṭa*, earrings, necklace, a large number of bangles and a beautiful drapery. One of her hand is held in *abhaya-mudrā*, the other placed akimbo and the remaining two holds a trident and a shield or *śakti.*[272]

Gupta Period

A two-armed figure of Durgā of Gupta period is in the State Museum, Lucknow. The deity with the right fore-arm broken is seated in *latitāsana* over a couchant lion. She wears a fine *sarī* with folds, *keyūra, kataka, nūpura* and *ekāvalī* and upper part of the body appears to be bare. She holds a spear in her left hand.[273]

Durgā is also represented on a pillar (on its one side already referred to above) discovered from Bhitarī. The goddess is seated on a lion walking to left. She is four-armed and holding a *triśūla, khaḍga*, shield and lotus clockwise. Halo (*prabhāmaṇḍala*) is seen around her head.[274]

DURGĀ MAHIṢĀSURAMARDINĪ

The earliest representation of Mahiṣāsuramardinī occurs on a terracotta plaque discovered from Sonkh, Mathurā belonging to the Ist century B.C.[275] One more terracotta plque of an early period, dated between Ist century B.C. to Ist century A.D. discovered from Nagar (ancient Karkotanagar), now preserved in the Museum at Āmer (Jaipur). The Nagar plaque made of Kaoline, depicts the goddess as four-armed, with lower right hand placed on the back of the buffalo, while upper right hand holds a trident.[276]

Kuṣāṇa Period

The images of Mahiṣāsuramardinī became popular in the Kuṣāṇa period. The sculptors of the Mathurā school of art carved out numerous images of this goddess (Pl. LII). The goddess is usually four or six-armed, with or without lion, holding different weapons and strangulating the neck of the buffalo demon.[277]

In one four-armed image goddess is shown holding a spear and trident (*triśūla*) and strangulating the buffalo demon (*Mahiṣā*). Her mount lion is also shown below, which is a rare feature in Kuṣāṇa period.[278]

In all these representations, buffalo is shown as being trampled by the goddess, but in none of them the throat of the demon is shown severed or his human form is shown coming out of the throat. It was a later feature that started with the compilation of *Devī-mahātmya*.[279]

Gupta Period

The iconography of Durgā Mahiṣāsuramardinī further developed during the Gupta age. Number of her hands multiplied and she was conceived having as many as twelve hands.

One of the remarkably early reliefs belonging to the Gupta period, unearthed at Bhīṭā, depicts the goddess subduing the buffalo demon, unaccompanied by her vehicle or any accessory figure. Carved out of local sandstone, the two-armed goddess with her left hand placed on waist, has a trident in her right hand which she is piercing into the neck of the demon in animal form.[280]

One more figure of early 4th century or of transitional phase is found from Kaṅkālī mound, Mathurā. The goddess is eight-armed and clasping the tail of Mahiṣāsura.[281] A fragmentary relief from Sārnāth also represents the goddess piercing the demon with her trident held in her right hand while she is trying to lift the buffalo by catching its tail. The goddess is carved having two hands and without her usual mount.[282]

A terracotta plaque of Mahiṣāsuramardinī from Gaṅgānagar district of Rājasthān, belonging to the early Gupta period, shows Devī in the act of killing the buffalo demon with a *triśūla* which she holds in her upper right hand. The upper left hand is broken, with the lower left she holds the head of the buffalo-demon. This plaque is now in the Bīkāner Museum.[283]

Durgā killing the buffalo demon is also depicted at Udaigiri caves (400 A.D.). Her three representations occurs in cave No. 4, 6, 13 and 17.[284]

The goddess (Cave No. 17) stands in full frontal pose (Pl. LIII) with the buffalo rearing before her, one of her left arms pressing stiffly down upon its back. The goddess has twelve arms. The front right hand is firmly placed on the animal's back, the second holds his tail, the third holds an arrow, the fourth holds the *śūla* with which the goddess is piercing the animal's haunch, and the last holds one end of garland held above her head. The other end of garland is held by her rear left hand. The only distinguishable emblem in her other left hands are the shield and the bow. A small attendant figure stood by her left foot.[285]

The splendid though badly damaged image of the goddess (Cave No. 6) shows her in a completely new pose from the above mentioned (Pl. LIV). Instead of rearing up, here, the buffalo is shown with his head pressed into the ground, with the goddess's foot proudly placed upon it. The same diagonal movement is maintained for the depiction of animal but, here, his haunches and hind legs are shown raised. The goddess holds in her left hands a chakra, a bow, a club and a large funnel-shaped object on the proper left with leaf patterns, which has not been identified. The object held above her head is a lotus garland. The attributes of right hands are not clearly visible.[286]

A beautiful image of goddess from Bhūmarā (500 A.D.) is now in the Allahabad Museum.[287] The goddess standing in the *pratyālīḍha*[288] pose is seen pressing the demons' head (in animal form) with her right leg, piercing the back with her trident in right hand and lifting the hind part of the demon by its tail with her left hand. She is four-armed, holding an unsheathed sword in her back right hand and a shield in the back left hand.[289] A dwarf attendant is accompanying her on her right. But Stella Kramrisch is of the view that the boy on her right may by Dundubhi, the son of Māyā.[290]

A four-armed sculpture of Devī of Gupta era is also reported from Sindūrī. Her hair are arranged in a trepoil parted by *sīmanta* ornament in the middle. Her upper right hand rests on a tapering three pronged spear piercing into the chest of the demon. Her lower right hand holds *khaḍga.* Her upper left hand holds a flaming shield by its strap. Her lower left hand is akimbo holding the pig-tail of the animal and lifting up his hind part. She has planted her right foot on the head of the prostrate animal. She wears *kuṇḍalas, graiveyaka* and *valayas.* The *mekhalā* claps her *sārī* bearing horizontal decorative strips, her left leg is straight and stiff which is hidden behind the chest of buffalo.[291]

These Gupta images of Mahiṣāsuramardinī were made in accordance to a description found in the *Devī-mahātmya*.[292]

SAPTA MĀTṚKĀS

The origin of the Mātṛkās are based on two different Pūraṇic versions. According to the *Mārkaṇḍeya Pūraṇa*[293] the Mātṛkās aided Aṁbā along with Chāmuṇḍā in causing death to the most powerful ally of the demon Śuṁbha named Raktabīja, who was endowed with the character of multiplying into secondary demons equal to himself in strength and powers no sooner drops of blood oozing from the wounds on person of the Asura touched the ground.[294] The other story is related to the demon Andhakāsura who fought against Śiva.[295] As soon as the drops the blood of Andhakāsura touched the ground, it gave birth to other demon. To stop the blood from falling on the earth, Śiva created, out of the flame issuing from his mouth, a *śakti* called Yogeśvarī. The other gods also issued their *śaktis* to serve the same purpose. They came to be designated as Brāhmī, Maheśvarī, Kaumārī, Vaiṣṇavī, Vārahī, Indrāṇī and Chāmuṇḍā. These female counterparts of the gods (Brahmā, Maheśa, Kaumāra, Viṣṇu, Varāha, Indra and Yama). These were recognisable through the arms and banners corresponding to their gods.[296]

The images of the Mātṛkās, however, do not represent them either engaged in assisting Śiva in his war against Andhakāsura or Ambikā against Raktabīja or devouring the secondary demons born out of the blood of any of the two demons; they are shown simply standing or seated at ease along with their respective characteristic features. It appears that the Mātṛakās had independent origin and existence but later as a result of religious syncretism were made associated with Śaiva or Śākta cults. In the extant images Mātṛkās are shown with two or four hands. Her normal hands are placed in the *abhaya* and the *varada* poses. They are also accompanied by the *vāhanas* of the gods. Sometimes they are also found accompanied by children in order to emphasis their 'Motherly aspect'.[297]

A stone slab of the early Kuṣāṇa period from Dhanagaon, near Mathurā, now housed in the Government Museum, Mathurā, represents the Mātṛkās as ordinary females, without any distinguishing symbol or vehicle. Standing in a row, these females have their right hand raised in *abhaya-mudrā*, while they have water-vessels held by their suspended left hands. All of them wear ear-pendants, bracelets, anklets and are attired in a skirt. These seven female figures flanked on either side by a male figure with his right hand in *abhaya-mudrā* and a long spear held in his left hand, the one on the proper left being lost.[298]

A stone slab of Ist-2nd century A.D., the provenance of which is not known, is stored in the State Museum, Lucknow. The fragment of a slab shows a mother seated with both legs stretched inwards resting on the same seat. She wears ear-pendants, torque, armlets and anklets and carries a cradle-like object in her left hand resting on her knee. It might have contained a boy in its original form, which is now worn out. Her right hand is in *abhaya-pose*. Traces of the figure of worshippers, are visible to her right.[299]

A relief of 2nd century A.D. from Mathurā now in the Lucknow Museum, shows a series of human figures. The one on the extreme left is a lion-headed female deity seated with both legs resting on the same seat, her right hand is raised above to the shoulder in *abhaya-mudrā*. A basket-like thing supposed to be a cradle, which is held in her left hand turned inwards and resting on two knees, has a baby with folded hands in it. She wears torque, armlets and bracelets. To her right stands Kārttikeya holding a spear (*śakti*) in left hand, his right hand being raised in *abhaya* pose. On the proper right corner four miniature figures are seen standing in *namaskāra mudrā*.[300]

In one more slab from Mathurā of 2nd century A.D. now in the State Museum, Lucknow, Mātṛkās are depicted with Kubera. (The slab shows four figures seated in a line). One to the extreme left is a figure of a pot-bellied Kubera holding probably a purse in his left hand, right is seen in *abhaya*-pose. He wears a turban with its crest to the left, a torque in his neck and pendants in the ears. Next to him is a female deity holding a cradle-like object containing a baby. Her right hand is in *abhaya* pose. She has got the canopy over her head. To her right is again a similar female divinity, but without a child, her left fist is simply clenched as if holding the hem of her garment. Fourth is, seated Lakṣmī with canopy over her head. She holds a stalked lotus, shown in profile, in her left hand. The extreme right of the slab shows two worshippers, one seated and the other standing.[301]

The existence of Sapta mātṛkās in the Kuṣāṇa art however remains a supposition due to non-availability of clear cut iconography which is found in subsequent period in Indian art.[302]

Gupta Period

The rudiments of the iconic form of the Sapta-mātṛkās can be seen in the Kuṣāṇa art but in those plaques there is little possibility of identifying them as Brāhmī, Maheśvari, Vaiṣṇavī and Kaumārī etc. It is only in the Gupta period the seven mothers were substituted by the female counterparts of the then important gods, viz. Brahmā, Viṣṇu, Śiva, Kārttikeya, Indra and Varāha.[303] And their icons within a securely dated context occur during the first decade of the 5th century A.D.[304]

The earliest representations of the Sapta-mātṛkās are located at Udaigiri (M.P.). The caves have three groups of Mātṛkās panels two in Cave No. 6 and one in Cave No. 4. The Cave No. 4, although Śaivite in character, has a Mātṛkā chapel of nine figures. The first icon, a seated figure on the chapel's left wall, is badly mutilated and only the torso with a thick sacred thread remains. Above the weathered figure and engaged to the wall, however, is a standard upon which the scant outline of the cock can be discerned. And because of the presence of the cock, one of the attributes of Skanda, the figure is identified with that deity. Along the back wall of the chapel are the remains of seven figures seated in western fashion. Only the thighs of the goddesses remain. Each figure sits on an individual bench. One of the goddesses has a child. And each deity has been carved with a staff and an identifying emblem. A trident attached with flying ribbons can be seen behind the second figure. Since a trident is the attribute of Maheśa or Śiva, the figure to be identified as of Maheśvarī. Above the first figure the outlines of a weathered circular shape has been recognized as a large full-blown lotus, and as such the figure may have represented Brāhmī. A badly mutilated figure engaged to the right chapel wall, has no distinguishing attributes, but in the light of the identification of Skanda at the head of the groups, this final figure either represented Śiva or a guardian.[305]

The Cave No. 6 has two continuous figures of the Mātṛkās. To the left of the first chapel ponderous and barely visible nimbus behind the head is indicative of a divinity probably representing Śiva. Along the back of the chapel wall are carved seven Mātṛkās. Few of the goddesses display remnants of a nimbus. The first figure to the left is badly damaged, only one leg is preserved. The torsos and heads of the next five are still intact, but the seventh has only one leg. The wall behind the figures is so rough that it is impossible to determine if the figures had staffs with identifying emblems. On the right of the chapel is another seated male figure. it is also in a poor state of preservation with attributes not discernible and therefore, difficult to be identified.

The second chapel is adjacent to Cave No. 6 and is separated from the first Sapta Mātṛkā group by a lateral wall. On the left wall is a large image of Skanda astride his vehicle. The peacock's body and long neck covered with a delicate cross-hatched pattern is still preserved. Eight badly damaged figures are seated in *latitāsana* along the chapel's back wall. Above each icon is a staff with an identifying emblem to which streamers or ribbons are attached. The first figure is of Śiva. The next figure has a staff with a circular emblem, might be a lotus, an attribute of Brāhmī. The staff of the next figure, Maheśvarī is embellished with a trident, and next to her Kaumārī, the next can be identified by her spear. ·The remains of a circular discus can be discerned on the staff above the head of the fourth deity, representing Vaiṣṇavī. The staff emblems of the next three figures, presumably those of Varāhī, Indrāṇī and Chāmuṇḍā, have been erased completely. The tenth figure on the right wall, is fragmentary, only the torso and head remain of a once tall and lithe standing male figure. A spear is carved on the wall immediately to his left, probably representing Skanda, Śiva or a guardian.[306]

A complete Sapta Mātṛkās panel of Gupta period is reported from a hill between the villages of Badoh and Patharī (M.P.) (Pl. LV). Each of the eight figures are seated on a bench and have two arms. To the far left is a figure of ithyphallic Śiva and Chāmuṇḍā on the far right recognized by her emaciated body, taut neck muscles and curly hair cascading from the crown of her head. In her left hand is a somewhat mutilated implement, possibly a knife or another kind of weapon. The first goddess on the far left, Brāhmī carries a lotus. The next figure holds a staff but the top is broken. According to proper Sapta Mātṛkā order, the second figure would be Maheśvarī. The third figure carries a staff (now borken top) may be Kaumārī. The fourth goddess lacks attributes and part of her head has been broken. The fifth has lost both arms, part of her face and the top of her head. The next also has her arms, but there are remnants of something to the right of her throne, possibly the feet of a child or part of a *Vāhana.* One interesting feature of the second, third, fourth and sixth goddesses is that each has a variation in hair style called *sikhandaka.* This hair-do is normally associated with Skanda and Kaumārī, whose locks of hair on either side of the head is divided. The strands are then pulled to the back to form pony tails.[307]

Ekānaṁśā

Ekānaṁśā, usually accompanied by Balarāma and Kṛṣṇa, was for the first time represented during the Kuṣāṇa period. The Mathurā Museum has many panels of this deity. In one panel a two-handed deity is depicted between two four-handed males (Fig. 17). The right hand of devi is in *abhaya-mudrā* and left hand is on waist. The male god on her right is Balarāma, standing and holding a mace is his upper right hand and plough surmounted with lion in upper left hand and normal right hand is in *abhaya-mudrā* and left is shown as *kaṭi-hasta.* The deity on her left is Kṛṣṇa, standing and having a mace, *chakra, śaṅkha* and one hand is in *abhaya-mudrā.*[308] One more sculpture from Mathurā is now in the National Museum, Karachi.[309] Separate Kuṣāṇa statues representing Saṁkarṣaṇa-Balarāma, Ekānaṁśā and Vāsudeva-Kṛṣṇa are known from Gayā district.[310]

A relief of Ekānaṁśā obtained from Sanghel is in Gurgaon district of Haryana shows the triad standing to front of pose. On the proper right of Ekānaṁśā is quadrumanous Balarāma wearing a typical early foliated *mukuṭa*, earring in the left ear only, necklace, armlets and bracelets. His normal right hand is raised to the level of the shoulder in *abhaya* pose and the left one is akimbo, holding a flask. The rare right and left hands not very clearly discernible in the relief, carried a mace and plough surmounted by a lion. Ekānaṁśā is two-handed. Her right hand is in *abhaya-mudrā* and the left rests on the waist. But for the lower garment, other items of jewellery on her person, are not clear.

On her proper left stands Vāsudeva-Kṛṣṇa with head broken. His normal hand is disposed in *abhaya-mudrā* and proper left is *kaṭyalambita* holding perhaps a conch which looks as *aṁrta-ghaṭa.* A part of the extra hand on the left indicates that the figure was originally four-handed. The broken back hands may have held mace and disc.[311]

The sculptures depicting Ekānaṁśā of the Gupta period have not yet been reported from any ancient site.

Gaṅgā-Yamunā

One of the novel features of the art of Gupta period is the depiction of the rivers Gaṅgā and Yamunā in personified forms[312] which became a regular decorative-motif for the door-jambs of a temple. It signifies that crossing the threshold of a temple flanked by images of the goddesses, Gaṅgā and Yamunā, devotees were probably symbolically cleansed in the purificatory waters of these rivers.[313]

The motif seems to have originated from the Yakṣī figures shown standing on the *makara* in the art of Bharhut and Mathurā.[314]

The goddesses are usually depicted as two-handed deities holding a water-vessel or a lotus flower. An umbrella is held over their head by a male or female attendants.[315]

The descend of Gaṅgā and Yamunā from heavens to the sea is beautifully sculptured in the Cave No. 4 at Udaigiri. (Pl. LVI).[316] On the right and left sides of the Mahāvarāha panel the river-goddesses are depicted at first in their natural form as two mighty streams taking their rise from heavenly world and are shown with divine dance and music and on the earth they again appear in their human form i.e. Gaṅgā standing on *makara* (crocodile) and Yamunā on *Kūrma* (tortoise), both holding in their right hand a *pūrṇa ghaṭa.*[317]

The image of Gaṅgā from Besnagar (c. 500 A.D.), now housed in the Museum of Fine Arts, Boston, shows her standing on a *makara.* The goddess is accompanied by a small figure to her right and second small figure below is subduing the rampant *makara.*[318]

The doorway of the temples of Bilsād[319] and Tigwā[320] (Pls. LVII, LVIII) contain the figure of goddess Gaṅgā standing on *makara* on right door jamb and Yamunā on *Kūrma* on the left jamb. In these temples goddesses are shown at the top of the jambs. But it is with the coming of the fifth century at Nachnā[321] for the first time, these goddesses were depicted on the lower parts of the jambs,[322] which become a rule as evidenced at Bhūmarā[323] Sakhor and BhīṂtargaon.[324] But at the same time at Deogarh the River-goddesses are depicted on the upper part of the jambs instead of lower which may indicate the survival of the earlier traditon.[325]

Gaṅgā is also depicted on a highly ornamental door-jamb acquired by the

Government Museum, Mathurā, from Śrī-Kṛṣṇa Janmasthāna. The figure of Yamunā on tortoise is carved on a pillar unearthed from Kaṅkālī mound and now displayed in the State Museum, Lucknow.[326] The figure stands on a tortoise with her dwarf parasol-bearer, below whose feet appears a lion's head. The figure wear earrings, short necklace, *mekhalā,* armlets and bracelets.[327]

But the most elegant and sophisticated images of the river goddesses of the 5th-6th century A.D. have been found from the excavated remains of a large brick temple at Ahichchhatrā (Pls, LIX, LX).[328] Now forming a prized-possession of the National Museum, Delhi. The goddesses are shown standing on their respective mounts *makara* and *kūrma.*

Vasudharā

Vasudharā or Bhūdevī, meaning goddess Earth, is also known as the consort of Viṣṇu. Possibly this association of the goddess Earth with Viṣṇu is due to his boar incarnation.[329] Her representation in art dates back to the pre-Mauryan period.[330] A gold leaf excavated at Lauriyā-Nandangarh has the figure of a female stamped upon it. Bloch described it as a representation of the Vedic Earth goddess.[331] The worship of Vasudharā was quite popular in Śuṅga period. She is not only found in terracotta art of this period but a few moulds of her figure have also been recovered from Mathurā region.[332]

Her representation is in the Kuṣāṇa art is also known.[333] She is usually depicted in this period along with a pair of fish and a pitcher.[334] A figure of Ist-2nd century A.D. of Vasudharā from Mathurā, now in the State Museum, Lucknow, shows her standing in *abhaya*-pose. She carries a pair of fish in her left hand below her hand is seen a high rimmed bowl placed on a jar with *mekhalā* at the centre. She wears a head-band, ear-pendants, torque, armlets, bracelets, anklets and a *dhotī,* the lower portion of the sculpture is missing.[335]

In the Gupta period we do not come across her independent figure but she is usually depicted with boar incarnation of Viṣṇu and can be seen tucked to his tusks at Udaigiri and Eran.

Others Deities

Yakṣas, Nāgas, Gandharvas and Kinnaras

YAKṢAS

The images of Yakṣas were the first anthropomorphic representation of a deity in stone,[336] and certainly it was the Yakṣa image which laid the foundation for the later Brahmaṇical and Buddhist iconography.[337]

The Yakṣas, basically the folk cult deities, seem to have been quite popular during the early historic India. The free standing stone images of the Yakṣas of the third-second centuries B.C. to the first century A.D., are known from different regions of northern and eastern India. Usually portrayed standing and meant to be viewed frontly, they are life size and corpulent, with swelling abdomens, their bulging masses with scarf and ornaments, conveying a great sense of power. Their backs on the other hand are flat, with the details simply suggested in low relief.[338]

A colossal image of Yakṣa of c. 3rd B.C. was found from Pārkham (Pl. LXI. Fig. 22.)[339] near Mathurā. The figure is slightly pot-bellied[340] both of his hands are mutilated and decked with torque, necklace with four knots behind and chest band. He is shown wearing a *dhotī* and a girdle fastened round the waist and the two fillets hanging from the knot between the thighs; and comparatively thin legs of the standing figure pay little or no heed to the back.[341] The fragment of a colossal figure of Yakṣa was found from Barodā near Mathurā, which is now in the Government Museum, Mathurā. The figure belonged to the Maurya period[342] or little earlier.

Two statues of the Yakṣas of 2nd century B.C. were found from Patnā now preserved in the Patnā Museum.[343] Both standing figures also are almost identical in form and appearance, vision and execution, dress and ornament etc. The two figures have a scarf on their shoulder, a line of *Brāhmī* inscription which has paleographically been dated round about the beginning of Christian era. Their weightly appearance and archaic heaviness of form and the conflict between fully rounded and modelled volume as noticed in the arms, chest and abdomen on the one hand, the flat surface of the back on the other seem to suggest their close affinity with the huge heavy and primitive Boddhisattvas of the Mathurā school. On the other hand the general shape and appearance of the upper part of their body and the character of plastic treatment seems to indicate a close relationship with the art of the eastern gate of the great *stūpa* at Sāñchī.[344]

The most beautiful and famous figure among the Yakṣa and Yakṣī series is Dīdārganj Yakṣī (Pl. LXII) now preserved in the Patnā Museum, Patnā. It is a work of Maurya or Śuṅga period.[345] The figure stands, and holds *chāmara* in right hand. The figure is carved round hence bound by no law of frontality. The treatment of the back, particularly the region along the spine is indicative of a superb craftmanship. The forward movement of the upper part of the body is helped by a slight bent of the right knee-joint, the waist is carved narrow and a necklace is hanging around rhythmically. The legs are executed in shape that can be witnessed by the gradually tapering down to the thin ankles shown as decorated by heavy and fully jewelled ornaments. The sensitiveness of the flesh as shown in the modelling of the lower belly and the abdomen, the chin and the region around the eyes is striking.[346]

On many of the *vedikā* uprights of Bharhut are seen Viruḍako Yakho, Kupiro

Yakho (Pl. LXIII), Ajakālko Yakho, Gāṅgeya Yakho, Sūchīlomo Yakho, Supavāso Yakho, of them Viruḍaka and Kubera Yakṣas are the guardians of the southern and northern quarters respectively, while the other four are not associated with any major or minor quarters.[347] All have (except one) their hands in *añjali* or *namaskāra-mudrā* a few are female. A male, in boots and tunic, with a diadem and short curls, is among the first of many such fugures in Indian art to be dressed in *udīchya* or Northern costume usually associated with Sun-god or with guardians of shrine *(dvārapālas)*.[348]

They also have different mounts beneath them. Kubera stands on the back of a malformed pot-bellied Yakṣa sitting on his haunches, Viruḍaka on a high rocky ground, Gaṅgito's right leg is placed on the back of a tusker, Sūchīloma stands erect on a coping stone of a rail and Supavāsa stands with right knee slightly bent on a caparisoned tusker trotting to right, Ajakālaka whose hands are shown in different poses his right hand holds a half-blossomed lotus flower and his left hand is held in the *kaṭi hasta* stands in a graceful pose on the back of a composite animal, with the tail of a *makara* and the fore-legs of a lion (or tiger).[349] It is an earliest example of the Indian custom of assigning an animal or a human as vehicle *(vāhana)* for individual deities.[350]

A statue of Maṇibhadra Yakṣa of 1st century B.C. hailing from Pāwayā near Gwālior was set up by a guild of *Maṇibhadrabhaktas.* It is now in the Gwālior Museum.[351]

One intact image of Yakṣa found from Vidiśā, (Pl. LXIV., Fig. 23) 6½ ft. tall, carrying a purse now preserved in the Vidiśā Museum. It belongs to the first century B.C. [352]

A four-faced Yakṣa of 2nd and 1st century B.C. was recovered from Bhiṭā in Allahabad district of U.P. The image is intended to be fixed at a spot visible from all the sides. On one side is seen crowned Yakṣa standing in *abhaya* pose. His right hand is raised to the shoulder in *abhaya* pose and the left hand by his side holds an ornamental jar, which can be seen at the back of the closed fist. He wears heavy ear-pendents, necklace and bracelets. His *uttrīya* has been beautifully shown over his shoulders. The *dhotī,* the folds of which are seen in front and on the left side, is tied with a heavy girdle, one end of which is seen over the right thigh. The figure, though muscular and heavy, is slightly leaner than the other at the back, which depicts another standing Yakṣa. He unlike the previous Yakṣa does not wear any crown. His hair, parted in the middle, fall on either shoulders in the form of braides. He wears no necklace, ear pendents or even *uttarīya.* However, the only ornament seen worn by him is a bracelet in his left hand. Right hand which was raised to the shoulder in *abhaya* pose is broken. In his left hand resting on belly holds a pot-like object. *Dhotī* is held fit with a heavy girdle the end of which are seen on the right thigh.

High adjacent side of the crowned figure : The face is completely damaged. Traces of ears and ear pendants and that of a 'V' shaped heavy necklace are visible. Below his face is a figure of a boar standing on a pedestal. His head is turned upwards, while the fore-paws are stretched upwards and joined together as if in *namaskāra-mudrā.* Left side of the crowned figure : Face of this side is also completely damaged. The angular portion below the chin suggests that it would have been a bearded figure. No further details of the face are available at present. Below the face is a figure of a sejant lion.[353]

Another image of this type, carved on different faces of a block, is deposited in the Bharat Kala Bhawan, Vārāṇasī. Agrawala describes it as representing a triple image on a three-sided block of stone which has a square pedestal below, each side is carved with a standing male figure in bold-relief. The figures are rather dwarfish in stature, plum and have their hands lifted up. [354]

Yakṣa's figure of Ist century B.C. discovered from Palwal in Gurgaon district of Haryana, is now in the State Museum, Lucknow (U.P) (Pl. LXV). The bust of a colossal Yakṣa figure wear a heavy turban under which thick locks of his hair are visible. He wears ear ornaments, collar, falt triangular torque and *sapatrakeyūra.* In his existing right hand with a badly disfigured conch-like object, appear four bracelets. Traces of his *uttarīya* are also visible near his right elbow. The face has been badly disfigured bearing no traces of eyes, nose or lips. The sculpture was carved in round.[355]

Characteristics of Early Yakṣa Images

The extant early Yakṣa images are colossal in size and massively built with pronounced emphasis on muscular strength.

They are usually carved in the round and therefore is standing freely; the main effect is frontal as if they were intended to be seen from the front side only.

The drapery consists of a turban on the head and upper scarf thrown on the shoulders and arms tied round the chest and *dhotī* hanging below up to the ankles and fastened with a girdle. the ornaments consist of heavy earrings, heavy torque, and a flat triangular, necklace and armlets.

There is also a tendency to depict the figure slighty pot-bellied as in the case of Pārkham and Maṇibhadra Yakṣa from Pāwayā.[356]

Sātavāhana and Kuṣāṇa Period

Sāñchī has supplied several images of the Yakṣas in two varied forms. In one form Yakṣas stand gracefully like their Bharhut counterparts and in the other they have dwarfish and grotesque features, which was a new development of this time.

The first category of the Yakṣas can be seen in the relief of Padmapāṇi Yakṣa on northern *toraṇa* (P. LXVI). He stands under a tree, holding a lotus *phalaka*. His dress and ornaments are tastefully shown.[357] It belongs to first half of the Ist century B.C.[358]

The other standing Yakṣa of same type can be seen on the upper part of Northern gateway holding a *chaurī* in his right hand. The date of its carving is also first half of Ist century B.C. [359]

The second type which was inaugurated during this period can be seen on the Western *toraṇa* as *bhāravāhaka* Yakṣa figures (Pl. LXVII), standing back to back, impressive in bulk and volume, but dwarfish in size. Their dress and ornaments are the same, although their patterns differ. Some Yakṣas are shown grinning. While others have controlled features all of them support the parts of *toraṇa* above.[360]

A unique image of Yakṣa is known from Ahichchhatrā. The iamge is carved on a rectangular block of stone whose upper side must have served as a seat. The knees and the arms and legs of the Yakṣa figure served as the legs of the seat. The Yakṣa is pot-bellied and is shown stretching the two ends of his mouth with the index figures of both of his hands. His hair is shown arranged in three parts, two on the sides and one in the middle of his scalp; the remaining portion in between the *simantas* partings. The figure has big bulging eyes, teeth peeping through the mouth, the moustaches, large ears and deep navel. He wears a *ghutanna*, and his ornaments consist of a garland around the neck and three bracelets. The image also carries an inscription.[361]

Characteristics of Kuṣāṇa Yakṣa

Yakṣas have given new attributes as lotus, staff and cup.

Generally, Yakṣas are depicted in sitting or standing or crouching postures with smiles or fierce expressions.

The Yakṣa images in this period are generally not provided with lables, in some cases there are inscriptions which indicate that they were worshipped.

The seated figures of Yakṣas in Kuṣāṇa art are comparatively less in number. [362]

Gupta Period

We do not find many sculptures of Yakṣas in the Gupta period. Although Kubera (chief of the Yakṣas) was a popular subject for images during this time but other Yakṣa and Yakṣī representation are rare. And they appear either as decorative motifs or in the form of Gaṇas.

This indicates that they had lost their independent status and merged in the personalities of greater cult gods such as Śiva, Gaṇeśa, Buddha and Bodhisattvas in the Kuṣāṇa and Gupta periods. Therefore, their iconography has not been described in contemporary iconographic texts which otherwise contain copious material about the other cult gods. It is not that the Yakṣas and Yakṣīs were entirely eliminated from the scene as it is proved by the emergence of 24 Yakṣa upāsakas and Yakṣī *śāsanadevatās* in Jain pantheon.[363]

NĀGAS

The antiquity of Nāga cult goes back to Indus Valley Civilization. In one seal a seated deity is shown as being worshipped on either side by a kneeling man and behind each of the worshippers a cobra, having its head raised and hood expanded. Nāga, here, appears as a protective diety.[364]

The Nāgas are usually depicted in three styles :

(1) The form of the serpent, usually many-headed, (2) the human form characterized by the polycephalous serpent hood, and (3) a combination of two, the upper part of a human body and lower part formed by snake's coil.

The simplest and the most primitive form in which the Nāgas appear in Indian art is the serpent form. And to show their divinity they are provided with many heads and the number varying to three, five or seven. It can be seen on the reliefs of Bharhut and Sāñchī.

In one relief from Bharhut (200 B.C) a five-headed serpent is shown conversing with an ascetic who is seated in front of his hut. The scene is perhaps an illustration of the *Maṇikaṇṭha* Jātaka.[365]

The central architrave of the Eastern gateway of Sāñchī (Ist century A. D.) bears a well-known relief representing the worship of a sacred tree by forest animals. Among the beasts of the jungle naturalistically treated, a five-headed Nāga along with his natural foe, the Garuḍa.[366]

On the same eastern gateway of Sāñchī, the scene of the Buddha subduing the venonous dragon is depicted (Pl. LXVIII). The presence of the Buddha is shown with an empty seat and the Nāga is plainly shown in the semblance of five-headed cobra.[367]

The Nāgas are also depicted in anthropomorphic form in the Buddhist art.

A figure of Nāgarāja Chakrāvaka is depicted on a railing pillar which stood in the corner of the south gate at Bharhut.[368] It is represented wholly in the form of human being, with the addition of a canopy of five snake-hoods attached behind the head, besides a heavy turban. The figure shown standing to front on a high rock by the side of a lotus lake in the attitude of calm with the hands crossed upon the breast in *namaskāra-mudrā* has the upper part of the body bare, but from the hips downwards, it is clad in *dhotī* the end of which reached the ground in a succession of very formal plaits. The Nāga chief is also wearing a number of jewellery like large earrings, necklaces, armlets, bracelets, besides strings of pearls and beads of embroidered cloth bound round the hair.[369]

An inscription on the Prasenjit pillar at Bharhut, informs about the worship of Lord Buddha by the Nāgarāja Elapatta or Airāvata. Buddha is portrayed through an empty seat at the foot of a sacred tree. The Nāgarāja, on the contrary, is depicted not less than three times. First, it appears as a five-headed serpent that emerged from the lake. Next he appears in human form with five-hooded serpent crest and accompanied by two nāgīs each wearing a single snake-emblem. And for the third time the Nāga-king is shown kneeling down in devotion before the stone seat under the tree, indicative of the Buddha's presence. Here, the crest of five snake heads issues from the side and not from the back of the turban.

Third variety can be seen on Bharhut's bas-relief carved in the shape of medallion, which shows Nāgarāja accompanied by two female *chaurī*-bearers. The Nāga is distinguished by the usual five-hooded serpent crest but here the five-serpent heads stand so wide apart as almost to present the appearance of a tree. The two Nāgīs show the hybrid form in which the upper part of human body ends in the coils of a snake.[370]

The popularity of Nāga cult in the Kuṣāṇa age can be gauged by their depiction in Graeco-Buddhist and Mathurā art. Moreover, at Mathurā a temple of early Kuṣāṇa period has been discovered in the excavations at Sonkh.[371]

In the Graeco-Buddhist art of Gandhāra, which flourished in the early centuries of the Christian era, Nāgas are shown in both styles, *i.e.* theriomorphic and anthropomorphic. In the famous scene of the fire-splitting dragon of Uruvilā tamed by the Buddha, the Nāga is invariably shown in true reptile form.[372] The submission of the Nāga king Apalala seems to be a favourite theme in the Gandhāra school. In the representation, the Nāga king is shown either standing at the Buddha's side or kneeling before him or rising from the waters of which he is supposed to be the presiding deity. In most cases, he as well as his female companions raise their hands joined in token of reverence to the Buddha. One relief from Loriyan Tangai, now in the Indian Museum, Calcutta, represents the story of Apalala, depicting the Nāga king and his two wives as coming out of waters with their hands joined reverentially.[373]

The temple at Sonkh in Mathurā have a medallion on a *stambha* which depicts a nāga, having human shape in the upper body while the lower part ends in a snake tail. The nāga is crowned with a canopy of seven cobras. He carries three lotus stalks in his uplifted right hand. Another fragment of a relief shows a Nāga with human legs end and a snake's upper body, from which again arms are sticking out, carrying a book in the hands.

There is one relief at Sonkh which contains as many as nineteen figures. In the centre are sitting a Nāga king and a Nāgī. The king is seated quite lazy in a throne, two legs of which are deliberately placed out of level. The Nāga king head is not in centre, just to create the impression of a slightly drunk Nāgarāja. The rather corpulent and a bit pot-bellied king is touching a garland, which is presented to him by a group of four children. With the gesture of touching the garland he accepts his salutation. On his right side sits a Nāga woman, looking like the real commanding person. With her right hand she has just passed on a pearl necklace to her servant, to be presented as a gift to the leader of a delegation approaching from the left. On the right side of the relief, servants of the Nāga court are depicted, each marked by a single cobra head. The two females among them carry the royal emblems, the *chaurī* and the *chhatra*.[374]

The most notable image of Mathurā art is from Chhargoan (Pl. LXIX) now preserved in the Mathurā Museum. The Nāga is shown standing with his right arm raised over the head. The left hand is broken, but probably held a cup in front of the shoulder. The head is surmounted by a seven-headed snake. From the well preserved inscription incised on the back of the image it appears that it was set up at a water tank in the fortieth year of the Kuṣāṇa era during the reign of king Huviṣka.[375]

One image from Mathurā of Ist century A.D. is now stored in the State Museum, Lucknow, shows Nāga as carrying a water-pot in the left hand, right hand raised to the shoulder. The deity has a snake canopy with seven hoods over his head. Coils of the serpent are also to be seen in the background. Portion below the knees is missing.

One more image of Nāga from Mathurā of Ist-IInd century A. D. is in the State Museum, Lucknow. The deity is shown standing in *abhaya* pose and carrying a vase in the left hand. The deity stands on the coils of a seven-hooded snake which provides the canopy and background.[376]

Gupta Period

The representation of Nāga during the Gupta period though remain vogue yet we do not find much independent figures of this deity. In this age the Nāgas were more or less associated as attendants or attributes of major deities e.g. Viṣṇu and Śiva.[377]

In the Cave No. 4 at Udaigiri (400 A.D.) (Pl. LXX) Śeṣa is depicted in hybrid from along with Varāha. The colossal figure of the boar-headed god, carrying the earth goddess on his left shoulder, is shown treading with his left foot on the coils of a human figure, with both hands joined in the attitude of reverence. It is surrounded by a canopy of thirteen snake heads, seven in front and six in the interval behind.[378]

On the north panel at Deogarh temple (6th century A.D.) the legend of the deliverence of the lord of elephants is depicted. In this legend, as known from literature, the aquatic monster from whose grasp the elephant is freed by Viṣṇu is described as a crocodile. But, here it assumes the shape of a Nāga, combining the human with serpent form and shows the feet of the elephant caught in the coils of snake tail. The seven-hooded Nāga is also accompanied by a single-hooded Nāgī and the hands of both of them are joined in the attitude of reverence.[379]

The southern panel of the Deograh temple depicts the Anantaśāyin Viṣṇu. The deity is shown here as sleeping on the folds of the serpent Ananta, whose seven-hooded heads form a canopy over him and each of the head is provided with the jewels.[380]

Excavations of the mound at Rajagṛha revealed the remains of a shrine which was dedicated to the worship of Maṇi Nāga. The shrine contained ten well-preserved figures, out of which five represented the Nāgas and one Nāgī. All the figures have been found portrayed as human beings, standing, two-armed, held in different positions and provided with usual snake-hoods varying in number form five to one.[381] From their style these images could be attributed to the Gupta epoch.[382]

GANDHARVAS AND KINNARAS

The Gandharvas survived from Vedic times as servants of Indra or heavenly musicians. In the time of the Buddha they seem to have been especially connected with the procreation of children. Associated with them and sometimes referred to as a sub-division of their order, were the Kinnaras the heavenly musicians with human heads and body of a horse, and thus resembling to centaurs with whom they may be connected.[383] There main function was singing, dancing, playing music and to do service of the principal deities by offering flowers, fruits etc. [384]

In the early Buddhist monuments at Bharhut and Sāñchī (Pl. LXXI) they are very often shown with bird like lower parts, with wings attached to their arms, with human heads and torso and adorned with crowns, earrings and other ornaments.[385]

A fragmentary sculpture in the Mathura Museum shows some divine or semi-divine beings in a worshipping attitude and flying as indicated by the position of their legs and carrying cabbage like bouquets from which they are showering flowers. They have muscular and robust figure wear garments below the navel upto the anklet, the plait of the *dhotī* flying in folds and the upper garment flying in the air over the shoulders with the swift movement of their body through the sky. Their hair is tied in knot into a tapering crown with braid on the edge and they are redecorated with necklace.[386]

In the Śiva temple at Bhūmarā (5th century A. D.) (Pl. LXXII), the top horizontal bar of the doorway of *garbhagṛha* shows six flying figures-three on each side of the bust of Śiva in the centre, carrying in their left hands a tray full of flowers. They wear a wig on their head and seem to have decorated it with garlands. They are equipped with waist band and an undergarment below the navel which is seen flying in the air.[387]

A representation of Gandharva or Kinnara couple belonging to the late Gupta period have been found at Deogarh. The pair stands facing each other on either side of a tall tree, their upper part is that of a with wings (the arms are not distinct, but the wings are), the legs below the knee are also of human being, the feet only being those of bird, they have goggle eyes like those of Garuḍa.[388]

A fine sculpture of flying Gandharvas of 6th century A.D. is preserved in the Gwālior Museum, Gwālior (Pl. LXXIII). Figures are represented as flying in the air. The motion of flying is shown by the drawn legs and wind swept draperies. The head-dress of the figures is highly decorative.[389]

References

1. Kramrisch, Stella, *The Art of India*, p. 9.
2. Ray, Niharranjan, *An Approach to Indian Art,* pp. 48-49.
3. *Ibid.*, p. 52.
4. *The Perennial Vivekananda : A Selection,* ed. by Swami Lokeswarananda, p. 91.
5. Marshall, J., Mohenjodaro and the Indus Valley Civilization, p. 49.
6. कः इमं दशभिर्ममेन्द्र क्रीणाति धेनुभिः।

   Ṛgveda, IV. 24.10
7. Banerjea, J. N., *DHI*, p. 45.
8. जीविकार्थे चापण्ये

   Aṣṭādhyāyī, 5.3.99
9. Bajpai, K.D., *Five Phases of Indian Art,* p. Intro. 7.
10. Joshi, N. P., *Catalogue of Brahmanical Sculptures in the State Museum, Lucknow*, p. 7.
11. *Samabhaṅga* is the position of equipose or perfect balance. It is used to show the calmer, more reposeful mood and attitude. The right and left of the figure are disposed symmetrically, the *sūtra* or plumb-line pressing through the navel, from the crown of the head to a point midway between the heels. In other words the figure, whether seated or standing, is poised firmly on both legs without reclining in any way to right or left. The disposition or attitudes of the limbs and organs on either side are made exactly similar except that the *mudrā* or symbolical posing of the fingers is different (Shukla, H. L. *Semiotica Indica.,* Vol. II, p. 502).
12. Bajpai, K. D., *Five Phases of Indian Art,* pp. 31-32.
13. Chaudhary, K., Dionysos of Indo-Greek Coins—A Study, *JNSI,* Vol. XLV, 1983, p. 125.
14. रुचिराग्रकर चास्य चक्रांङ्कित इवेक्षते।

    द्वितीय उद्यतश्चापि गदासंयोगमिच्छति।

    Harivaṁśa, II, Ch. 25, S. 26.

15. Chaudhary K, *op. cit.* p. 127.
16. Joshi, N. P., *Catalogue of Brahmanical Sculptures in the State Museum, Lucknow.* p. 11.
17. Agrawala, V. S., *Studies in Indian Art,* p. 183.
18. *Abhaya-mudrā* is a symbol of protection or shelter. In this posture the right hand is shown as slightly elevated and bent with palm turned outwards, the fingers being stretched out and raised. Shukla, H. L. *(Semiotica Indica, Encyclopaedic Dictionary of Body Language in Indian Art and Culture,* p. 33.)
19. Agrawala, V. S., *op cit.,* p. 184.
20. Joshi, N. P., *Catalogue of the Brahmanical Sculptures in the State Museum, Lucknow.* p. 79, Pl. 1.
21. Singh, S. B., *Brahmanical Icons in Northern India,* p. 52.
22. *ASI,* Vol. VI, p. 20 cit. Joshi, N. P., *op. cit.,* p. 13.
23. Singh, S. B., *loc. cit.,* p. 52.
24. *Ibid.,* p. 51.
25. Agrawala, V. S., *op. cit.,* p. 184.
26. Singh, S. B., *loc cit.,* p. 51.
27. Joshi, N. P., *op. cit.,* p. 80, Fig. 1.
28. शंखचक्रगदापाणिं गरुडस्योपरि स्थितम्।
    Harivamśa Purāṇa, II, 99, 11.
29. Harle, J. C., *The Art and Architecture of the Indian Sub-continent,* p. 66.
30. Singh, S. B., *Brahmanical Icons in Northern India,* p. 54.
31. *Harivamśa Purāṇa,* Bhaviṣya Parva, Ch. 33-39.
32. Joshi, N. P., *Mathurā Sculptures,* Appendix 2, p. 4.
33. Joshi, N. P., *कुछ अप्रकाशित कलाकृतियां,* BMA, No. 4, 1969, p. 13; Cit.
    Joshi, N. P. *Catalogue of Brahmanical Sculptures in the State Museum, Lucknow,* p. 13.
34. Khan, Abdul Wahid, *An Early Sculptures of Nṛsimha,* pl. I, Cit.,
    Desai, Kalpana, *Iconogrpahy of Viṣṇu* , p. 87.
35. नरस्य कृत्वार्धतनुं सिहंस्यार्धतनुं प्रभुः।
    Harivamśa Purāṇa, I, 41.76.
36. *Ibid.,* I. 41. Bhaviṣya Parva, Ch. 33-39.
37. Joshi, N. P., *Catalogue of Brahmanical Sculptures in the State Museum, Lucknow,* p. 15.
38. Sharma, R. C., *The Splendour of Mathurā Art and Museum,* p. 131.
39. Joshi, N. P., *Mathurā Sculptures,* p. 52.
40. Joshi, N. P., *loc, cit.,* p. 16.
41. *Ibid.,* p. 17
42. Agrawala, V. S., *Studies in Indian* Art, p. 186.

43. Joshi, N. P., *Catalogue of Brahmanical Sculptures in the the State Museum, Lucknow,* p. 91.
44. Desai, Kalpana, *Iconography of Viṣṇu,* p. 134.

    तस्या मध्ये सहस्त्रास्यं हेमतालोच्छ्रितध्वजम्
    लाङ्गलासक्तहस्ताग्रं मुसलोपाश्रितोदरम
    असिताम्बरसंवीतं पाण्डुरं पाण्डुरासनम्।
    कुण्डलैकधरं मत्तं सुप्तमम्बुरूहेक्षणम्।
    Harivaṁśa Purāṇa, II, Ch.26, S. 49-50.
45. Desai, Kalpana, *op. cit., p.* 134.
46. Joshi, N. P., *Catalogue of Brahmanical Sculptures in the State Museum, Lucknow,* pp. 7-10.
47. Joshi, N. P., *Mathurā Sculptures,* p. 23.
48. Sharma, R. C., *The Splendour of Mathurā Art and Museum,* p. 146.
49. Sharma, R. C., Buddhist and Brahmanical Gupta Sculptures from Mathurā, *Mārg,* Vol. 42, No., 3, 1988-89, p. 21.
50. Sharma, R. C., *op. cit,* p. 28.
51. Williams, J. G. *The Art of Gupta India, Empire and Province,* p. 60.
52. Srivastava, V.S., The Gupta Art of Mathurā, *Mārg,* Vol. XV, No. 2, 1961-62, p. 50.
53. Coomaraswamy, A.K., *History of Indian and Indonesian Art,* p. 72.
54. William, J. G., *loc., cit.,* p. 9.
55. Sharma, R. C., Buddhist and Brahmanical Gupta Sculptures from Mathurā. *Mārg,* Vol. 42, No. 3, 1988-89, p. 21.
56. Desai, Kalpana, *op. cit.,* p. 8.
57. Harle, J. C., *op. cit.,* p. 34.
58. *Pralamba-bāhu* or *hasta* is a single hand gesture. (Shukla, H. L., *Semiotica Indica,* Vol. I, p. 303).
59. Joshi, N. P., *Catalogue of Brahmanical Sculptures in the State Museum, Lucknow,* pp. 82-83, pl. 2.
60. Sharma, R. C., Gupta Sculptures from Mathurā, *BMC,* No. 27-28, 1981, p. 95.
61. Sharma, R. C., *op. cit.,* pp. 95-96.
62. Harle, J. C., *The Art and Architecture of the Indian Sub-Continent,* p. 97, Fig. 96.
63. William, J. G., *loc. cit.,* p. 91.
64. Harle, J. C., *Gupta Sculpture,* p. 46.
65. Desai, Kalpana, *op. cit.,* p. 8.
66. Harle, J. C., *op. cit.,* p. 46.

    According to Kalpana Desai (*op. cit.,* p. 8) the date of this image is 4th century A. D.
67. Desai, Kalpaṇa, *op. cit.,* p. 8.
68. Williams, J. G., *loc. cit.,* p. 142.

69. Desai, Kalpana, *op. cit.*, p. 26.
70. Coomaraswamy, A.K., *Catalogue of the Indian Collection in the Museum of Fine arts, Boston,* Pts. I and II, p. 60, pl. XIX.
71. Joshi, N.P., *Catalogue of Brahmanical Sculptures in the State Museum, Lucknow.* p. 23.
72. Sharma, R. C., Buddhist and Brahmanical Gupta Sculptures fromMathurā, *Mārg,* Vol. 42, No. 3, 1988-89, p. 22.
73. शापान्तो मे भुजगशयनादुत्थिते शार्गांपाणौ।

    Meghadūta, ii, 50.
74. नाभिप्ररूढाम्बुरूहासनेन संस्तूयमानः प्रथमेन धात्रा।

    Raghuvaṁśa, XIII, 6.
75. Williams, J. G., *op. cit.*, p. 46.
76. *Ibid.*, p. 47.

    योगनिद्रां यदा विष्णुर्जगत्येकार्णवीकृते।

    आस्तीर्य शेषमभजत्कल्पांते भगवान्प्रभुः।

    तदा द्वावसुरौ घोरौ विख्यातौ मधुकैटभौ।

    विष्णुकर्णमलोद्भूतौ हंतुं ब्रह्माणमुद्यतौ।

    स नाभिकमले विष्णोः स्थितो ब्रह्मा प्रजापतिः।

    दृष्ट्वा तावसुरौ चोग्रौ प्रसुप्तं च जनार्दनम्।

    तुष्टाव योगनिद्रां तामेकाग्रहृदयस्थितः।

    प्रबोधनार्थाय हरेर्हरिनेत्रकृतालयाम्।

    Mārkaṇḍeya Purāṇa, 78, S. 49-52.
77. Williams, J. G., *op. cit.,* p. 47.
78. Cunningham, A., *ASIR*, Vol. X, Bundelkhand and Malwa, 1874-75 and 1876-77, p. 108.
79. Agrawala, V. S., *Gupta Art*, p. 37.
80. Anand, Mulk Raj, Bhitargoan Art and Architecture of Humanism, *Mārg.* Vol. 22, No. 2, p. 22.
81. Joshi, N. P., *Catalogue of Brahmanical Sculptures in the State Museum,* Lucknow, p. 23.
82. Agrawala, V. S., *Gupta Art,* p. 36.
83. वामार्धे माधवं विद्याद् दक्षिणे शूलपाणिनम्।

    The Matsya Mahā Purāṇa, Part II, Ch. 260, Ś. 22-27.
84. Desai, Kalpana, *Iconography of Viṣṇu,* pp. 52-53.
85. Williams, J. G., *op. cit.* p. 83.
86. Ibid, p. 54.
87. तेनादीचीं दिशमनुसरेस्तिर्यगायामशोभी श्यामःपादो बलिनियमनाभ्युद्यतस्येव विष्णोः।

    Meghadūta, i. 60.

88. Williams, J. G., *op. cit.*, p. 53.
89. Harle, J. C., *op. cit.*, p. 45.
90. Harle, J. C., *op.*, *cit.*, pp. 95-96.
91. Agrawala, V. S., *Gupta Art.* p. 105, See Also Cunningham, A., *ASIR*, Vol. X, p. 48.
92. Williams, J. G., *op. cit.*, p. 45.
93. Agrawala, V. S., *Gupta Art*, p. 30.
94. Harle, J. C., *op. cit.*, p. 98.
95. Williams, J. G. *op. cit.*, p. 91.
96. Williams, J. G., *op. cit.* p. 91, Figs. 126 and 127.
97. Harle, J. C., *op. cit.*, p. 98.
98. Williams, J. G., *op. cit.*, pp. 129-130, Fig. 198.
99. Desai, Kalpana, *op. cit.*, p. 75.
100. *Ibid.*, p. 112.
101. *Ardha-paryaṅkāsana* or seated stance, described as 'half-seated on the hams' is assumed by the kings in a relaxed mood (hence also some times called mahārajālilā), or by ascetics while practising meditation. Both the legs are on the same pedestal but one is bent with knee raised up while the other is bent with the knee remaining horizontal. The terms occur in Buddhist iconography. (Shukla, H. L., Semiotica Indica, Vol. I, p. 45).
102. Desai, Kalpana, *op. cit.* pp. 86-87.
103. *Ibid.*, p. 87.
104. Williams, J. G., *op. cit.*, p. 47.
105. *Ibid.*, p. 122.
106. *Ibid.*, p. 113.
107. Agrawala, V. S., *Gupta Art*, p. 14.
108. Williams, J. G., *op. cit.*, p. 56.
109. *Ibid.*, p. 116.
110. Agrawala, V. S., Gupta Art, pp. 13-14.
111. Joshi, N. P., *Mathurā Sculptures*, Fig. 90.
112. Anand, Mulk Raj, Bhītargaon-Art and Architecture of Humanism, *Mārg*, Vol. 22, 1969, p. 20, Fig. 31.
113. Harle, J. C., *op. cit.*, p. 105.
114. Williams, J. G., *op. cit.*, p. 141.
115. *Vyākhyāna-mudrā* is also known as the gesture of the exposition; or discourse on truth. In this gesture, the hands are held on the chest and joined. The thumb and the fore-finger of the right hand are joined, and the palm is held at a level lower than the right hand and turned towards the chest.
116. Agrawala, V.S., *Gupta Art*, p. 36.
117. Joshi, N. P., *Catalogue of Brahmanical Sculptures in the State Museum, Lucknow*, p. 18.
118. *Ibid.*, pp. 20-21.

119. Altekar, *CGE*, pp. 145-146, Pl. IX, 8-9.
120. Rao, T.A.G., *Elements of Hindu Iconography*, Vol. 11, Part I, p. Intro. 1.
121. Marshall, John, Mohenjodaro and the Indus Civilization, p. 52.
122. Joshi, N.P., *op. cit*, pp. 29-30.
123. Sharma, I. K., The Development of Early Śaiva Art and Architecture, p. 39.
124. Coomaraswamy, A. K., *HIIA*, p. 39.
125. Sharma, I. K., *loc. cit.*, pp. 54-55.
126. Joshi, N. P., *op. cit.*, pp. 99-100.
127. Joshi, N. P., *op. cit.*, p. 30.
128. Joshi, N. P., *Mathurā Sculptures*, pl. 10.
129. Joshi, N.P., *op. cit.*, p. 103.
130. *Ibid.*, pp. 35-36.
131. Coomaraswamy, A. K., *HIIA*, p. 67.
132. Joshi, N.P., *op. cit.*, *p.* 32.
133. Joshi, N. P., *op. cit.*, p. 103.
134. *Ibid*, p. 103.
135. *Ibid.*, pp. 34-35.

द्वे तनू तस्य देवस्य वेदज्ञ ब्रह्मणा विदुः ।
घोरामन्यां शिवामन्यां ते तनू बहुधा पुनः ।
उग्रा घोरा तनूर्यास्य सोऽग्निर्विद्युत्स भास्करः ।
शिवा सौम्या च या तस्य धर्मस्त्वापोऽथ चन्द्रमाः ।

Mahābhārata, Ch. 46, Śloka 3-6.

136. Joshi, N. P., *op. cit.*, p. 31.
137. Singh, S. B., *Brahmanical Icons in Northern India*, p. 6.
138. Cunningham, A., *Coins of Ancient India*, p. 98.
139. Sharan, Mahesh Kumar, *Tribal Coins—A Study of the Yaudheyas, the Mālavas, the Audumbaras and the Kuṇindas*, p. 283.
140. Whitehead, R. B., *Catalogue of Coins in the Punjab Museum, Lahore*, Vol. I, p. 101, pl. X.
141. *Ibid.*, p. 151, pl. XV 43.
142. Singh, S. B., *loc. cit.*, p. 7.
143. Whitehead has, however, traced out a few coins in the British Museum on which Śiva is shown having five heads (*loc, cit.*, p. 208, pl. xix).
144. Gardner, Percy, *The Coins of the Greek and Scythic kings of Bactria and India in the British Museum*, p. 125, pl. xxv 8.
145. *Ibid.*, p. 132, Pl. XXV. 8.
146. *Ibid.*, p. 147, Pl. XXVIII 132.
147. *Ibid.*, p. 159, Pl. XXIX.

148. Gardner, Percy, *The Coins of the Greek and Scythic Kings of Bactria and India in the British Museum,* p. 124, Pl. XX.6, p. 159, P. 1. XXIX. 10. See also Whitehead, R. B., *op. cit.*, p. 208, pl. xix.

149. Cunningham, A., *Coins of the Indo-Scythian, Śakas and Kuṣāṇas,* p. 65, pl. xxiii. 1.

150. Joshi, N. P., *Catalogue of Brahmanical Sculptures in the State Museum. Lucknow,* pp. 38-39.

151. *Ibid.*, p. 44.

152. *Ibid., op. cit.*, p. 39.

153. Gardner, Percy, *op. cit.* p., 148, Pl. XXVIII.

154. Banerjea, J. N., *DHI,* pp. 123-124.

155. Joshi, N. P., *op. cit.*, p. 39.

156. Joshi, N. P., *op. cit.*, p. 33.

157. Fleet, J. F., *CII,* Vol. III, No. 6, Pl. IVA.

158. Williams, J. G., The Art of Gupta India, Empire and Province, p. 29.

159. *Ibid.*, p. 114.

160. *ASI Monuments* (*Datia*) 1976, File No. 1015. M. Cit. Mishra, S. N., *Gupta Art and Architecture,* p. 166.

161. Williams, J. G., *loc. cit.*, p. 121.

162. *Ibid.*, p. 86.

163. Agrawala, V. S., *Gupta Art,* p. 32.

164. Williams, J. G., *loc. cit.*, p. 163.

165. Mishra, S. N., *Gupta Art and Architecture (With Special Reference to Madhya Pradesh),* p. 163.

166. Williams, J. G., *loc. cit.*, p. 121.

167. Agrawala, V. S., *loc. cit.*, p. 32.

168. *Viṣṇudharmottara Purāṇa,* III, Ch. 48, S. 1-19.

169. Sharma, R. C., Gupta Sculpture from Mathurā, *BMC,* No. 27-28, p. 98.

170. Joshi, N. P., *Catalogue of Brahmanical Sculptures in the State Museum,* Lucknow, pp. 36-37.

171. *Ibid.*, p. 41.

172. *Ibid.*, p. 106.

173. Sharma, R. C., *The Splendour of Mathurā Art and Museum,* p. 154.

वागर्थाविव संपृक्तौ वागर्थप्रतिपत्तये।
जगत: पितरौ वन्दे पार्वतीपरमेश्वरौ।

Raghuvaṁśa, I. 1.

174. Sharma, R. C., Gupta Sculpture from Mathurā, *BMC,* No. 27-28, p. 99.

175. Sharma, R. C., *The Splendour of Mathurā Art and Museum,* p. 156.

वागर्थाविव संपृक्तौ।

Raghuvaṁśa, 1.1.

176. Singh, S. B., *Brahmanical Icons in Northern India,* pp. 16-17.
177. Sharma, R. C., *op. cit.*, p. 98.
178. Sharma, R. C., Gupta Sculpture from Mathurā, *BMC,* No. 27-28, p. 98.
179. Dixit, S. K., *A Guide to the Central Archaeological Museum. Gwalior,* 1962, p. 31 cit. Mishra, S. N., *Gupta Art and Architecture,* p. 159.
180. *Ibid.*, p. 161.
181. Sharma, R. C., *op. cit.*, p. 98.
182. Joshi, N. P., *Catalogue of Brahmanical Sculptures in the State Museum,* Lucknow, p. 108, pl. 36.
183. Coomaraswamy, A. K., *The Dance of Śiva,* p. 68.
184. Rao, T. A. G., *EHI,* Vol. 2, Pt. 1, p. 223.
185. Malaiya, Sudha, Naṭeśa Sculptures in the Early Art of Central India, *Purātattva,* No. 16, 1985-86, p. 48.
186. Agrawala, V. S., *Gupta Art,* p. 34.
187. Williams, J. G., *op. cit.*, p. 123.
188. Agrawala, V. S., *op. cit.*, pp. 33-34.
189. William, J. G., *op. cit.*, p. 123.
190. Prāchya Pratibhā, A Journal of Art, History and Culture, Vol. 2, pp. 128-30, Mishra, S. N., *Gupta Art and Architecture,* pp. 169-70.
191. Sharma, R. C., Buddhist and Brahmanical Gupta Sculptures from Mathurā, *Mārg,* Vol. 42, No. 3, March 1991, p. 18.
192. Williams, J. G., *The Art of Gupta India, Empire and Province,* p. 36.
193. Sharma, R. C., *loc. cit.*, p. 18.
194. Williams, J. G., *loc. cit.*, p. 71.
195. Sharma, R. C., Gupta Sculpture from Mathurā, *BMC,* No. 27-28, 1981, pp. 98-99.
196. Mishra, S. N., *op. cit.*, p. 159.
197. Williams, J. G., *loc. cit.*, p. 177.
198. In *samapāda* the foot rests on the ground in a natural way. Walking in steadily equip-distant steps. Feet are obliquely placed when the whole feet is placed on the ground with the leg in normal position, then, it is called *sama-pāda.* (Shukla, H. L. *Semiotica Indica.* Vol. II, p. 502).
199. Mishra, S. N., *op. cit.*, pp. 168-69.
200. The various boons bestowing aspects of Śiva are called the *anugrahamūrtis.* (Rao, T. A.G. *EHI,* Vol. II, Part I, p. 145.).

     गत्वा चोर्ध्वं दशमुखभुजोच्छ्वासितप्रस्थसन्धेः ।

     Meghadūta, I. 61.
201. Sharma, R.C., Gupta Sculpture from Mathura, *BMC,* No. 27-28, pp. 98-99.
202. Rao, T.A.G., *EHI,* Vol. II, Part I, p. 217.
203. Sharma, R. C., *op, cit.*, p. 156.

204. Williams, J. G., *The Art of Gupta India, Empire and Province*, p. 128.
205. Harle, J. C., *Gupta Sculptures*, p. 56.
206. Singh, S. B., *Brahmanical Icons in Northern India*, p. 18.
207. Joshi, N P., *Catalogue of Brahmanical Sculptures in the State Museum*, Lucknow, p. 41.
208. Rao, T. A. G., *EHI*, Vol. II, Part I, pp. 149-150.
209. *Ibid.*, Vol. I, Part II, p. 379.
210. Williams, J. G., *loc. cit.*, p. 141.
211. Mishra, S. N., *Gupta Art and Architecture*, p. 103.
212. Harle, J. C., *Gupta Sculptures*, p. 39.
213. Rao, T. A. G., *EHI*, Vol. I, Part I, p. 287.
214. Mishra, S. M., *Gupta Art and Architecture*, p. 103.
215. Joshi, N. P., *op. cit.*, p. 107.
216. Sharma, R. C., Gupta Sculpture from Mathurā, *BMC*, No. 27-28, p. 99.
217. Joshi, N. P., *op. cit.*, p. 40.
218. Sahai, B., *Iconography of Minor Hindu and Buddhist Deities*, p. 41.
219. Banerjea, J. N., *DHI*, pp. 277-78, Pl. XVII, Fig. 3.
220. Joshi, N. P., *Catalogue of Brahmanical Sculptures in the State Museum*, Lucknow, p. 128, Fig. 62.
221. Bajpai, K. D., *Five Phases of Indian Art*, p. 62.
222. Banerjea, J. N., *DHI*, p. 378.
223. Bajpai, K. D., *op. cit.*, p. 64.
224. Sahai, B., *Iconography of Minor Hindu and Buddhist Deities*, pp. 145-46.
225. Altekar, *CGE* p. 328.
226. Thaplyal, K.K., *Studies in Ancient Indian Seals*, p. 189, Pl. XXI, Fig. 3.
227. Allan, J., *Catalogue of Ancient Indian Coins*, p. 252, Pl. XXXVIII.
228. Cunningham, A., *Coins of Ancient India from the Earliest Times down to the Seventh Century*, p. 74, Pl. V, Fig. 9.
229. Banerjea, J. N. *DHI*, p. 110.
230. Cunningham, A., *op. cit.*, p. 92, Pl. IX, Fig. 6.
231. Whitehead, R. B., *Catalogue of Coins in the Punjab Museum*, Lahore, p. 135, Pl. XIII.
232. Cunningham, A., *op. cit.*, p. 86, Pl. VIII, Fig. 4.
233. *Ibid.*, Fig. 5.
234. Gardner, Percy, *The Coins of the Greek and Scythic kings of Bactria and India in British Museum*, p. 9, Pl. III. 9.
235. *Ibid.*, p. 9, Pl. IV.9.
236. Jaiswal, K. N., *Uttara Bhārata Ki Prāchīna Hindu Devī Mūrtiyān*, p. 51.
237. Kar, C., *Classical Indian Sculpture, 300 B. C. to 500 A. D.*, p. 29, Pl. 14, Fig. 14.
238. Singh, O. P., *Iconography of Gaja-Lakṣmī*, pp. 26-27.

239. Singh, O. P., *Iconography of Gaja-Lakṣmī*, p. 33.
240. Sahai, B., *op. cit.*, pp. 166-167.
241. Singh, *O.P., op. cit.*, p. 35.
242. *Ibid*, p. 41
243. Coomaraswamy, A. K., *Yakṣas,* Part II, p. Pl. 44.
244. Sahai, B., *op. cit.*, p. 168.
245. No. 80.2, Sharma, R. C., *The Splendour of Mathurā Art and Museum,* p. 112.
246. Joshi, N. P., *Catalogue of Brahmanical Sculptures in the State Museum,* Lucknow, p. 125, Fig. 57.
247. *Ibid.*, pp. 125-26, Fig. 58.
248. Coomaraswamy, A. K., *HIIA*, p. 65, Pl. XX, Fig. 74.

     Coomaraswamy, A. K., *Yakṣas,* Part II, Pl. 49.
249. Jaiswal, K. K., *Uttara Bhārata Ki Prāchīna Hindu Devī Mūrtiyān,* p. 55,
250. Joshi, N. P., *op. cit.*, p. 63.
251. Sharma, R. C., *op. cit.*, p. 131.
252. Joshi, N. P., *op. cit.*, p. 124.
253. Sharma, R. C., *op, cit.*, p. 131.
254. Joshi, N. P., *op. cit.*, pp. 126-127, Fig. 60
255. निविष्टमुदधेः कूले तं प्रपेदे विभीषणः।

     स्नेहाद्राक्षसलक्ष्म्येव बुद्धिमाविश्य चोदितः।

     Raghuvaṁśa, XII, 68.
256. Sahai, B., Iconography of Minor Hindu and Buddhist Deities, p. 175.
257. *Padmāsana* is a type of *Yogāsana.* The right leg is placed on the left thigh, similarly the left is placed on the right thigh and the heels should be adjusted in such a way that they almost meet in front of and each foot possess the position of the abdomen adjacent to it. (Shukla, H. L., *Semiotica Indica,* Vol. I, p. 261).
258. Singh, S. B., *Brahmanical Icons in Northern India,* p. 173.
259. Joshi, N. P., *op. cit.,* p. 127, Fig. 61.
260. Thaplyal, K. K., *Studies in Ancient Indian Seals,* pp. 179-183.
261. *Ibid.*, p. 181.
262. Mukherjee, B. N., *Nānā on Lion,* p. 13.
263. Gardner, P., *The Coins of Greek and Scythic Kings of Bactria and India in the British Museum,* p. 85, Pl. XIX. 5.
264. Mukherjee, B. N., *loc. cit.*, pp. 16-17.
265. Cunningham, A., *Coins of the Indo-Scythic, Śakas and Kuṣāṇas,* p. 63, Pl. XXII. 19.
266. *Ibid.*, pp. 65-66, Pl. XXIII. 1.
267. Mukherjee, B. N., *loc. cit.*, pp. 16-17.
268. *Ibid.*, p. 19.

269. Singh, S. B., *Brahmanical Icons in Northern India*, p. 154.
270. Mukherjee, B. N., *Nānā on Lion*, p. 119, Pl. XI, Fig. 42.
271. *Ibid.*, pp. 19-20, Pl. XII, Fig. 43.
272. Singh, S. B., *loc. cit.*, p. 54.
273. *Ibid.*, p. 154.
274. Joshi, N. P., *op. cit.*, p. 120, Fig. 52.
275. Sharma, R. C., *The Splendour of Mathurā Art and Museum*, p. 37.
276. Srivastava, M. C. P., *Mother Goddess in Indian Art, Archaeology and Literature*, p. 112.
277. Sharma, R. C., *The Splendour of Mathurā Art and Museum*, p. 37.
278. *Ibid*, No. 33.2317, p. 118.
279. Sahai, B., *Iconography of Minor Hindu and Buddhist Deities*, p. 185.
280. Banerjea, J. N., *DHI*, p. 498.
281. Sharma, R. C., *op. cit.*, p. 147, No. D-12,
282. Sahni, D. R. *Cat. of the Museum of Archaeology at Sarnath*, p. 167, No. B. (h) 12. cit. Sahai, B., *Iconography of Minor Hindu and Buddhist Deities*, p. 185.
283. Bhattacharya, N. N., *The Indian Mother Goddess*, p. 161.
284. *Ibid.*, p. 14
285. Harle, J. C. *Gupta Sculptures*, pp. 35-36.
286. *Ibid.*, p. 36.
287. Kramrisch, Stella, *Indian Sculpture*, p. 172, Pl. XIII.
288. In *pratyālịdha* the right leg is bent and the left one is spread. The posture in which the legs prominently involved: the left leg is thrown forward and kept firmly while the right leg is slightly bent. It is the reverse posture, known as *ālịdha*. (Shukla, H. L., *Semiotica Indica*, Vol. I, pp. 300-301).
289. Sahai, B., *loc. cit.*, p. 185.
290. Kramrisch, Stella, *loc. cit.*, p. 172, pl. XXII.
291. Mishra, S. N., *Gupta Art and Architecture*, p. 164.
292. एवमुक्ता समुत्पत्य सारूढा तं महासुरम्।

     पादेनाक्रम्य कंठे च शूलेनैनमताड्यत्।

     Mārkaṇḍeya Purāṇa, Ch. 80 Ś. 38.
293. *Mārkaṇḍeya Purāṇa*, Ch. 85, 86, 87.
294. Sahai, B., *loc. cit.*, p. 208.
295. *Ibid.*, p. 208.
296. Rao, T. A. G., *EHI*, Vol. I, Part II, pp. 380-381.
297. Sahai, B., *op. cit.,*, p. 210.
298. *Ibid.*, p. 210.
299. Joshi, N. P., *Catalogue of Brahmanical Sculptures in the the State Museum*, Lucknow, p. 220, Fig. 53.

300. Joshi, N. P., *op. cit.*, p. 122, Pl 8.
301. *Ibid.*, p. 124, Fig. 55.
302. Harper, Katherine Anne, The Iconography of the Sapta-Mātṛkās-Seven Hindu Goddesses of Spiritual Transformation, *Studies in Women and Religion,* Vol. 28, p. 69.
303. Joshi, N. P., *op. cit.,* p. 72.
304. Harper, K. A., *loc. cit.,* p. 73.
305. *Ibid.*, p. 76.
306. *Ibid.*, pp. 77-78.
307. *Ibid.*, pp. 79-80.
308. Jaiswal, K. K., *Uttara Bhārata Ki Prāchina Hindu Devi Mūrtiyān,* p. 233.
309. Agrawala, R. C., Krṣṇa-Balarāma as Attendant Figures, *Indian Historical Quarterly,* Vol. 38, No. 1, 1963, pp. 86-87.
310. *Ibid,* p. 41.
311. Handa, Devendra, A Kusāṇa Ekānaṁśā Relief from Haryana, *BMA,* No. 29-30, 1982, pp. 41-42.
312. मूर्ते च गङ्गायमुने तदानीं सचामरे देवमसेविषाताम्।

     समुद्रगारूपविपर्ययेऽपि संहसपाते इव लक्ष्यमाणे।

     Kumarasaṁbhavam, vii, 42.
313. Kinsley, David, *Hindu Goddesses, Vision of the Divine Feminine in the Hindu Religious Tradition,* p. 192.
314. Coomaraswamy, A. K., *Yakṣas,* Part I, p. 39, Pl. 6, Fig. 1 and 2.
315. Jaiswal, K. K., *op. cit.,* p. 239.
316. Cunningham, A., *ASIR,* Vol. X, p. 48, Pl. XVIII.
317. Agrawala, V. S., *Gupta Art,* p. 105.
318. Roy, C. Craven, *Indian Art, A Concise History,* p. 118, Fig. 78.
319. Williams, J. G., *The Art of Gupta India, Empire and Province,* p. 76.
320. *Ibid.*, p. 93.
321. *Ibid.*, p. 109.
322. Joshi, N. P., *op. cit.*, p. 71.
323. Williams, J. G., *op. cit.*, p. 120.
324. *Ibid.*, p. 123.
325. *Ibid.*, p. 75.
326. Sharma, R. C., Gupta Sculptures from Mathura, *BMC.,* No. 27-28, 1981, pp. 101-102.
327. Joshi, N. P., *op. cit.*, p. 130, Figs. 66, 67.
328. Harle, J. C., *The Art and Architecture of Indian Sub-continent,* p. 117.
329. Rao, T. A. G., *EHI, Vol. I,* Part, II, p. 375.
330. Sahai, B., *Iconography of Minor Hindu and Buddhist Deities,* p. 158.

331. Banerjea, J. N., *DHI,* p. 96. See also Coomaraswamy, A. K., *HIIA*, p. 65.
332. Joshi, N. P., *op. cit.*, p. 67.
333. Joshi, N. P., *Mathurā Sculptures,* p. 25.
334. Jaiswal, K. K., *Uttara Bhārata Ki Prāchīna Hindu Devī Mūrtiynā,* p. 245.
335. Joshi, N. P., *op. cit.*, p. 129, Fig. 63.
336. Mishra, R. N., *Yaksha Cult and Iconograhy,* p. Intro. 7.
337. Coomaraswamy, A. K., *Yakṣas,* Part I, p. 37.
338. Harle J. C., *The Art and Achitecture of Indian Sub-continent,* p. 29.
339. Agrawala, V. S., *Studies in Indian Art,* p. 61. The historians hold different views regarding the execution of Pārkham Yakṣa. Coomaraswamy dates it in Maurya or earlier period (Coomaraswamy, A. K., *HIIA*, p. 229, Pl. V. Fig. 9) and J. C. Harle places in 1st century B.C. (Harle, J. C., *The Art and Architecture of Indian Sub-continent,* p. 30). There are some who do not indulge in the controversy and simply assign in the beginning of Christian era (Ray, Niharranjan, *Maurya and Post Maurya Art,* p. 39).
340. Agrawala, V. S., *Studies in Gupta Indian Art,* p. 61.
341. Sharma, *R. C., The splendour of Mathura Art and Museum, p. 66.*
342. Ray, Niharranjan, *Maurya and Post Maurya Art,* p. 39.
343. Coomaraswamy, A.K., *Yakṣas,* Part I, p. 38, pl. 2, Fig. I and II.
    See also Coomaraswamy, A. K., *HIIA,* p. 232, Pl. XVIII, Fig. 67.
344. Ray, Niharranjan, *loc. cit.*, p. 107, Fig. 16 and 17.
345. Coomaraswamy, A. K., *HIIA,* p. 230, Pl. V, Fig. 17. The art historians have diverse opinion regarding the age of this sculpture. Niharranjan Ray thought it as the work of 4th century (Ray, Niharranjan, *loc. cit.*, p. 106) and Harle opines the figure is of 1st century A.D. (Harle, J. C., *The Art and Architecture of Indian Sub-continent,* p., 30, Fig. 15).
346. Ray, Niharranjan, *Maurya and Post Maurya Art,* pp. 105, 106 and 40, Fig. 11.
347. Banerjea, J. N., *DHI,* PP. 342-343.
348. Harle, J. C., *The Art and Architecture of Indian Sub-continent,* p. 28.
349. Banerjea, J. N., *DHI,* pp. 342-43.
350. Harle, J. C., *loc. cit.*, p. 29.
351. Coomaraswamy, A. K., *Yakṣas,* Part I, p. 38, Pl. I, Fig. 2.
352. Harle, J. C., *loc, cit.*, p. 29, Fig. 13.
353. Joshi, N.P., *Catalogue of Brahmanical Sculptures in the State Museum, Lucknow,* pp. 115-116.
354. Mishra, R. N., *Yaksha Cult and Iconography,* pp. 112-13.
355. Joshi, N.P., *op. cit.*, pp. 116-117, Fig. 44.
356. Agrawala, V. S., *Studies in Indian Art,* pp. 60-61.
357. Mishra, R. N., *Yaksha Cult and Iconography,* p. 122.
358. Coomaraswamy, A. K., *Yakṣas,* Part I, p. 39, Pl. ix.
359. *Ibid.*, p. 40, Pl. 10, Fig. 2.

360. Mishra, R. K., *op. cit.*, p. 122.
Coomaraswamy, A. K., *Yakṣas,* Part I, p. 40, Pl. 10, Fig. 1.
361. Mishra, R. N., *op. cit.*, p. 125.
362. *Ibid.*, p. 125.
363. *Ibid.*, pp. 125-126.
364. Marshall, J., *Mohenjodaro* and *the Indus Civilization,* Part I, p. 68.
365. Vogel, J., Ph., *Indian Serpent Lore or The Nāgas in Hindu Legend and Art*, p. 38.
366. Fergusson, *Tree and Serpent-Worship,* p. 104, pl. ix.
367. Grunwedel, *Buddhist Art in India,* p. 62, Fig. 35 and 36 Vogel, J. Ph., *loc. cit.*, p. 38.
368. Vogel, J. Ph., *loc., cit.*, p. 39.
369. Sahai, B., *Iconography of Minor Hindu and Buddhist Deities,* p. 77.
370. Vogel, J. Ph., *The Indian Serpent Lore or the Nāgas in Hindu Legend and Art,* p. 39.
371. Hartel, Herbert, A Kuṣāṇa Nāga Temple at Sonkh, *BMA*, No. 11-12, 1973, p.1.
372. Vogel, J. Ph., *loc., cit.*, p. 40, Pl. IX. b.
373. Shahai, B., *Iconography of Minor Hindu and Buddhist Deities,* p. 79. See also Grunwedel, *Buddhist Art in India,* p. 106, Fig. 58.
374. Hartel, Herbet, A Kuṣāṇa Nāga Temple at Sonkh, *BMA*, No. 11-12, 1973, pp. 4-5.
375. Vogel, J. Ph., *Indian Serpent Lore,* p. 42.
376. Joshi, N. P., *Catalogue of Brahmanical Sculptures in the State Museum,* Lucknow, p. 118.
377. Vogel, J. Ph., *loc. cit.*, p. 195.
378. Cunningham, A., *ASIR*, Vol. X, *Bundelkhand and Malwa,* p. 48.
379. Vogel, J. Ph., *loc. cit.*, p. 195.
380. Cunningham, A., *ASIR*, Vol. X, p. 107.
381. Sahai, B., *loc cit.*, p. 83.
382. Vogel, J. Ph., *loc. cit.*, p. 219, pl. XXIV.
383. Basham, A.L., *op. cit.*, p. 320
384. Panchmukhi, R. S., *Gandharvas and Kinnaras in Indian Iconography,* p. 19.
385. Banerjea, *DHI*, p. 352. See Also Fergusson, *Tree and Serpent Worship,* p. 108.
386. Panchmukhi, R. S., *loc. cit.*, p. 32.
387. *Ibid.*, pp. 33-34.
388. Banerjea, J. N., *DHI*, p. 353.
389. Kar, C., *Classical Indian Sculpture (300 B. C. to A. D. 500),* p. 38., Fig. 86.

Conclusion

6

The cults, today, have sound root in Indian society. But to reach the pinnacle of height, it took long time and had to face many upheavals and setbacks in the foregoing centuries.

All the popular cults of present time had their roots in the proto-historic India. The rudiments of cult-practices in India are traceable as early as the Indus Valley Civilization (c. 2500 B.C). Śiva-Paśupati, Mother-goddess, Nāgas and trees were highly revered divinities of the dwellers of the Indus Civilization. The number of deities remained increasing and it reached to 33 in Vedic times. The popular deities of Christian era i.e. Viṣṇu and Śiva, have a very insignificant position in Vedic literature. But gradually, from the time of Post-Vedic literature they started gaining momentum. The two major cross-currents of this period were the assimilation of the personalities of the Vedic Viṣṇu with Nārāyaṇa of the Brāhmaṇas and Paśupati-Śiva of Indus Valley with Vedic Rudra Śiva.

The first major turning point in the religious history of India came in *c.* 6th century B.C. in the form of Buddhism and Jainism. These were, launched against the superiority of Vedas and *Yajñas.* This revolt resulted in the proliferation of cults in *c.* 4th century B.C.

The period of present study, *c.* 400 B.C. to A.D. 600, particularly rich in varied sources for understanding the origin and growth of various Brahmanical cults and their iconography. The coins, inscriptions, archaeological relics, Brahmanical, Buddhist and Jaina literature help us to trace the developmental stages of the cults during this period. The development of the Brahmanical cults have been studied under four phases in a chronological order.

The first phase (*c.* 4th to 2nd century B.C.) saw the existence of many cults and divinities as mentioned in the *Mahāniddeśa.* These were the Ājivika, Nirgranṭha, Jaṭila, Paribhājakas, Avaruddhaka, and the worshippers of the elephant, horse, cow, dog, crow, Vāsudeva, Baladeva, Puṇṇabhadra, Maṇibhadra, Mahārājas (the four Lokapālas), Chandra, Sūrya, Indra, Brahmā, Deva and Dik. This evidence is corroborated by two other sources of this period viz. the *Aṣṭādhyāyī* of Pāṇini and the *Arthaśāstra* of Kauṭilya. But the prominent deities of this period were the Yakṣas and Yakṣīs, Nāgas and Nāgīs and tree-divinities which are represented in the sculptures and reliefs on the *stūpas* discovered from Pārkham, Mathurā, Besnagar, Vidiśā, Dīdārganj and Bharhut etc.

During the second phase (c. 2nd century B.C. to the beginning of the Christian era) which was characterised by a revolt against the pro-Buddhist policies of Mauryan rulers proved quite crucial for the development of Brahmanical cults, as it, certainly gave impetus to Vaiṣṇavism and Śaivism along with Buddhism. The evidences in the *Mahābhāṣya, the Rāmāyaṇa* and *the Mahābhārata* as well as the archaeological sources stand as proofs of it. The erection of an inscribed Garuḍa pillar raised at Besnagar (Madhya Pradesh) in the honour of Vāsudeva by a Greek devotee, the construction of a stone enclosure *(pūjā-śilā-prākāra)* at Ghosundi (Rājasthān) and the mention of the five Vṛṣṇi heroes in the Morā Well inscription near Mathurā (Uttar Pradesh) provide ample testimony to the popularity of Vaiṣṇavism. In the first century B.C. or in the beginning of Christian era Vāsudeva-Kṛṣṇa (the son of Vāsudeva and Devakī) of the famous Yadu clan, who became the leader of the Vāsudeva-Bhāgavata cult, was identified with the Vedic Viṣṇu and Brāhmaṇa's Nārāyaṇa and henceforth religion came to be known as Vaiṣṇava *dharma.* The early Vaiṣṇavism believed in the worship of *chatur-vyūha* and *pañcha-vīras* (five heroes). On these Saṁkarṣaṇa was associated with agriculture.

The prevalence of the Śiva cult is evident from the several indigenous coins containing theriomorphic, phallic, and anthropomorphic forms of Śiva. On the coins of Ujjainī (c. 3rd and 2nd century B.C.) Śiva has been depicted in all the three forms. Besides, the coins of Indo-Scythian ruler Maues the Indo-Pārthian ruler Gondophares also depict Śiva in anthropomorphic form. Though Śiva was worshipped in anthropomorphic forms yet the plain *liṅgas* and *mukha-liṅgas* (Gudimallam and Bhīṭā) also seems to be the popular objects of worship.

The cult of Mother-goddess gave rise to several important female divinities around which later on the Śākta cult developed. The Durgā Mahiṣāsuramardinī form of the mother-goddess have been quite popular in Mathurā and adjoining Rājasthān area since early times, which is proved by the findings of terracotta plaque of 2nd century B.C. and 1st century B.C. from Sonkh (Mathurā) and the coins of Azes I on which goddess is seated on a lion.

The cult of Śrī or Lakṣmī, the goddess of prosperity, also came into existence during the Śuṅga period. The earliest representation of her as a woman of mature beauty seated on a lotus and often with a lotus in her hand attended by two elephants who sprinkle water on her from their trunks is seen on the tribal coins of Ujjainī *(c.* 3rd and 2nd century B.C.) Kauśāmbī, Ayodhyā (*c.* Ist century A.D.) and on the coins of alien rulers Azes I, Azilises, Rājuvula and Soḍāsa.

The cult of Sūrya was also becoming popular in the society. The symbolic representation of Sūrya on the coins of Mitras of Pāñchāla (c. 2nd century B.C. and end of Ist century B.C.) Taxila, Audumbaras as well as the anthropomorphic representation of the coins of Avantī (*c* 2nd century B.C. and 2nd century A.D.) and Indo-Greek coins of Plato and Philoxenus are ample proof of it.

The cult of Skanda-Kārttikeya also originated in this period. The device peacock on hill on punch-marked coins and cock on top of post on Devamitra and Vijaymitra coins, the local rulers of Ayodhyā, and deity holding spear on the coins of Audumbaras (c. Ist century B.C. and Ist century A.D.) are testimony of it.

The third phase (*c.* Ist century A.D. to 3rd century A.D.) was an era dominated by the Kuṣāṇas, a tribe from Central Asia. Various earlier cult, not only remained flourishing during this period with same vigour but exercised a great influence on the rulers of the Kuṣāṇa dynasty. The adoption of name Vāsudeva by Huviṣka for his son and successor proves the popularity of Vaiṣṇavism in Kuṣāṇa times. Ekānaṁśā, the sister of Baladeva and Vāsudeva, was also highly revered in this period for having protected Kṛṣṇa-Vāsudeva.

The most popular deity of this period seems to be Śiva. He is depicted with trident, water-pot and Nandī on the coins of all the Kuṣāṇa rulers including Wema Kadphises, Kaniṣka, Huviṣka, and Vāsudeva.

Skanda-Kārttikeya seems to be the other popular deity of this period. The coins of Huviṣka depicted the figure of Skanda, Mahāsena, Kumāra, Śākha and Viśākha with their names in Greek script. Skanda was also a tutelary deity of Yaudheyas and found depiction on their coins (*c.* 2nd century A.D.) having a single or six faces.

The cult of Durgā or Aṁbikā was also in flourishing condition. She is usually depicted in the name of Nānā or Nānia on the coins of Kaniṣka, Huviṣka and Vāsudeva. On one coin of Huviṣka she is shown standing with Śiva.

Ardoksho, the Persian goddess of fortune, depicted on the coins of Kaniṣka and Huviṣka is considered to be a counterpart of Indian goddess of fortune Lakṣmī, was also a revered deity of this period.

Sun-god usually depicted in the name of Mihira (which is a corrupt form of Mithra or Mitra) on the coins of Kaniṣka and Huviṣka seems to be a well-known deity of the times.

During the fourth phase (c. 3rd century A.D. to 6th century A.D. better known as the Gupta period, the Brahmanical cults emerged as sole representative of the people's faith leaving behind all other sects. It is evident from literary works *the Amarakośa, the Raghuvaṁśa, the Kumārasaṁbhavam, the Pratimānātakam, the Bālacharita* and few the *Purāṇas* and also from inscriptions, coins and sculptural remains of this period. The reason behind it were the patronage of the Gupta monarchs, the support of priestly class and the adoption of syncretistic and tolerant attitude. In this period Brahmanical cults spread not only in most parts of the country but also in the Indian colonies of Jāvā and Bālī. The Guptas were quite generous towards Vaiṣṇavism as they styled themselves as *parambahāgavatas* and the inscriptions found at Udaigiri, Bhītarī, Mehraulī, Junāgarh and Eran bespeak this truth and certainly prove the superiority of Vaiṣṇava cult over Śiva cult in the Gupta period. A Vaiṣṇava family of the deities, Viṣṇu as its chief, developed in this period. The concept of ten incarnations of Viṣṇu and Lakṣmī's association as a consort of Viṣṇu was the outcome of this period. Although Lakṣmī has also been worshipped independently. The coins of the Gupta rulers provide ample testimony.

The Śaiva cult centred around the personality of Śiva with his retinue Pārvatī as wife and Gaṇeśa and Kārttikeya as sons was fully established in this era. Pārvatī, the consort of Śiva, depicted on the coins of Chadragupta II, shows that the deity seated on lion as an individual divinity was fast gaining ground in the society. After the fall of the Gupta empire she emerged as a great cult goddess. Of the two sons of Śiva, Gaṇeśa and Kārttikeya, the former was not a popular deity of the period who has to play a great role in the coming centuries. Kārttikeya remained popular since 2nd century B.C. to Gupta period but vanished from north India but his cult made its way to south India under the name of Subramanya.

The Mandsor inscription and copper plate inscriptions found at Indore speaks about the popularity of Sūrya cult.

The cults of Brahmā and Sarasvatī have been formalised in the preceding centuries but these could not make grounds among the masses. The cult was specially related with the Brāhmaṇas.

The two new divinities, Gaṅgā on crocodile and Yamunā with tortoise, decorated almost all the door-frames of the temples of Gupta period shows that their cults were fast gaining grounds in Gupta society.

No image of Brahmanical deity is older than c. 2nd century B.C. so far as the plastic arts in India is concerned. Only figures of Mother-goddesses in terracotta of earlier periods are known. A few Yakṣa images, attributed to Maurya-Suṅga period served as models for the Brahmanical and other sects. The earliest image of Viṣṇu as well as Balarāma of c. 2nd century B.C. have been found from Malhār and Mathurā respectively. The Kuṣāṇas certainly stimulated the practice of image-making in the country through two famous schools of art, better known as Gāndhāra and Mathurā. It were the artists of Mathurā who not only made maiden attempt in carving out the images of Brahmanical deities but also their early iconographic forms.

During this period Viṣṇu was usually depicted as four-armed deity holding *śaṅkha, chakra, gadā* and *kamaṇḍalu.* Some of his incarnations were also depicted in the art. The depiction of Kṛṣṇa is found in the reliefs from Mathurā. He was also depicted with Ekānaṁśā and Balarāma. Śiva is represented through symbolic and anthropomorphic forms. Many of his forms, Śiva-Pārvatī, Ardhanārīśvara and Hari-Hara, were the outcome of this century.

The Mātṛkās or Mother-goddesses were represented in a variety of forms. Either they were shown with a human head or that of an animal but always carrying a child in her lap. These stand either independently or in a row of five or seven figures. Goddess Lakṣmī is seen with a bloomed lotus, at times, seated in European style and sometimes associated with Kubera. One example of goddess Sarasvatī with *akṣamālā* and book is known in the Kuṣāṇa art of Mathura. In several images Mahiṣāsuramardinī is seen strangulating the demon Mahiṣāsura with her hands. The Nāgas were usually depicted with the human body and crest of five or seven hoods over the head.

In the Gupta period Indian art was freed from the foreign influences of the Śaka-Kuṣāṇa times and became indianised. The most important contribution of the Gupta art is the evolution of the divine images of perfect type based on Śāstric lines of the *Bṛhat Saṁhitā*, the *Matsya Purāṇa* and the *Viṣṇudharmottara Purāṇa.* Viṣṇu and his ten incarnations, Śiva and his various forms, Durgā, Lakṣmī, Mother-goddess, Yakṣa, Nāga etc. were depicted in art. The idea of depicting the river goddesses, particularly Gaṅgā on the crocodile and Yamunā on the tortoise,was given a visual form in the sculptural art of this period.

The images of the gods and goddesses were installed in the temples and small shrines built for the purpose. Patañjali refers to the temples of Kubera, Balarāma and Keśava in which bells were sounded to perform rituals. The excavations have thrown light on the existence of simple brick temples at Nāgarī, Besnagar, Sonkh (Mathurā), having apsidal plan and a niche for keeping the cult image. A further development is noticed in the temples of Gupta phase which were constructed with elaborate plan consisting of the *maṇḍapa, garbhagṛha* etc. and their outer walls decorated with religious themes elaborating the exploits of the deity. Flower, garland etc. were offered to appease the deities. The evidence of temples suggests that the institution of priesthood related to temples had come into existence. It seems that during the early period rituals were of simple nature which with the passage of time became elaborate and complicated.

Appendix

Rituals, Pūjā and Temples

It is ritual that gives life to a cult, without it a cult is a moribund and cannot sustain long. In other words, if a cult has to last long it has to rely more and more on rituals. The discovery of sealings and figurines from Indus Valley more or less prove that the practice of image worship in India has been popular since the prehistoric times. But no evidence of a temple has been found in the Harappan context. The images of gods and goddesses were installed in the temples and small shrines which began to be constructed during the historical period. Patañjali refers to the temples of Dhanapati (Kubera), Rāma (Balarāma) and Keśava (Viṣṇu) in which bells were sounded to perform rituals.[1]

Jarl Charpentier is of the view that the word *pūjā,* meaning worship has been derived from the Tamil word *pūśu* or the Kanarese *pūsu,* to smear or daub. He has further remarked that the most characteristic feature of the *pūjā* is washing and sprinkling of a image with water, honey or curd or daubing it with red paint. This view is, however, disputed by some scholars who are of the opinion that the word is formed by the combination of the Dravidian words *pū* and *cey* or *gey* meaning a flower-act or *puṣpa-karma.*[2]

During the early period the mode of worship was quite simple as a passage in the *Rāmāyaṇa* refers to Lakṣmana offering flowers *(puṣpa-bali)* to the gods.[3]

The *Viṣṇusmṛti*[4] gives one of the earliest description of the ritual *pūjā.* It includes an invocation and welcome of the deity, the offering of *arghya* or water for washing hands and feet, and for sipping and bathing (of the deity).[5]

The *Viṣṇusmṛti* further refers to various items such as incense, flowers, cloth, food and lamp to be used in the worship of a deity.[6] The *Viṣṇudharmottara Purāṇa* added the use of betel (*tāmbūla*) in the worship of a deity.[7]

The *Bṛhat Saṁhitā* also mentions various articles viz. perfumes, garlands, scented pastes, eatables and dishes of various kinds as well as a varieties of roots, fruits and meat and attractive drinks such as liquor, milk and wine to be used for the worship of deities like Rudra, Skanda, Viṣṇu, seven Mothers and Viśākha..[8] In another passage Varāhamihira precisely refers to various objects to be used to please the minor deities. These include flesh, rice and wine as an offering to the Piśāchas and goblines; the hymns of the *Ṛg, Yajur* and *Sāmaveda;* perfumes, incense and garlands to the seers; unmixed colours and *tri-madhura* (honey, clarified butter and sugar) to the Nāgas; perfumes, garlands and other fragrant articles to the Gandharvas and divine nymphs.[9]

The other popular ritual was the *japa* or repeated recitation of sacred syllables, formulae or names of the deity. The *Viṣṇusmṛti* states that the japa-yajña is ten times more meritorious than the ritualistic sacrifice *(vidhi-yajña).*[10] And this emphasis on simple *japa* instead of costly rituals of the Vedic period certainly contributed in popularising the Vaiṣṇavism and Śaivism.[11] The *Viṣṇusahasranāma*[12] and *Śivasahasranāma* [13] further prove the importance of the sacred names.

The singing and dancing in front of the deities, especially on festival days, became an integral part of image worship during the Gupta period. As the *Bṛhat Saṁhitā* states the consecration of image should be accompanied by songs, dance and sounds of musical instruments.[14] The *Viṣṇudharmottara Purāṇa* explicitly states that the dedication of a dance, song or musical instrument is far more meritorious than of flowers and food (*naivedya*) as it fulfils all desires and is equal to performance of a sacrifice.[15]

These references indicate that the practice of attaching courtesans or dancing girls *(devadāsis)* to temples had come into existence in the time of Guptas. It is supported by the *Meghadūta* which refers to courtesans dancing and holding flywhisks at the Mahākāla temple of Ujjainī.[16]

The rite of *daivata* or *surayātrā,* a kind of religious procession in which the idol of a particular god or goddess is taken in a cart or chariot (better known as *Ratha-yātrā* at present), mentioned in the *Bṛhat Saṁhitā* [17] is highly praised in the *Viṣṇudharmottara Purāṇa* (Ch. 117). One who performs such *yātrās* regularly every year gets all his desires fulfilled in this world as well as goes to the abode of Viṣṇu.[18]

The sanctity of *Tīrthas* has been fully established by the time of Guptas. *Tīrtha* was not only considered as venue for religious rites like *Puṣya-snāna* [19] and bathing an image with *tirtha water* [20] but also to die there in the (*tīrtha*) was considered meritorious.[21]

The custom of fasts *(vratas),* total or limited abstinence from food and the execution of certain acts of worship,[22] has become a part and parcel of ritualistic worship since the time of first century B.C. In the Nānāghāṭa inscription queen Nayanikā is referred to as devoted to the observance of the *vratas,*[23] and Nāsik epigraph speaks of queen Balaśrī as one eagerly engaged in the observance of fasts.[24] The *vratas* were also held in high esteem in the Gupta period as Kālidāsa mentions in the *Abhijñana Śākuntalam* that the mother of Duṣyanta observed a fast (*upavāsa*) which was to end on the fourth day. It is probable that some of the numerous *vratas* mentioned in the *Viṣṇudharmottara* and other *Purāṇas* were known and observed in the Gupta period.[25]

We do not find the mention of popular festivals as *Janmāṣṭamī* the birthday of Kṛṣṇa, *Rāmanavamī,* the birthday of Rāma and *Śivarātri* upto the time of Gupta phase. But the festival of *Chaturmāsya* especially related to Viṣṇu had become quite popular.[26] The Purāṇas like *the Harivaṁśa* [27] and *the Viṣṇudharmottara* [28] narrate that the god Viṣṇu goes to sleep on the eleventh of the bright fortnight of the month of Āṣāḍha for four months and wakes up again on the eleventh of the bright fortnight of the month of Kārttika and during his sleep the rain-god Indra does his work.[29] This festival was quite well-known in the Gupta period as it is referred in the *Bṛhat Saṁhitā.* [30] An inscription of A.D. 424 alludes to the awakening of Madhusūdana (Viṣṇu) in the month of Kārttika. It bears the date of the thirteenth of the bright fortnight of the month of Kārttika and records the erection of the Viṣṇu temple, which was apparently completed on that sacred date.[31] An elaborate description of this festival is given in the *Viṣṇudharmottara Purāṇa* [32] in connection with king Bharata. The celebrations began on the eleventh of the bright fortnight of *Āṣāḍha* and continued for five days during which Bharata made land gifts and worshipped Janārdana. Large scale festivities were again indulged in for five days at the approach of the end of the bright fortnight of Kārttika, and these culminated on the full-moon day. There are many epigraphic records which showed the practice of giving land-grants and the performance of other pious deeds at the beginning and the end of the festival during the Gupta period.[33] The earliest record giving liberal donations on the full-moon night of Kārttika is the Nāsik cave inscription of the Śaka chief Uṣavadāta of the years 41 and 45 of his reign.[34] The Eran stone pillar inscription (485 A.D.) of the Gupta period records the dedication of a flag-staff of Viṣṇu by Matṛviṣṇu on the twelfth of the bright fortnight of the month of Āṣāḍha.[35]

Any place or edifice dedicated to the worship of deity is regarded[36] as temple or in other words temple is the seat and dwelling of God.[37] There is no evidence of the survival of temple buildings prior to the first century B.C. The excavation have thrown light on the existence of simple brick temples at Nāgarī (middle of Ist century B.C.),[38] Besnagar[39] and Sonkh (early Kuṣāṇa period),[40] having apsidal plan and a niche for keeping the cult image. The development of temples took great strides during the Gupta period. The temples of early phase consisted of *maṇḍapa* and *garbhagṛha* as seen at the sites of Sāñchi (temple No. 17), Tigwā and Eran. Further elaboration of temples was done adding the *pradakṣhiṇāpatha,* outer decoration of walls (with religious themes elaborating the exploits of the deities) and *śikhara* which germinated at Nachnā (M.P.), and took its final shape at Deograh (M.P.). The existence of temples dedicated to various cult deities belonging to the Gupta period have been attested.

The evidence of temples suggest that the institution of priesthood related to the temples had come into existence. The terms *Sāttvatas* and *Āchāryas* found in the *Manu smṛti,* [41] as explained by Govindraja indicate that Sāttvatas were the people living on image-worship.[42] The *Matsya Purāṇa* mentions a rule that the priests, incharge of an idol in a temple *(mūrtipaḥ)* should number either thirty two or sixteen or eight[43] and should be well-versed in the *Vedas, Purāṇas* and belong to *dvija* class of high descent (*kulīna*).[44]

References

1. Jaiswal, S., *The Origin and Development of Vaiṣṇavism*, p. 155.
2. *Ibid.*, p. 155.
3. स गत्वा लक्ष्मणः श्रीमान्नदीं गोदवरीं तदा। स्नात्वा पद्मानिचादाय सफलः
   पुनरागतः। ततः पुष्पबलिं कृत्वा शान्ति च स यथाविधि। III, 15, 24-25.
4. *Viṣṇusmṛti*, Ch. 65, S 1-13.
5. Jaiswal, S., *loc. cit.*, p. 155.
6. *Viṣṇusmṛti*, Ch. 66.
7. निवेद्य पश्चात्ताम्बूलं देवं वह्नौ समर्चयेत्।
   VP, I, 63. 28.
8. ग्रहांश्च सर्वनक्षत्रै रुद्रांश्च सह मातृभिः।
   स्कन्दं विष्णुं विशाखं च लोकपालान् सुरस्त्रियः।
   वर्णकैर्विविधैः कृत्वा हृद्यैर्गन्धगुणविन्तैः।
   यथास्वं पूजयेद्विद्वान् गन्धमाल्यानुलेपनैः।
   भक्ष्यैरन्नैश्च विविधैः फलमूलामिषैस्तथा।
   पानैश्च विविधैर्हृद्यैः सुरक्षीरासवादिभिः।
   Bṛhat Saṁhitā, XL VIII, 26-28.
9. Shastry, Ajay Mitra, *India as seen in the Bṛhat Saṁhitā of Varāhamihira*, p. 179.
   मांसौदनमद्याद्यैः पिशाचदितितनयदानवाः पूज्याः।
   सामयजुर्भिर्मुनयस्त्वृग्भिर्गन्धैश्च धूपमाल्ययुतैः।
   Bṛhat Saṁhitā, XL VIII, 30-31.
10. विधियज्ञाज्जपयज्ञो विशिष्टो दशभिर्गुणैः।
    Viṣṇusmṛti, Ch. 55, Ś. 19.
11. Jaiswal, S., *loc. cit.*, p. 162.
12. *Mahābhārata., Anuśāsana Parva*, Ch. 135
13. *Ibid., Anuśāsana Parva*, Ch. 17.

14. सुप्तां संगीतनृत्यैर्जागरणैः ....

.... अभ्यचर्य, कुसुसवस्त्रानुलेपनैः शङ्खतूर्यनिर्घोषैः।

Ch. LX, Ś 15-16.

15. Jaiswal, S., *op. cit.,* p. 162.

पुष्पनैवेद्यदानेभ्यों नृत्तदानं विशिष्यते।
स्वयं नृत्तेन यः कुर्याद्देवदेवस्य पूजनम्।
स सर्वकामनाप्नोति मोक्षोपायं च विन्दति।

VP, III 34, 25-29.

16. Shastry, Ajay Mitra, *India as seen in the Bṛhat Saṁhitā of Varāhamihira.* 179-180.

पादन्यासैः क्वणितरशनास्तत्र लीलावधूतै।
रत्लच्छायाखचितबलिभिश्चामरैः क्लान्तहस्ताः
वेश्यास्त्वत्तो नखपदसुखान्प्राय।

Meghadūta, i, 38.

17. Shastry, Ajay Mitra, *loc. cit.,* p. 180.
18. Shah, Priya Bala, *Viṣṇudharmottara Purāṇa,* Vol. II, p. 191.
19. पुण्येष्वायतनेषु च तीर्थेषूद्यानरम्यदेशेषु।
पूर्वोदक्प्लवभूमौ प्रदक्षिणाम्भोवहायां च।

Bṛhat Saṁhitā. XLVIII, 15.

20. द्विपवृषभोद्धतपर्वतवल्मीकसरित्समागमतटेषु।
पद्मसरःसु च मृद्भिः सपञ्चगव्यैश्च तीर्थजलैः।

Bṛhat Saṁhitā, LX 9.

21. Shastry, Ajay Mitra, *loc. cit.,* p. 187.
22. Jaiswal, S., *op. cit,* p. 165.
23. Sircar, D.C., *SI,* Vol. I, No. 82, p. 192.
24. *Ibid.,* No. 86, p. 203.
25. Jaiswal, S., *op. cit.,* p. 166.
26. Jaiswal, *op. cit.,* p. 163.
27. तस्मिन् सुप्ते न वर्न्तन्ते मन्त्रपूताः ऋतुक्रियाः। शरत्प्रवृत्तयज्ञोऽय
जागर्ति मधुसूदनः। तदिदं वार्षिकं चक्रं कारयत्यम्बुदेश्वरः।

Harivaṁśa, I, 50, 25-26.

28. अथाषाढस्य मासस्य शुक्लपक्षावसानिकम्।
उत्सवं त्रिदेशेन्द्राणां समाप्तं दिनपञ्चकम्।
क्षीरोदशेषशयने भगवानमधुसूदनः।
योगनिद्रां तदा भेजे लोकानां हित काम्यया।
भरतोऽप्युत्सवं कृत्वा पूजयित्वा जनार्दनम्।

महीदानं तथा कृत्वा नक्ताशीदिनपञ्चकम्।
उत्सवं विपुलं चक्रे संप्राप्य दिनपञ्चकम्।
प्रबोधं देवदेवस्य त्रिदशानां महोत्सवे।
तेषु दत्त्वा गहादानं कार्तिक्यां च विशेषतः।
पूजयित्वा जगन्नाथ शङ्खचक्रगदाधरम्।
Viṣṇudharmottara Purāṇa, I, Ch. 269.

29. Jaiswal, *op. cit.*, p. 186.
30. *Bṛhat Saṁhitā*, Ch. XLIII, S 23-24.
31. Fleet, *CII*, Vol. III, No. 17, Line 21.
32. *VP III*, Ch. 153.
33. Jaiswal, S., *op. cit.*, p. 164.
34. Sircar, *SI*, Vol. I, No. 58, p. 164.
35. Fleet, *CII*, Vol. III, No. 37, pl, XXIII B, p. 161.
36. *Encyclopaedia of Religion*, ed by Vergilius Ferm, p. 765.
37. Kramrisch Stella, *The Hindu Temples*, Vol. I, p. 135.
38. Sircar, D.C. *SI*, Vol. I, No. 3, p.
39. Sharma, I.K., *The Development of Early Śaiva Art and Architecture*, p. 53.
40. Hartel, Herbert, A Kuṣāṇsa Nāga temple of Sonkh, *BMC*, No. 11-12, 1973, p. 1.
41. *Manu Smṛti*, II, 148.
42. Jaiswal, S., *op. cit.*, p. 148.
43. द्वात्रिंशत् षोडशाथापि अष्टौ वा श्रुतिपारगाः।

    Matsya Mahā Purāṇa 265, 6.
44. *Ibid.*, 265, 1-5.

Bibliography

PRIMARY SOURCES

Literary

Agni Purāṇa, Trans. by N. Gangadharan, Part I, Delhi, 1984.

Amarakośa of Amarasiṁha, ed. by Brahmanand Tripathi, Second Edition, Vārāṇasī, 1982.

Arthaśāstra of Kauṭilya, ed. by R. Shamasastry, Eighth Edition, Mysore, 1967.

- - ed. by T.A.G. Shastry 3 Vols. Reprint, Delhi, 1984.

Aṣṭādhyāyī of Pāṇini, Trans. by Sumitra, M. Katre, Delhi, 1989.

Bhagavad Gītā, ed. by Vasudev Laxman Shastry Pansikar, Delhi 1984.

Bṛhat Saṁhitā of Varāhamihira, ed. by Ram Krishna M. Bhat, 2 Vols. Delhi, 1981.

Charaka-Saṁhitā ed. by Priyavrat Sharma, Varanasi, 1984.

Divyāvadāna, ed. by P.L. Vaidya, Darbhaṇgā, 1959.

Harivaṁśa Purāṇam, ed by Nag Saran Singh, 2 Vols, Delhi, 1985.

Kumārasaṁbhavam of Kālidāsa, ed. by Vedaprakash and Dharmdeva, Ambālā, 1973.

Lalitavistara, ed. by P.L. Vaidya, Darbhaṅgā, 1958.

Mahābhārata, ed. by Damodra Satvlekar, Vol. I (Ādi Parva, 1963), Vol. II (Āraṇyaka Parva, 1969), Vol. VII (Droṇa Parva, 1975), Vol. IX (Śalya Parva, 1973), Vol. XII (Śānti Parva, 1979), Vol. XIII (Anuśāsana Parva, 1978), Pāraḍī.

Mahābhārata with commentary of Nīlakaṇṭha, Vol. 4 : Virāta Parva,

- - Vol. 6 : Bhīṣma Parva, Pune, 1931.

Manu Smṛti, ed. by Narayana Ram Āchārya, Tenth, Edition Bombay, 1946.

Mārkaṇḍeya Purāṇa ed. by Nag Saran Singh, Delhi, N.D.

Matsya Mahā Purāṇam, Arranged by Nag Saran Singh, 2 Parts, Delhi, 1983.

Meghadūta of Kālidāsa, ed by Shivaraj Shastry, Fourth Edition, Meerut, 1976.

Nāṭya Śastra of Bharata Muni, ed. by Babulal Shukla, Second Edition, Vārāṇasī, 1984.

Raghuvaṁśa of Kālidāsa, ed. by Shrikrishnamani Tripathi, Third Edition., Vārāṇasī, 1983.

Ṛgveda with the Commentary of Sayana, Second Edition, Pune, 1972.

Rāmāyaṇa ed. by Shrinivasa Kati Mudholakara, Vol. III, Āraṇya Kāṇḍa, Delhi, 1983, Vol. VII, Uttara Kāṇḍa, Delhi, 1983.

Śatapatha Brāhamaṇa ed. by A. Weber, 3 Vols., Delhi, 1988.

Vedic Index, ed. by Vishva Bandhu, Hoshiarpur, 1958.

Viṣṇudharmottara Purāṇa, ed by Nag Saran Singh, 2 Vols., Delhi, 1985.

Viṣṇu Smṛti, ed. by J. Jolly, Vārāṇasī, 1962.

Archaeological Sources

Allan, John, *Catalogue of the Coins of Ancient India,* New Delhi, 1975.

Altekar, A.S., *Coinage of Gupta Empire,* Vārāṇasī, 1957.

Cunningham, A., *Coins of Ancient India, From The Earliest Times Down to the Seventh Century A.D.*, Vārāṇasī, 1971.

- - Coins of the *Indo-Scythians, Śakas and* Kuṣāṇās 1971.

Fleet, J.F, *Corpus Inscriptionium Indicarum,* Vol. III, 1888.

Gardner, Percy, *The Coins of the Greek and Scythic Kings of Bactria and India in the British Museum,* Reprint, Delhi, 1971.

Lüder, H., *Appendix to Epigraphica Indica and Record of the Archaeological Survey of India,* Vol. X, *A List of Brāhmī Inscription : From the Earliest Times to About 400 A.D. with the Exception of those of Aśoka,* Calcutta, 1912.

Rapson, E.J., *Sources of Indian History : Coins,* Vārāṇasī, 1966.

Seminar Papers on the Local Coins of Northern India (c. 300 B.C. to 300 A.D.), ed. by A.K. Narain, Vārāṇasī, 1968.

Smith, V.A., *Coins of Ancient India, Catalogue of the Coins in Indian Museum, Calcutta,* Vol. I, Vārāṇasī, 1972.

Sircar, D.C., *Select Inscriptions, Bearing on Indian History and Civilization,* Vol. I, Calcutta, 1965.

Whitehead, *Catalogue of the Coins in Punjab Museum,* Lahore, Vol. I, Vārāṇasī, 1971.

Journals, Bulletins and Reports

Archaeological Survey of India Report, Vol. X, *Bundelkhand and Malwa,* 1874-75 and 1876-77 by A. Cunningham, Vārāṇasī, 1966.

Bulletin of Museum and Archaeology in U.P., Vol. 11-12, 27-28, 29-30, Lucknow.

Indian Culture : Journal of the Indian Research Institute, Vol. VIII, Patnā, Reprint, Delhi.

Journal of Numismatic Society of India, Vols. XLV, Vārāṇasī.

Lalit Kalā : A Journal of Oriental Art Chiefly Indian, Nos. 18, 20, 22, New Delhi.

Mārg : A Magazine of the Arts, Vols. 22, 42, Bombay.

Purātattva; Bulletin of the Indian Archaeological Society, No. 16, New Delhi.

SECONDARY SOURCES

Agrawal, Bhanu and Rai, Subhas, *The Punch-Marked Coins,* Delhi, 1994.

Agrawala, V.S., *Evolution of the Hindu Temple and Other Essays,* Vārāṇasī, 1965.

- - , *Gupta Art,* Vārāṇasī, 1971.

- - , *ndia As Known to Pāṇini,* Vārāṇasī, 1969.

- - , *Matsya Purāṇa : A Study,* Vārāṇasī, 1963.

- - , *Śiva-Mahādeva,* Vārāṇasī, 1966.

Agrawala, V.S., *Studies in Indian Art,* Vārāṇasī, 1965.

Anderson, John, *Catalogue and Hand-Book of the Archaeological Collection in the Indian Museum,* 2 Parts Reprint, Patnā, 1971.

Bajpai, K.D., *Five Phases of Indian Art,* Jodhpur, 1991.

Banerjea, J.N., *The Development of Hindu Iconography,* Calcutta, 1956.

Basham, A.L., *The Wonder that was India,* Reprint, New Delhi, 1990.

Basu, Jogiraj, *India in the Age of Brāhmaṇas,* Calcutta, 1969.

Bhandarkar, R.G., *Vaiṣṇavism, Śaivism and Minor Religious Systems,* Poona, 1982.

Bhardwaj, O.P., *Ancient Kurukshetra, Studies in Historical and Cultural Geography,* New Delhi, 1991.

Bhattacharya, B., *Śaivism and The Phallic World,* 3 Vols., New Delhi, 1975.

Bhattacharya, N.N., *The Indian Mother Goddess,* Second Edition, New Delhi, 1977.

Chakraborty, Swati, *Socio-Religious and Cultural Study of Ancient Indian Coins,* Delhi, 1986.

Chattopadhyay, B. *Age of the Kushāṇas,* Calcutta, 1967.

Chattopadhyay, B. Coins and Icons, *A Study of Myth and Symbols in Indian Numismatic Art,* Calcutta, 1977.

Coomaraswamy, A.K., *Catalogue of the Indian Collection in the Museum of Fine Art,* Boston, 3 Parts, Delhi, 1978.

- -, *Dance of Śiva,* New York, U.S.A., 1957.

- -, *History of Indian and Indonesian Art,* Dover ed. New York, U.S.A., 1965.

- -, *Yakṣas,* 2 Parts, New Delhi, 1971.

Dandekar, R.N., *Age of Guptas and Other Essays,* Select Writings IV, Delhi, 1982.

- -, *Vedic Mythological Tracts,* Select Writings I, Delhi, 1979.

Desai, Kalpana, *Iconography of Viṣṇu In Northern India Upto the Medieval Times,* New Delhi, 1973.

Dwivedi and Bhatt, *The Jātakamālā of Āryaśura,* Delhi, 1966.

Encyclopaedia of Religion, ed. by Vergilius Ferm, London, N.D.

Fergusson, James, *Tree and Serpent Worship,* Reprint, Delhi, 1971.

Geity, Alice, *Gaṇeśa, A Monography on the Elephant-Faced God,* New Delhi, 1971.

Gonda, J., *Aspects of Early Viṣṇuism,* Utrecht, 1954.

- - , *Viṣṇuism and Śaivism, A Comparison,* New Delhi, 1976.

Grunwedel, *Buddhist Art in India,* Vārāṇasī, 1974.

Gyani, S.D., *Agni Pūraṇa—A Study,* Vārāṇasī, 1964.

Hackin, J., et. al., *The Mythologies of the East,* 2 Vols., New Delhi, 1996.

Haldhar, J.R., *Early Buddhist Mythology,* New Delhi, 1977.

Harle, J.C., *The Art and Architecture of the Indian Sub-continent,* England, 1986.

- - , *Gupta Sculptures,* New Delhi, 1996.

Harper, Katherine, Anne, *The Iconography of the Sapta Mātṛkās, Seven Hindu Goddesses of Spiritual Transformation, Studies in Women and Religion,* Vol. 28, New York, U.S.A., 1989.

Hopkins, E.W., *Epic Mythology,* Reprint, Delhi, 1986.

Jaiswal, K.K., *Uttara Bhārata Kī Prāchīna Hindu Devī Mūrtiyān,* Delhi, 1992.

Jaiswal, Suvira, *Origin and Development of Vaiṣṇavism,* Delhi, 1981.

Joshi, J.R., *Some Minor Divinities in Vedic Mythology and Ritual,* Pune, 1977.

Joshi, N.P., *Mathurā Sculptures,* Mathurā, 1965.

- - , *Catalogue of the Brahmanical Sculptures in the State Museum Lucknow.* Lucknow, 1972.

Kar, C., *Classical Indian Sculptures,* 300 B.C. to 500 A.D., London, 1956.

Khosla, *Sarla, Aśvaghoṣa and His Times,* New Delhi, 1986.

Kinsley, David, *Hindu Goddesses, Vision of the Divine Feminine in the Hindu Religious Tradition,* Delhi, 1986.

Knappert, Jan, *Indian Mythology,* London, 1995.

Kramrisch, Stella, *The Art of India,* Delhi, N.D.

- - , *The Hindu Temples,* 2 Vols. Reprint, Delhi, 1979.

- - , *Indian Sculpture,* Delhi, 1981.

- - , *The Presence of Śiva,* New Jersey, U.S.A., 1981.

Krishnamachariar, M., *History of Classical Sanskrit Literature,* Third Edition, Delhi, 1974.

Limaye, V.P., *Critical Studies on the Mahābhāṣya,* Hoshiarpur, 1974.

Lokeswarananda, ed, by *The Perennial Vivekananda, A Selection,* Reprint, New Delhi, 1992.

Macdonell, A., *Vedic Mythology,* New Delhi, 1971.

" *A Vedic Reader for Students,* Eleventh Edition, Madras, 1981.

Marshall, John, *Mohenjodaro and the Indus Civilization,* 2 Vols., Delhi, 1973.

Martin, E.Q., *Gods of India, Their History, Character and Worship,* New Delhi, 1988.

Mathothu, Kurian, *The Development of the Concept of Trimūrti In Hinduism,* Palai (Kerala), 1974.

Mishra, Indumati, *Pratimā-Vijñāna,* Bhopal, 1972.

Mishra, R.N., *Yaksha Cult and Iconography,* New Delhi, 1981.

Mishra, Rajni, *Brahmā Worship : Tradition and Iconography,* Delhi, 1989.

Mishra, S.N., *Gupta Art and Architecture, with Special Reference to Madhya Pradesh,* Delhi 1992.

Mukherjee, B.N., *Nānā on Lion, A Study in Kuṣāṇa Numismatic Art,* Calcutta, 1969.

Mukerjee, Chhanda, *Gupta Numismatic Art, An Artistic and Iconographic Study,* Delhi, 1991.

Nariman, J.K., *Literary History of Sanskrit Buddhism,* Delhi, 1972.

Navaratnam, Ratna, *Kārttikeya the Divine Child (The Hindu Testament of Wisdom),* Bombay, 1973.

New Encyclopaedia Britannica, Chicago, U.S.A., 1984.

Pandeya L.P., *Sun-Worship in Ancient India,* Delhi, 1971.

Panchmukhi, R.S., *Gandharvas and Kinnaras in Indian Iconography,* Dharwar, 1951.

Pratimā-Kośa, ed, by S.K. Ramachandra Rao, Bangalore, 1994.

Puri, B.N., *India in the Time of Patañjali,* Bombay, 1959.

Rajeshwari, D.R., *Śakti Iconography,* New Delhi, 1989.

Ram Gopal, *Kālidāsa, His Art and Culture,* New Delhi, 1984.

Rao, T.A.G., *Elements of Hindu Iconography,* 2 Vols., Second Edition, Vārāṇasī, 1971.

Ray, Niharranjan, *An Approach to Indian Art,* Chandigarh, 1974.

- - , *Maurya and Post Maurya Art, A Study in Social and Formal Contrasts,* New Delhi, 1975.

Raychaudhri, H.C., *Materials for the Study of the Early History of Vaiṣṇava Sect,* Second Edition, New Delhi, 1975.

Rosenfield, J.M., *The Dynastic Arts of the Kuṣāṇas,* New Delhi, 1993.

Roy, C. Craven, *Indian Art, A Concise History,* Reprint, London, 1993.

Sadhu Ram, *Essays on Sanskrit Literature,* New Delhi, 1965.

Sahai, B., *Iconography of Minor Hindu and Buddhist Deities,* New Delhi, 1975.

Sharma, I.K., *The Development of Early Śaiva Art and Architecture,* Delhi, 1982.

Sen, Benoychandra, *Studies in the Buddhist Jātakas, Tradition and Polity,* Calcutta, 1974.

Shah, Priya Bala, *Viṣṇudharmottara Purāṇa,* 2 Vols., Baroda, 1961.

Sharma, J.P., *Jaina Yakṣa,* Meerut, 1989.

Sharma, R.C., *The Splendour of Mathurā Art and Museum,* New Delhi, 1994.

Shastry, Ajay Mitra, *India as Seen in the Bṛhat Saṁhitā of Varāhamihira,* Delhi, 1969.

Shukla, H.L., *Semiotica Indica, Encyclopaedic Dictionary of Body Language in Indian Art and Culture,* 2 Vols., New Delhi, 1994.

Singh, O.P., *Iconography of Gaja-Lakṣmī,* Varanasi, 1982.

Singh, S.B., *Brahmanical Icons in Northern India,* New Delhi, 1977.

Sinha, Kanchan, *Kārttikeya in Indian Art and Literature,* Delhi, 1979.

Sircar, D.C., ed. by *Bhakti Cult and Ancient Indian Geography,* Calcutta, 1970.

Sivaramamurti, C., *Naṭarāja in Art, Thought and Literature,* Reprint, New Delhi, 1994.

- - , *Sculptures Inspired by Kālidāsa,* New Delhi, 1984.

- - , *Sources of History Illuminated by Literature,* New Delhi, 1979.

Srivastava, M.C.P., *Mother Goddess in Indian Art, Archaeology and Literature,* Delhi, 1979.

Srivastava, V.C., *Sun-Worship in Ancient India,* Allahabad, 1972.

Thakur, Upendra, *On Kārttikeya,* Vārāṇasī, 1981.

Thaplyal, K.K., *Studies in Ancient Indian Seals,* (A Study of North Indian Seals and Sealings from Circa Third Century A.D. to Mid-Seventh Century A.D.), Lucknow, 1972.

Thomas, P., *Epics, Myths and Legends of India, A Comprehensive Survey of the Sacred Lore of Hindu, Buddhist and Jain,* Bombay, 1961.

Tyagi, I.C., *Shaivism in Ancient India,* Meerut, 1982.

Vettam, Mani, *Purāṇic Encyclopaedia,* Reprint, Delhi, 1979.

Vogel, J., Ph., *Indian Serpent Lore or Nāgas in Hindu Legend and Art,* Vārāṇasī, 1972.

Wilkins, *Hindu Mythology,* 25 Edition, New Delhi, 1994.

Williams, Jonna, G., *The Art of Gupta India, Empire and Province,* New Delhi, 1983.

Wilson, H.H., *Analysis of the Purāṇas,* Delhi, 1979.

Winternitz, M., *A History of Indian Literature.* Vol. I, Part II (*Epics and Purāṇas*), Third Edition, Calcutta, 1978.

- - , *A History of Indian Literature (Buddhist and Jaina Literature)* Vol. II Delhi, 1983.

- - , *History of Indian Literature,* Vol. III, Reprint, Delhi, 1985.

Zimmer, Heinrich, *The Art of Indian Asia, Its Mythology and Transformation.* ed. by Joseph Campbell, 2 Vols., New Jersey, U.S.A., 1983.

Index

Figures and Plates

1

2

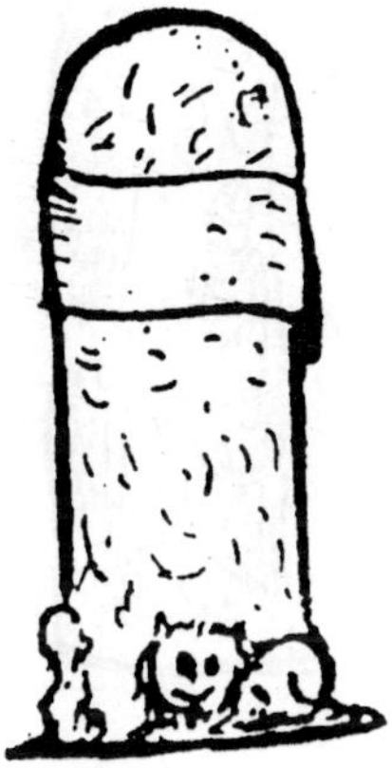

3

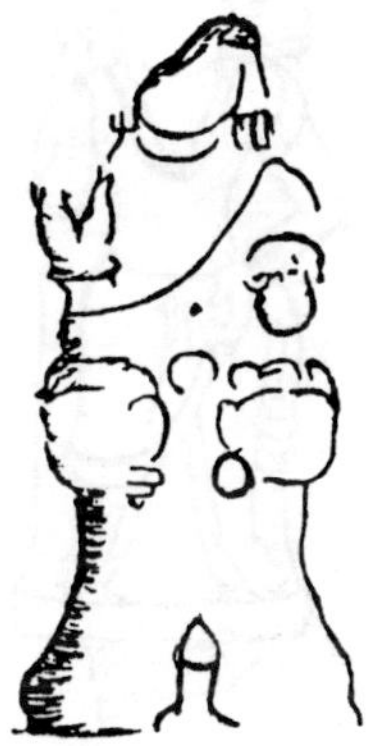

4

5

6

Fig. : 1-2 Mathurā, 3-Chaumā, 4-Bhīṭā, 5-Khoh, 6-Bhīṭā,

7

8

9

10

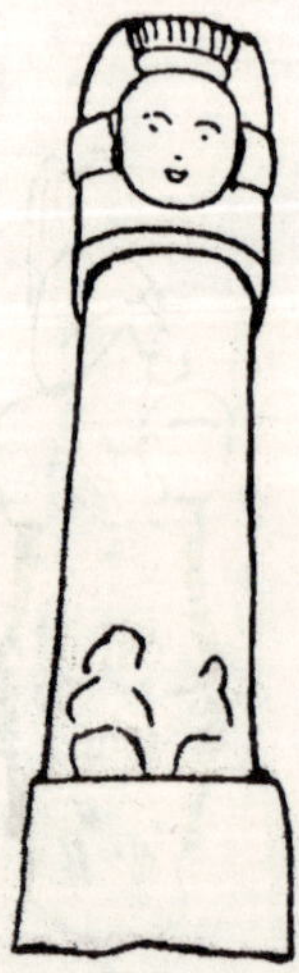

11

12

Fig. : 7-Gudimallam, 8-Mathurā, 9-Mathurā, 10-Nandā, 11-Mathurā, 12-Mathurā

13

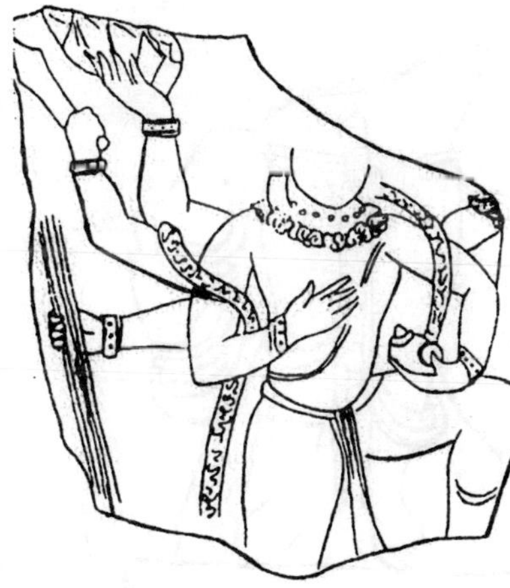

14

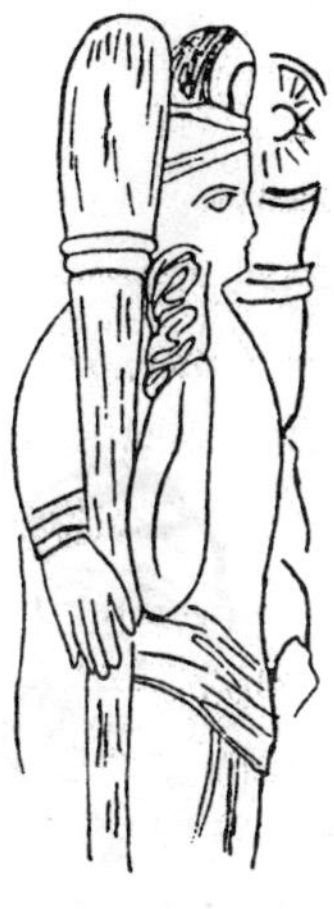

15

16

17

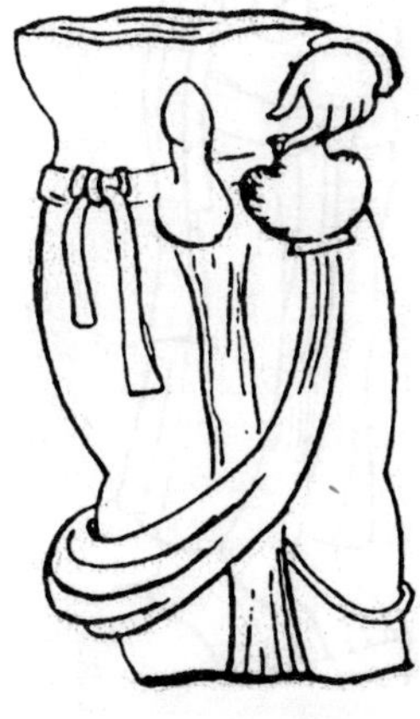

18

Fig. : 13-Bhūmarā, 14-Eight-armedViṣṇu, 15-Four-armed-Viṣṇu, Mathurā, 16-Back view Mathura of Viṣṇu Image, Mathurā, 17-Balarāma-Ekānaṁśā-Kṛṣṇa, Mathurā, 18-Śiva Image, Mathura

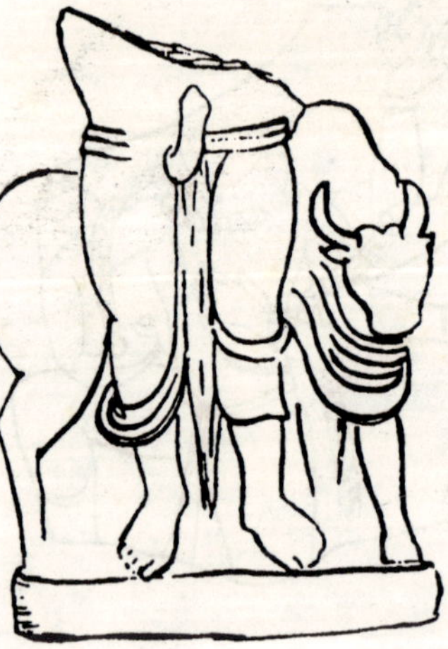

19

20

21

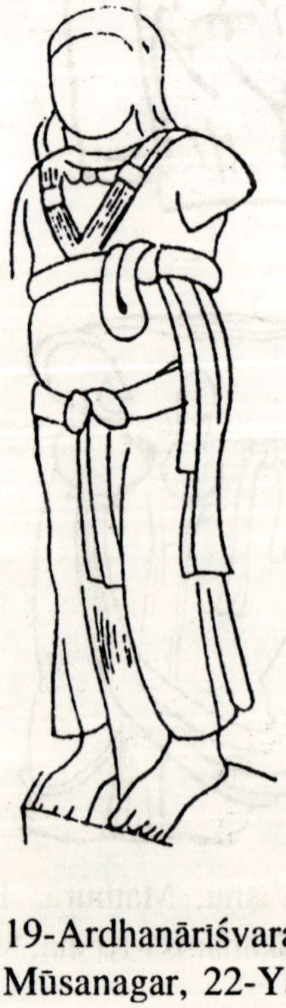

22

23

Fig. : 19-Ardhanārīśvara, Mathurā, 20–Śiva with a lion, Mūsanagar, 21-Śiva from Mūsanagar, 22-Yakṣa, Pārkham, 23-Yakṣa, Vidiśā

Plate I : Viṣṇu, Malhār, c. 2nd century B.C.

Plate II : Chatur-Vyūha, Mathurā, 3rd century. A.D.

Plate III : Varāha, Mathurā, 2nd century. A.D.

Plate IV : Viṣṇu, Unchadih, c. mid 5th century A.D.

Plate V : Viṣṇu, Jhusī, c. 510-20

Plate VI : Viṣṇu, Deogarh, c. 500-25 A.D.

Plate VII : Vaikuṇṭha Viṣṇu, Mathurā, c. 5th century A.D.

Plate VIII : Viśvarūpa Viṣṇu, Gaḍhwā, c. 5th century A.D.

Plate IX : Anantaśāyīn, Udaigiri, Cave Number 6, c. 401-02 A.D.

Plate X : Anantaśāyīn, Deogarh, c. 500-25 A.D.

Plate XI : Gajendramokṣa, Deogarh,
c. 500-25 A.D.

Plate XII : Harihara, Kuṭarī, last half of 5th and beginning of 6th century A.D.

Plate XIII : Churning of Ocean, Udaigiri (Cave Number 19)

Plate XIV : Vāmana Story, Pāwayā, c. 400-410 A.D.

Plate XV : Trivikrama Viṣṇu, Mathurā, c. 5th century A.D.

Plate XVI : Vāmana Viṣṇu, Rājaghāṭā pillar, c. 478 A.D.

Plate XVII : Varāha, Udaigiri, Cave Number 6, c. 401-02 A.D.

Plate XVIII : Varāha, Eran, end of 5th or beginning of 6th century A.D.

Plate XIX : Varāha, Eran, c. 490 or 510 A.D.

Plate XX : Nṛsiṁha, Deogarh, c. 5th century A.D.

Plate XXI : Nṛsiṁha, Rājaghāṭa pillar, c. 478 A.D.

Plate XXIII : Redemption of Ahalyā, Deogarh, c. 5th century A.D.

Plate XXII : Nṛsiṁha, Marhia, c. late 6th century A.D.

Plate XXIV : Rāma, Sītā and Śūrpaṇakhā, Deogarh, c. 5th century A.D.

Plate XXV : Lakṣmaṇa punishing Śūrpaṇakhā, Deogarh, c. 5th century A.D.

Plate XXVI : Kṛṣṇalīlā Scene Mandor, c. 400 A.D.

Plate XXVII : Devakī, Vāsudeva and Kṛṣṇa, Deogarh, c. 5th century A.D.

Plate XXVIII : Kṛṣṇa kicking at milk-cart Deogarh, c. 5th century A.D.

Plate XXIX : Kṛṣṇa stealing butter, Bharat Kala Bhawan, Vārānasī, c. 5th century A.D.

Plate XXX : Govardhanadhārī, Mathurā Museum, c. 5th century. A.D.

Plate XXXI : Nara-Nārāyaṇa, Deogarh, c. 500-25 A.D.

Plate XXXIII : Pañcha-mukha liṅga, Bhītā, c. 2nd century A.D.

Plate XXXII : Gudimallam Śiva-liṅga, Gudimallam, c. 2nd century B.C.

Plate XXXIV : Chatur-mukha liṅga, Kauśāmbī, c. 2nd century A.D.

Plate XXXV : Eka-mukha liṅga, Khoh, c. 500 A.D.

Plate XXXVI : Eka-mukha liṅga, Bhūmarā c. 5th century A.D.

Plate XXXVII : Chatur-mukha liṅga, Nachnā, c. 500 A.D.

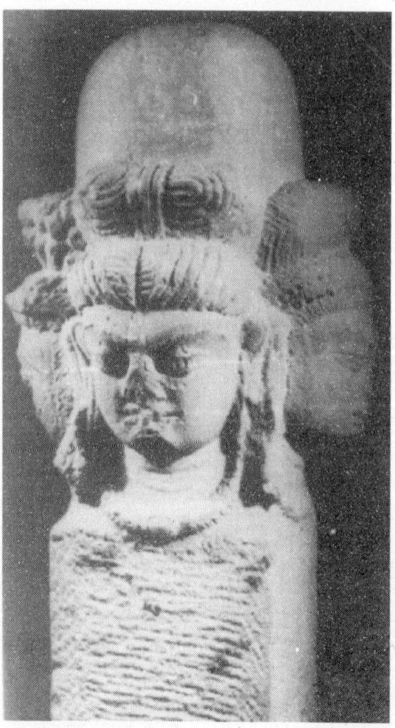

Plate XXXVIII : Chatur-mukha liṅga,
Kosam, c. 5th century A.D.

Plate XXXIX : Ardhanārīśvara, Mathurā
c. 5th century A.D.

Plate XL : Lakulīśa (dwarfish), Mathurā, c. 5th century A.D.

Plate XLI : Lakulīśa, Nachnā, c. 500 A.D.

Plate XLII : Naṭarāja, Nachnā, early 5th century

Plate XLIII : Naṭarāja, Adbhar, c. late 6th century

Plate XLIV : Umā-Maheśvara, Kauśāmbī, early 3rd century A.D.

Plate XLV : Śiva-Pārvatī, Bharat Kala Bhawan, Vārāṇasī, c. 5th century A.D.

Plate XLVI : Vīrabhadra, Badoh-Paṭharī, c. 5th century A.D.

Plate XLVII : Śiva with Triśūla-puruṣa, Allahabad, c. 5th century A.D.

Plate XLVIII : Sarasvati, Mathurā

Plate XLIX : Gaja-Lakṣmī (standing), Bharhut, c. 200 B.C.

Plate L : Lakṣmī, Mathurā, c. 2nd century A.D.

Plate LII : Mahiṣāsuramardinī, Mathurā, c. 2nd century A.D.

Plate LI : Kubera, Hāritī and Lakṣmī, Mathurā. c. 2nd century A.D.

Plate LIII : Mahiṣāsuramardinī, Cave Number 17, Udaigiri, c. 400 A.D.

Plate LIV : Mahiṣāsuramardinī, Cave Number 6, Udaigiri, c. 400 A.D.

Plate LV : Saptamātṛkā, Badoh-Paṭharī, c. 5th century A.D.

Plate LVI : Gaṅgā,-Yamunā, Udaigiri, c. 400 A.D.

Plate LVII : Gaṅgā, Tigwā, c. 5th century A.D.

Plate LVIII : Yamunā, Tigwā, c. 5th century A.D.

Plate LIX : Gaṅgā, Ahichchhatrā, c. 5th-6th century A.D.

Plate LX : Yamunā, Ahichchhatrā, c. 5th-6th century A.D.

Plate LXI : Yakṣa, Pārkham, c. 3rd-2nd century B.C.

Plate LXII : Yakṣī, Didārganj, c. 2nd century B.C.

Plate LXIII : Kubera Yakṣa, Bharhut, c. 2nd century B.C.

Plate LXIV : Yakṣa carrying purse, Vidiśā, c. 1st century B.C.

Plate LXV : Yakṣa, Palwal, c. 1st century B.C.

Plate LXVI : Padmapāni Yakṣa, Sāñchī, c. 1st century B.C.

Plate LXVII : Bhārvāhaka Yakṣa, Sāñchī, c. 1st century A.D.

Plate LXVIII : Buddha Subdues Nāga, Sāñchī, c. 1st century A.D.

Plate LXIX : Nāga, Chhargaon, c. 2nd century A.D.

Plate LXX : Nāgarāja, Cave Number 6, Udigiri,
c. 401-02 century A.D.

Plate LXXI : Gandharvas and Kinnaras, Sāñchī,
c. 1st century A.D.

Plate LXXII : Gandharvas and Kinnaras, Bhūmarā, c. 5th century A.D.

Plate LXXIII : Flying Gandharvas, Gwālior, c. 6th century A.D.